STUDENT WORKBOOK
FOURTH GRADE EDITION

The Kingdom of Shadows

ROBERT G. WAUGH

MURIEL WAUGH
EDUCATIONAL PRESS

MURIEL WAUGH
EDUCATIONAL PRESS

Library of Congress Control Number:

IBSN: 979-8-9988497-2-5

Cover design by R. G. Waugh

CONTENTS

WELCOME PAGE

WELCOME TO YOUR HERO'S WORKBOOK!

"Your teacher has a special guide that matches this workbook. You'll work together as a team — and your voice matters every step of the way!"

Get ready for an unforgettable journey!

This workbook goes along with the novel **Unleashing Greatness: The Kingdom of Shadows** and it's your guide through every step of the story.

- ☑ Build strong reading and thinking skills
- ☑ Connect deeply with the characters and story
- ☑ Grow your voice and confidence
- ☑ Discover the greatness inside YOU!

HOW TO USE THIS WORKBOOK

- **After each chapter:** Complete the pages for vocabulary, comprehension, reflection and creative thinking.

• ✍ **Write in your best full sentences** and take your time to share your ideas—your ideas matter!

• 💭 **Use the CER pages (Claim–Evidence–Reasoning)** to grow your thinking and prove your ideas like a real hero!

• 🖐 **Express yourself:** Draw, predict, connect, and imagine with your whole heart!

• . **Reflect:** Think about what each chapter teaches you—in the story and in your real life.

"Your teacher might help guide you through these pages, or you might do them on your own during reading time."

📓 YOUR READER'S JOURNAL

Welcome to your personal Journal section!

After every 4–5 chapters, you'll get a chance to pause, reflect, and respond. These pages are just for YOU — to think deeply, make connections, and even get a little creative.

Use the space to:
 • Reflect on how the story is changing your thinking
 • Connect the characters' journey to your own life
 • Write poems, doodle symbols, or answer journal prompts
You don't need to get it "perfect"—just be honest and thoughtful.

Use sentence starters like:
 • "I used to think... but now I think…"
 • "This chapter made me realize…"
 • "If I were Scatter, I would have…"
 . **TIP**: These pages can be kept private, shared with your teacher, or even turned into part of your final project!

☑ HELPFUL HINTS FOR HEROIC WORK

• Go at your own pace — this is *your* journey.

• Revisit the chapter when you need help finding answers.

• Ask for help — great heroes support one another!

✎ This Workbook Belongs To:

_____

(Sign your name proudly!)

✦ WORKBOOK RULES FOR HEROES

Before you begin your journey, remember these simple rules:

1 Be Kind — to Yourself and Others
• Cheer yourself on when things get tricky.
• Respect your classmates' ideas and efforts—teamwork makes magic.

2 Try Your Best — Every Time ✐
• Neat handwriting and full sentences show pride.
• Mistakes are part of learning — just keep going!

3 Use Your Imagination — Be Bold and Brave ✐
• Think big. Be curious. Make wild, wonderful connections.
• Dream, draw, and take risks — just like a real hero.

Every hero's journey is different — and yours is amazing.

◎ MY GOAL TRACKER

What do YOU want to grow while reading this story?
(Check all that apply!)

✅ Become a stronger reader 📚
    ✅ Grow my creativity 🎨
    ✅ Practice kindness and teamwork 💬
    ✅ Build my leadership skills 🦁
    ✅ Stay determined, even when it's hard 💪
    ✅ Learn to think deeply and explain my ideas 🧠
    ✅ Finish what I start and feel proud! 🏆

Each page you complete brings you closer to discovering your own greatness!

🌐 MORE ADVENTURES AWAIT ONLINE!

Want games, challenges, bonus quests, and tools to help you grow as a reader and leader? Our brand new website is coming soon!
    unleashinggreatnessedu.org

It will be your next step into Wakaduo — with printable activities, interactive tools, and new surprises coming soon!

PRE-TEST: SHOW WHAT YOU KNOW

"This is just to see what you already know. Try your best!"

✎ STUDENT PRE-TEST

◆ Section 1 – Vocabulary in Context (Multiple Choice)

1. What does the word **"portal"** most likely mean in this sentence?

"The glowing portal shimmered in the park sky like a wound in space."

    A. A magical doorway
    B. A bright light
    C. A loud noise
    D. A type of animal

2. In the sentence below, which clue helps you understand the word **"prophecy"?**

"Zara stared at the eclipse, thinking about the prophecy that spoke of four protectors."

    A. The word "thinking"
    B. The idea of the eclipse

C. The mention of four protectors

D. The word "Zara"

3. The word **"hesitate"** means:

    A. To run quickly

    B. To pause or be unsure

    C. To jump in excitement

    D. To whisper softly

4. Which word best describes **Adira's** actions when she risks helping a stranger?

    A. Selfish

    B. Careless

    C. Courageous

    D. Confused

5. Which word best completes this sentence?

    "Even though she was small, Scatter believed it was her _____ to lead the journey."

    A. accident

    B. mistake

    C. destiny

    D. vacation

◆ **Section 2 – Morphology (Multiple Choice + Matching)**

6. What does the word **"transformation"** mean based on its parts?

    A. A quiet moment

    B. The act of changing form

    C. A kind of symbol

    D. The end of a story

7. Match the word part to the correct meaning:

    Write the correct letter (A, B, or C) next to each word part.

    Word Parts

cor _____

guard _____

-ian _____

Meanings

A. one who protects

B. heart

C. to watch or keep safe

8. Which word includes the prefix **"uni-"**?

A. Universe

B. Reaction

C. Separate

D. Together

◆ **Section 3 – Short Passages & Literal Comprehension**

Read the short passage below and answer the questions.

"Scatter clutched the Sacred Ring, her tail trembling. She stepped forward, though every eye in the valley was fixed on her. Behind her, Henry stood silent but proud."

9. What does this passage tell you about Scatter?

A. She is used to being in charge.

B. She is afraid but brave.

C. She wants to give up.

D. She doesn't trust Henry.

10. What role does Henry seem to play in this moment?

A. He is unsure of Scatter.

B. He is angry about her choice.

C. He quietly supports her.

D. He wants the ring for himself.

◆ **Section 4 – Inference & Theme**

11. What can you infer from this quote by Adira?

"True strength is not found in size but in spirit."

A. Only large animals are wise

B. Strength is about muscles

C. Even small animals can lead

D. Leaders should be silent

12. Which theme is most clear in Chapter 1?

A. Teamwork helps people grow

B. Don't talk to strangers

C. Always believe in magic

D. Stay indoors during storms

◆ Section 5 – Sequencing

13. Put these events from the early chapters in the correct order (1–4):

-     ___ The children are called by a mysterious voice
-     ___ Adira helps a man tied in front of a hut
-     ___ Scatter discovers the Sacred Ring
-     ___ A portal opens in the sky

◆ Section 6 – Constructed Response (2–3 sentences each)

14. In your own words, what does the word **"guardian"** mean?

What does it mean to be a guardian in Wakaduo?

✎ Your Response:

15. Why do you think the author chose to make Scatter—someone small—the leader of a great journey?

✎ Your Response:

16. What does the proverb "A single bracelet does not jingle" mean? Use an example from your life or the story.

✎ Your Response:

◆ Section 7 – Extended Written Response (Optional or Challenge)

17. Prompt: Based on what you've read so far, which character shows the most growth—Zara, Adira, or Scatter?

Use one quote or moment to support your answer.

✍ Your Answer:

Claim: I think _____ shows the most growth because...

Evidence: One moment that proves this is...

Reasoning: This shows that...

HERO'S CODE OF HONOR

Hero's Code of Honor

This is your story. Your journey. Your voice.
Be brave, be kind, and most of all… be you.
Let's begin.

EMBRACING THE UNKNOWN

E mbracing the Unknown

NAME: _____

Date: _____

CHAPTER QUEST

⬤ CHAPTER 1 – *Embracing the Unknown*

📖 CORE READING SKILL FOCUS:

📖 **Skill:** *Cause and Effect + Context Clues*

◎ **WHY IT MATTERS:** HELPS STUDENTS UNDERSTAND HOW ACTIONS lead to consequences and decode new vocabulary.

· · ·

🔍 **Focus in This Chapter:** Maya and the group make choices that lead to an unfolding mystery. Students track emotional tone shifts and use surrounding text to decode unfamiliar words like *eclipse*, *prophecy*, and *portal*.

"You'll find Journal pages after every 4–5 chapters. Look for this: 📖 **Journal #: After Chapter # "**

📖 CHAPTER SUMMARY

In this chapter, we meet four ordinary kids—Zara, Jalen, Maya, and Malik—whose after-school lives are changed forever when a mysterious voice calls to them in the park. A strange tear opens in the sky, inviting them into a world unknown. Though afraid, the children step through and find themselves transformed into animals in the magical land of Wakaduo. Their decision to go forward shows early signs of courage and unity.

📚 VOCABULARY PRACTICE

(Need help with a word? Check out the Glossary.)

DIRECTIONS: MATCH EACH WORD TO ITS CORRECT MEANING, THEN complete the Morphology and Challenge Word activity below.

1. PORTAL

2. COURAGE

3. PROPHECY

4. HESITATE

5. DESTINY

WORD MEANINGS:
- A magical opening or doorway
- To stop or pause because of uncertainty
- What is meant to happen in the future
- The ability to face fear bravely
- A prediction about what will happen

MORPHOLOGY BREAKDOWN

WORD: PROPHECY
Root: *phecy* (from Greek "to speak")
Prefix: *pro-* (before)

→ **Prophecy** means "to speak about something before it happens."

. . .

WORD: COURAGE

Root: *cor* (Latin for "heart")

→ Originally, *courage* meant "strength of heart."

MORPHOLOGY MATCH (WORD PARTS IN ACTION)

Match each word part to the vocabulary word it helps build:

- **pro-** means "before" → _____
- **phecy** means "to speak" → _____
- **cor** means "heart" → _____
- **portal** comes from Latin *porta*, meaning "gate" →

_____

NOW YOU TRY:

Pick one word and explain how its parts help you understand it.

My Word: _____

WORD PARTS I SEE: _____ + _____

WHAT IT MEANS TO ME:

[_____]
[_____]
[_____]
[_____]

CHALLENGE WORD: PORTAL

THINK ABOUT THE "PORTAL" IN THIS CHAPTER. HOW IS IT BOTH literal and symbolic?

. . .

WRITE 2–3 SENTENCES EXPLAINING:

"What does it mean to step through a portal in real life—not just in fantasy stories?"

[_____]
[_____]
[_____]
[_____]
[_____]

🔍 READING COMPREHENSION CHECK

Directions: Answer the questions after reading Chapter One.

1. Who are the main characters introduced in this chapter?

2. What unusual event happens in the park?

3. Why do the children hesitate before entering the tear in the sky?

4. What transformation occurs after they cross into Wakaduo?

[_____]
[_____]
[_____]
[_____]
[_____]
[_____]
[_____]
[_____]
[_____]
[_____]
[_____]
[_____]
[_____]
[_____]
[_____]
[_____]
[_____]

. . .

INFERENTIAL QUESTION:

Why do you think the mysterious voice chose Zara, Jalen, Maya, and Malik instead of any other kids in the park?

[_____]
[_____]
[_____]
[_____]

☑ PREDICTION LADDER

Directions: Based on this chapter, make two predictions.

• I think the heroes will encounter...

[_____]
[_____]

• I THINK THEIR ANIMAL FORMS WILL HELP THEM...

Explain what clues in the story helped you make these predictions.

[_____]
[_____]
[_____]
[_____]

⌯ THEME TRACKER: TEAMWORK & BRAVERY

As you read, track moments when the characters show bravery or work as a team.

Example:

• When the kids step through the portal together → *Teamwork* and *Bravery*

Try to find at least two more examples from Chapter One.

[_____]
[_____]
[_____]
[_____]

❧ CREATIVE CORNER: WHAT DO YOU SEE?

Drawing Prompt:

Draw what you imagine the sky tear looks like as it opens over the city park. Who or what might be peeking through?

[_____]
[_____]
[_____]
[_____]
[_____]
[_____]
[_____]
[_____]
[_____]
[_____]

DRAWING PROMPT 2: DRAW WHAT YOU IMAGINE THE KIND OF magical animal protector you would become.

Feeling & Color Guide:
- Purple = Mystery
- Red = Danger or fear
- Gold = Courage
- Blue = Calm or peace
- Green = Hope

Use colors to show what emotions the scene gives you.

[_____]
[_____]
[_____]
[_____]
[_____]
[_____]
[_____]
[_____]
[_____]
[_____]

⊙ REFLECT & RESPOND

Choose **one** of the reflection questions below. Write **3–4 thoughtful sentences** to share your ideas and feelings.

YOU CAN ALSO DRAW A PICTURE IF THAT HELPS YOU EXPRESS YOUR answer.

■ MY REFLECTION QUESTION: (CHOOSE ONE OR WRITE YOUR own!)

WHAT WOULD YOU HAVE DONE IN THIS CHAPTER'S BIG MOMENT?

HOW DID THE CHARACTERS SHOW KINDNESS, COURAGE, OR leadership?

WHAT LESSON CAN YOU USE IN YOUR OWN LIFE?

DESCRIBE A TIME WHEN YOU NEEDED OTHERS TO HELP YOU succeed.

✍ **My Answer:**

[_____]
[_____]
[_____]
[_____]
[_____]
[_____]
[_____]
[_____]
[_____]

. . .

✏ (OPTIONAL: DRAW A SMALL SKETCH BELOW!)
📷 ✏ [Drawing Space]

[_____]
[_____]
[_____]
[_____]
[_____]
[_____]
[_____]
[_____]
[_____]
[_____]
[_____]

🧠 REFLECTION QUESTION
Write 3 sentences:

What does the proverb "For tomorrow belongs to those who prepare for it today" mean to you?

[_____]
[_____]
[_____]
[_____]
[_____]
[_____]
[_____]
[_____]

🪙 3. OPTIONAL: DRAWING PROMPT WITH WRITING TIE-IN
Caption Challenge:

Draw the sky portal. Then write a sentence starting with:
"Even though I didn't know what was ahead, I chose to..."

. . .

📷 ✏️ [Drawing Space]

[_____]
[_____]
[_____]
[_____]
[_____]
[_____]
[_____]
[_____]
[_____]

△ PARENT TIP (OPTIONAL DISCUSSION AT HOME):

Ask your child: *What do they think bravery looks like?* Talk about a time your family faced something unknown.

POETRY PACK

Poetry Focus Activity for Chapter One

🪨 CHAPTER 1: *"THE HEROES"*
Poetry Activity Sheet — Narrative Poem (City Magic & Dreams)
✏️ **Poem Text:**
The Heroes

In the heart of the city, where the trees whisper of mysteries,
Four friends embrace the unknown, with hearts wild and free.
Maya dances with the wind, braids flying like kites,
Jalen dribbles dreams on the court, under the morning light.
Malik draws worlds in the dust, a map to hidden treasures,
While Zara weaves tales of knights, her words are quiet pleasures.

. . .

☞ STUDENT POETRY ACTIVITIES
ACTIVITY 1: Dream Catcher Art 🪶

☑ Create a *"dream catcher"* poster showing what dreams Maya, Jalen, Malik, and Zara each chase.

☑ Use small drawings or key words ("basketball," "adventure," "stories") around their names!

ACTIVITY 2: MAGIC IN THE CITY 🏙

☑ Write 3 sentences describing where *you* find magic in your city or neighborhood.

☑ Bonus: Draw a little scene (park, court, library, tree!) that feels *"magical"* to you.

[_____]
[_____]
[_____]
[_____]
[_____]
[_____]
[_____]

ACTIVITY 3: WORD WEB

☑ Pick a powerful verb from the poem (examples: *dance, dribble, draw, weave*).

☑ Build a Word Web:

• Put the verb in the center circle.

• Draw lines outward and add 4 more action words you connect to it!

(*Example: dribble → bounce → race → leap → spin!*)

[_____]
[_____]
[_____]
[_____]
[_____]
[_____]

. . .

ACTIVITY 4: "HERO THOUGHT BUBBLE" ✎

☑ Pick Maya, Jalen, Malik, or Zara.
☑ Create a "thought bubble" for them:
"Today, I dream of _____ because
_____."

✿

✎ CER WRITING (CLAIM–EVIDENCE–REASONING)

Write Like a Hero
✎ CER Writing Challenge – Chapter 1
Prompt:
Why did the friends decide to step through the tear in the sky, even though they were afraid?

📣 CLAIM
✎ Starter: I believe the friends stepped into the unknown because...

[_____]
[_____]

📚 EVIDENCE
✎ Starter: In the story it says...

[_____]
[_____]

REASONING
✎ Starter: This shows that...

[_____]
[_____]

. . .

Bonus CER Prompt:

Why is it important to prepare—even when you're afraid?
How does that connect to what the kids did?

[_____]
[_____]
[_____]
[_____]
[_____]
[_____]
[_____]
[_____]
[_____]
[_____]

Quick Checklist

☑ Clear answer?
☑ Strong evidence?
☑ Good explanation?

☑ End of Student Workbook – Chapter One

Great work! You're just getting started on an amazing journey.

❧ 2 ❧

ADIRA'S AWAKENING

A dira's Awakening

Name: _____

Date: _____

CHAPTER QUEST

📖 **CORE READING SKILL FOCUS:**

📖 **Skill:** *Character Development + Symbolism*

◎ **WHY IT MATTERS:** BUILDS COMPREHENSION BY ANALYZING HOW characters change and what objects or moments represent.

🔍 **FOCUS IN THIS CHAPTER:** ADIRA TRANSFORMS THROUGH magical symbolism (potion, shell, light). Students explore what makes someone a leader and track internal character change.

⬭ CHAPTER SUMMARY

In the African savanna, a wise tortoise named Adira senses something strange—a mysterious hut surrounded by dangerous predators. When a man is dragged from the hut, Adira makes a courageous decision to help him. The man is revealed to be a forest wizard named Eze. He gives Adira a magical drink that grants her new powers: the ability to understand humans, see hidden truths, and heal others. As she transforms, a leopard reappears—but Adira, no longer afraid, stands tall. She has become the new Guardian of Wakaduo.

⬛ VOCABULARY PRACTICE

Match the word to its meaning:
1 Guardian
2 Instinct
3 Enchantment
4 Lurk
5 **Transformation** *(Challenge Word)*

Definitions:
– A magical spell or power
– A person who protects something important
– To hide and move secretly
– A natural feeling that helps guide actions
– A big change in form or identity

. . .

FILL IN THE BLANKS:

1 The hyena began to _____ in the grass, waiting to strike.

2 Eze placed an _____ over the hut to hide it from predators.

3 Adira acted on pure _____ when she helped the man escape.

4 Eze told Adira she would now be the _____ of Wakaduo.

🔠 MORPHOLOGY FOCUS

WORD: GUARDIAN

Root: *guard* (to watch or protect)
Suffix: *-ian* (one who)
→ *One who protects or watches over others*

WORD: ENCHANTMENT

Prefix: *en-* (to put into)
Root: *chant* (to sing or speak)
Suffix: *-ment* (state of being)
→ *The state of being under a magical influence*

WORD: INSTINCT

Prefix: *in-* (inward)
Root: *stinct* (Latin *stinguere*, to prick or urge)
→ *An inner urge or feeling*

CHALLENGE WORD: TRANSFORMATION

Prefix: *trans-* (across, beyond)
Root: *form* (shape)
Suffix: *-ation* (the act or process of)
→ *The act of changing shape, form, or nature*

🪨 BUILD-A-WORD ACTIVITY

Can you rebuild each word from its parts?
Draw lines or arrows to match the parts with the correct words:

Word Parts:
- **en-** (to put into)
- **chant** (to sing/speak)
- **-ment** (state of being)
- **trans-** (across)
- **form** (shape)
- **-ation** (the process of)

WORDS TO BUILD:

- Enchantment
- Transformation

Now write:

I built the word: _____

It means:

[_____]
[_____]

Because the parts tell me:

[_____]
[_____]

🪨 3. MINI "LEADERSHIP WORD WEB" FOR CHARACTER Vocabulary

Since leadership is the theme, create a vocabulary web to describe Adira:

· · ·

WORD WEB ACTIVITY:

Write the word **"Leader"** in the center.

Now add 4 words or phrases around it that describe Adira.

(Examples: *Brave, Listens, Thinks before acting, Helps others*)

[Drawing Space]

[_____]
[_____]
[_____]
[_____]
[_____]
[_____]
[_____]
[_____]
[_____]
[_____]
[_____]

READING COMPREHENSION

Multiple Choice:

1 WHAT MAKES ADIRA FEEL SOMETHING IS WRONG?

    A. The grass is too tall

    B. A storm is coming

    C. A strange hut appears with predators nearby

    D. She hears birds chirping

2 HOW DOES ADIRA HELP THE MAN ESCAPE?

    A. She fights the leopard

    B. She roars at the predators

    C. She bites through the branch he is tied to

    D. She runs away to get help

. . .

SHORT ANSWER:

What special powers does Adira gain from the enchanted brew?

[_____]
[_____]
[_____]

INFERENTIAL QUESTION:

Why do you think Eze chose Adira instead of another animal to become the Guardian of Wakaduo?

[_____]
[_____]
[_____]

∕ PREDICTION LADDER

1 What do you think will happen next in Adira's journey?

2 WHAT CLUES TELL YOU THAT HER JOB AS GUARDIAN WILL BE difficult?

3 WHO MIGHT HELP HER ALONG THE WAY?

MY PREDICTION:

[_____]
[_____]
[_____]
[_____]
[_____]
[_____]

⟨⟩ THEME TRACKER: COURAGE AND LEADERSHIP

Write ONE thing Adira did in the story that shows she's becoming a leader.
Action Adira Took:

[_____]

WHAT IT SHOWS ABOUT HER CHARACTER:

[_____]
[_____]

🎨 CREATIVE CORNER: MAGICAL MOMENT

Drawing Prompt:

Draw the moment when Adira drinks the enchanted brew and begins to glow with new magic.

📷 ✏️ [Drawing Space]

[_____]
[_____]
[_____]
[_____]
[_____]
[_____]
[_____]
[_____]
[_____]

COLOR/FEELING GUIDE:

- Purple = Mystery
- Orange = Courage
- Gold = Wisdom
- Green = Healing
- Red = Danger
- Blue = Calm

Use 2+ colors to show what Adira might be feeling (Brave and nervous or wise and unsure) as she transforms!

REFLECT & RESPOND – CHAPTER 2

Choose ONE question and answer in 3–4 complete sentences.

Why do you think Adira stayed silent for so long before speaking?

What makes Adira a wise leader?

How would YOU respond if you were chosen to protect a magical land?

[_____]
[_____]
[_____]
[_____]
[_____]
[_____]
[_____]
[_____]
[_____]
[_____]
[_____]

SENTENCE STARTER:

"If I were chosen to protect a magical land, I would feel

———————————————————————————,

BECAUSE _____.

BUT I WOULD STILL CHOOSE TO

[_____]

[_____]
(Optional Sketch Below)

[_____]
[_____]
[_____]
[_____]
[_____]
[_____]
[_____]

PROVERB REFLECTION

Proverb: *"A single bracelet does not jingle."*

What does this mean, and how does it connect to the story?

Write 2–3 sentences:

[_____]
[_____]
[_____]
[_____]
[_____]
[_____]

FOLLOW-UP PROMPT:

"A single bracelet does not jingle" means we need others.

How does Adira's journey show that leaders don't work alone?

[_____]
[_____]
[_____]
[_____]
[_____]
[_____]

✐ CER WRITING CHALLENGE – CHAPTER 2

Prompt: Why is Adira's wisdom important to the animals of Wakaduo?

CLAIM – What do you believe?

✎ I believe that Adira's wisdom is important because...

[_____]
[_____]

EVIDENCE – FIND A QUOTE OR MOMENT FROM THE STORY.

✎ One example is when...

✎ In the story it says...

[_____]
[_____]

REASONING – EXPLAIN HOW THIS PROVES YOUR POINT.

✎ This shows that...

✎ This means...

[_____]
[_____]

☑ USE YOUR STRONGEST WRITING TO SHOW HOW ADIRA'S ACTIONS reveal true leadership and wisdom.

BONUS (Optional):

✎ Draw Adira standing beneath the stars, glowing with magic and courage.

[_____]
[_____]
[_____]
[_____]
[_____]
[_____]
[_____]

POETRY PACK – *THE AWAKENING*

Poetry Style: Haiku Sequence

GOLDEN SAVANNA
Old tortoise stirs, sensing change—
Wind whispers secrets.
•• Curious eyes glance,
Danger prowls, hidden whispers—
Leopard's shadow looms.
Branch snaps, river's arms,
Safety in water's embrace—
Stranger's grateful gaze.
Magic fills the air,
Wise words brew, understanding—
New power awakens.

STUDENT POETRY ACTIVITIES
ACTIVITY 1: Painting the Scene

PICK YOUR FAVORITE HAIKU. SKETCH THAT MOMENT.

(Draw)

[_____]
[_____]
[_____]
[_____]
[_____]
[_____]
[_____]
[_____]
[_____]
[_____]

. . .

ACTIVITY 2: HAIKU DETECTIVE!

CHOOSE ONE HAIKU. COUNT SYLLABLES IN EACH LINE.
Example:
Golden savanna (5)
Old tortoise stirs, sensing change (7)
Wind whispers secrets (5)
Now your turn:
Syllable counts:

1.
[_____]

2.
[_____]

3.
[_____]

ACTIVITY 3: EMOTIONAL VOCABULARY HUNT
Find two words or images from the haikus that create strong feelings.

1 WORD/IMAGE: _____ → FEELING: _____

2 WORD/IMAGE: _____ → FEELING: _____

. . .

ACTIVITY 4: WRITE YOUR OWN HAIKU!

Topic: A New Adventure OR A Hidden Danger
(Remember 5–7–5 syllables.)

My Haiku:

[_____]
[_____]
[_____]
[_____]
[_____]
[_____]

ACTIVITY 5: CHARACTER'S THOUGHTS

Imagine you are Adira just before or after she drinks the potion.
Write a thought that might be in her mind.

EXAMPLE STARTER:

"I can feel the winds shifting. Change is near..."

[_____]
[_____]
[_____]
[_____]

✔ END OF STUDENT WORKBOOK – CHAPTER TWO

👋 Keep going—you're becoming a true Wakaduo Word Wizard!

❧ 3 ❧

THE MYSTERIOUS QUEST

Title: **The Mysterious Quest – The Enigmatic Ring**
Name: _____
Date: _____

CHAPTER QUEST

▨ CORE READING SKILL FOCUS:

▨ **Skill:** _Interpreting Proverbial Language + Figurative Meaning_

◎ **WHY IT MATTERS:** STRENGTHENS ABSTRACT THINKING BY encouraging students to interpret layered language.

🔍 **FOCUS IN THIS CHAPTER:** THE PROVERB "IF YOUR ONLY TOOL IS a hammer…" drives the theme of problem-solving and leadership diversity. The ring becomes a metaphor for vision, and students must consider multiple perspectives.

⊘ CHAPTER SUMMARY

In the heart of Wakaduo Valley, Scatter the pouched mouse uncovers a powerful artifact: the Sacred Ring of Journeys. During a gathering beneath the Council Tree, she bravely presents the ring and its mysterious history. Though some, like Sally the mandrill, doubt her story, others begin to rally behind her—especially Henry the honey badger and Adira the wise tortoise. Scatter's courage sparks something new in the animals: belief. A great journey is declared—but far beyond the valley, unknown dangers begin to stir.

📣 Proverb Reflection Prompt
Prompt:

The poem and story repeat the line: *"If your only tool is a hammer, you see each problem as a nail."*

What do you think this means in real life?

Write about a time you solved a problem in a new way.

[_____]
[_____]
[_____]
[_____]
[_____]
[_____]
[_____]
[_____]
[_____]

✎ VOCABULARY PRACTICE

Match the word to its meaning:

1 Quest
2 Unity
3 Skeptical
4 Enigmatic

Definitions:

– A long journey to reach an important goal
– Being united or working as one group
– Mysterious and hard to understand
– To be unsure or have doubts

FILL IN THE BLANKS:

1 The animals began a _____ to find a safe place to live.

2 Sally was _____ about the power of the ring.

3 The _____ ring was covered in symbols no one could explain.

4 Scatter reminded everyone that _____ makes them strong.

▦ MORPHOLOGY FOCUS

WORD: QUEST

Root: *quest* (to seek or search)
→ *A search or long journey to find something important*

WORD: UNITY

Root: *uni-* (one)
Suffix: *-ty* (state or quality of)
→ *The state of being together as one*

· · ·

WORD: SKEPTICAL

Root: *skept-* (to look or examine)

Suffix: *-ical* (related to)

→ *Doubtful or questioning*

CHALLENGE WORD: ENIGMATIC

Root: *enigma* (riddle or mystery)

Suffix: *-tic* (having the nature of)

→ *Mysterious or difficult to understand*

⬤ WORD BUILDER CHALLENGE – CHAPTER 3

Match the parts to the words they help create:

• **quest** (to search) → _____

• **uni-** (one) + **-ty** (state of) → _____

• **skept-** (to examine) + **-ical** (related to)

→ _____

• **enigma** (mystery) + **-tic** (nature of)

→ _____

NOW TRY THIS:

Pick one word and explain what its parts tell you.

✎ My Word: _____

✎ What I learned from its parts:

_____

⬤ 3. ADVANCED LEARNER OPTION

This is a small "deep dive" activity for early-finisher students:

Bonus Challenge: Enigmatic = Mysterious

Can you think of another word that uses one of these parts?

• **-ic** (like *heroic, scientific*)

• **-tic** (like *realistic, poetic*)

. . .

WRITE THE WORD AND WHAT YOU THINK IT MEANS:

_____ → _____

⚲ READING COMPREHENSION

Multiple Choice:

1 WHAT IS THE SACRED RING OF JOURNEYS BELIEVED TO DO?
   A. Call the rain
   B. Start a fire
   C. Guide animals to safety
   D. Make someone invisible

2 WHY IS SALLY UNSURE ABOUT THE RING?
   A. She doesn't believe in magic
   B. She wanted to find the ring herself
   C. She is afraid of Scatter
   D. She wants to leave the valley alone

SHORT ANSWER:

1 How does Scatter try to convince the animals that the ring is real?

[_____]
[_____]

INFERENTIAL QUESTION:

Why do you think Scatter's size makes some animals question her leadership?

[_____]
[_____]

⟳ SEQUENCING ACTIVITY

Put these events in order (1–6):

___ Scatter finds the ring in the Hollow Tree of Elders.

___ The animals gather under the Council Tree.

___ Scatter introduces the Sacred Ring.

___ Sally questions the ring's magic.

___ Henry supports Scatter's leadership.

___ Adira announces they will begin the journey.

🐾 CHARACTER TRAITS CHART

Character: Scatter

Trait: Brave

What the Character Does:

[_____]
[_____]

CHARACTER: SALLY

Trait: Skeptical

What the Character Does:

[_____]
[_____]

CHARACTER: HENRY

Trait: Supportive

What the Character Does:

[_____]
[_____]

CHARACTER: ADIRA

Trait: Wise

What the Character Does:

[_____]
[_____]

✎ THEME REFLECTION

What lesson does Scatter teach the animals (and us) about leadership and trust?

[_____]
[_____]
[_____]
[_____]
[_____]
[_____]

✎ CREATIVE CORNER: SACRED RING DESIGN

Design your own version of the Sacred Ring of Journeys!
   Color/Feeling Guide:
   • Gold = Wisdom
   • Blue = Calm guidance
   • Red = Risk or warning
   • Purple = Mystery
   • Green = Protection
   Power of the Ring: (Add ancient-looking symbols or patterns)

[_____]
[_____]
[_____]
[_____]
[_____]
[_____]
[_____]
[_____]
[_____]
[_____]
[_____]

⚲ SCATTER'S TOOLBELT

Directions: "Draw 3 tools a leader should carry—and what they stand for."
- Listening Ear = Active listening
- Compass = Wisdom or guidance
- Feather = Kindness

[_____]
[_____]
[_____]
[_____]
[_____]
[_____]
[_____]
[_____]
[_____]
[_____]
[_____]
[_____]
[_____]

⟋ PREDICTION LADDER

What might happen next?

[_____]
[_____]

STEP 1 – WHAT THE ANIMALS EXPECT:

[_____]
[_____]

STEP 2 – A SURPRISE:

[_____]
[_____]

. . .

STEP 3 – MY PREDICTION:

[_____]
[_____]

✎ CER WRITING CHALLENGE – CHAPTER 3

Prompt: Why does the Sacred Ring matter so much to the animals of Wakaduo?

🐾 CLAIM – WHAT DO YOU BELIEVE?

✎ I believe that the Sacred Ring is important because...

[_____]
[_____]

📚 EVIDENCE – FIND A QUOTE OR MOMENT FROM THE STORY.

✎ One example is when...
✎ In the story it says...

[_____]
[_____]
[_____]
[_____]

REASONING – EXPLAIN HOW THIS PROVES YOUR POINT.

✎ This shows that...
✎ This proves that...

[_____]
[_____]
[_____]
[_____]

. . .

✅ Make sure your claim, evidence, and explanation are all clear and strong.

BONUS (Optional):

🐾 Draw Scatter holding the Sacred Ring beneath the Council Tree.

[_____]
[_____]
[_____]
[_____]
[_____]
[_____]
[_____]
[_____]
[_____]
[_____]
[_____]

🧩 PARENT TIP:

Ask your child: "What do you think the ring represents? How do we build trust in our family?"

📜 POETRY PACK – *THE ENIGMATIC QUEST*

Poetry Style: Villanelle

🖋 *The Enigmatic Quest*

In the heart of the valley, beneath skies wide and vast,
Little Scatter stood brave, the Sacred Ring held fast.
If your only tool is a hammer, you see each problem as a nail.
Hope and worry mingled, as thunderclouds amassed,
Magic whispered of journeys, of legends from the past.
In the heart of the valley, beneath skies wide and vast.
"The ring speaks of safety," Scatter's voice cast,
Promises of shelter, from dangers so vast.
If your only tool is a hammer, you see each problem as a nail.
Adira questioned the truth, her tone overcast,

Is this ring true, will its guidance last?
In the heart of the valley, beneath skies wide and vast.
With a tale of old fires and paths long surpassed,
Scatter's faith in the ring, a contrast so vast.
If your only tool is a hammer, you see each problem as a nail.
Under starlit whispers, their fates forecast,
Together they'd journey, no doubts to outlast.
In the heart of the valley, beneath skies wide and vast,
If your only tool is a hammer, you see each problem as a nail.

☺ POETRY ACTIVITIES
ACTIVITY 1: Explore the Refrain
Find the two lines repeated throughout the poem:

1. [_____]

2.
   [_____]

WHY DO YOU THINK THEY ARE REPEATED?
   [_____]
   [_____]

ACTIVITY 2: FEELING THE RHYTHM
Read the poem aloud. Underline powerful or emotional words.
Circle words that feel like a *drumbeat* or *echo*.

ACTIVITY 3: FAMOUS QUOTE FOCUS
The line: *"If your only tool is a hammer, you see each problem as a nail."*
– What do you think this means?

– Have you ever seen someone solve a problem the wrong way?
Write your thoughts in 2–3 sentences:

[_____]
[_____]
[_____]
[_____]
[_____]
[_____]

ACTIVITY 4: FIND THE MOOD

Choose one mood: *Hopeful, Mysterious,* or *Worried*

Mood: _____

Proof from the poem:

[_____]
[_____]
[_____]
[_____]
[_____]
[_____]

ACTIVITY 5: WRITE YOUR OWN MINI VILLANELLE

CHOOSE TWO LINES TO REPEAT IN YOUR OWN 3-STANZA POEM.

Repeated Line 1:

[_____]
[_____]

REPEATED LINE 2:

[_____]
[_____]

. . .

MY MINI VILLANELLE:

[_____]
[_____]
[_____]
[_____]
[_____]
[_____]
[_____]
[_____]
[_____]
[_____]
[_____]
[_____]
[_____]
[_____]
[_____]

☑ END OF STUDENT WORKBOOK – CHAPTER THREE

AWESOME WORK! YOU'RE THINKING LIKE A TRUE READER AND leader. Keep turning the page—your journey is just beginning.

❧ 4 ❧

SCATTER'S STORY

Name: _____
Date: _____

SCATTER'S STORY

CHAPTER QUEST

▥ CORE READING SKILL FOCUS

📖 **Skill:** Character Development + Symbolism

◎ **WHY IT MATTERS:** HELPS STUDENTS RECOGNIZE HOW PERSONAL stories, symbols, and identity shape leadership and transformation.

🔍 **FOCUS IN THIS CHAPTER:** SCATTER USES STORYTELLING TO transform pain into pride. Students analyze how her self-worth evolves and track key symbols like the Sacred Ring and her tail. They connect this to real-life themes of belonging, identity, and voice.

📖 CHAPTER SUMMARY

In the moonlit valley of Wakaduo, a small pouched mouse named Scatter holds high the Sacred Ring of Journeys—an ancient artifact said to guide the brave. Many animals doubt her, thinking her too small to lead. But Scatter, with trembling courage, shares both the legend of the ring and her own painful past. Her honesty, along with support from Adira and others, helps unite the valley. By the end, Scatter becomes something more than small—she becomes a true leader.

Proverb: "A single bracelet does not jingle"

🐚 Proverb Expansion Prompt

(This is an excellent proverb for unity and support. Let's build a bridge to real life)

.   .   .

THINK ABOUT A TIME WHEN YOU NEEDED OTHERS TO HELP YOU succeed.

WHY IS IT HARD TO DO BIG THINGS ALONE?

HOW DO SCATTER'S FRIENDS HELP HER FEEL STRONG?

[_____]
[_____]
[_____]
[_____]
[_____]
[_____]
[_____]
[_____]
[_____]

1 VOCABULARY PRACTICE

Match the Word to Its Definition:
    1 Destiny
    2 Unity
    3 Ancestors
    4 Mosquito

Definitions:
    − A. Working together as one
    − B. Family from long ago
    − C. A fate or future meant to happen
    − D. A tiny insect that can still cause big trouble

FILL IN THE BLANKS:

    1. The animals were reminded that even a _____ can be powerful.

    2. Scatter believed it was her _____ to lead the

animals to safety.

    3. The ring was passed down by their _____.

    4. The animals chose _____ over fear.

▦ MORPHOLOGY FOCUS

WORD: DESTINY

    Root: *destin-* (to determine or set apart)

    Suffix: *-y* (state or quality)

    → The state of being meant for something

CHALLENGE WORD: ANCESTORS

    Root: *ante-* (before) + *cess* (to go)

    → Those who came before you in your family

☁ WORD PART CHALLENGE – CHAPTER 4

CAN YOU BUILD OR DECODE THESE WORDS?

MATCH THE PARTS BELOW TO THE CORRECT WORD:

    • **destin-** (to determine) + **-y** (state of)

    → _____

    • **ANTE-** (BEFORE) + **CESS** (TO GO)

    → _____

NOW WRITE:

    ✎ My Word: _____

. . .

✎ WHAT THE PARTS MEAN:

_____

✎ THE FULL WORD MEANS:

[_____]
[_____]

2 COMPREHENSION CHECK

Multiple Choice:

1. WHY DID SOME ANIMALS DOUBT SCATTER?
   A. She was too old
   B. She had no ring
   C. She was small
   D. She couldn't speak loudly

2. WHAT DID ADIRA SAY ABOUT TRUE STRENGTH?
   A. It's found in muscles
   B. It comes from surprising places
   C. It's something you're born with
   D. Only large animals have it

SHORT ANSWER:

1. What personal story did Scatter share that helped change the animals' minds?

[_____]
[_____]
[_____]
[_____]

. . .

2. WHY WAS IT IMPORTANT FOR SCATTER TO SPEAK HER TRUTH?

[_____]
[_____]
[_____]
[_____]

INFERENTIAL QUESTION:

Why do you think Scatter's honesty helped unite the animals more than the ring itself?

[_____]
[_____]
[_____]
[_____]
[_____]

⬛ SEQUENCING ACTIVITY

Put these in order (1–6):

___ Scatter stands before the animals with the Sacred Ring.
___ Some animals, like Ms. Guinea Fowl, doubt her.
___ Scatter explains the ring's history and power.
___ Scatter shares her personal story of being alone and judged.
___ Adira supports Scatter's leadership.
___ The animals prepare to follow her into the unknown.

⬛ CHARACTER TRAITS CHART

Scatter

Traits: Brave, Honest

What She Does: Shares her painful story and speaks up, even when scared

. . .

ADIRA

Traits: Wise, Encouraging

What She Does: Reminds everyone that leadership can come from surprising places

MS. GUINEA FOWL

Traits: Doubtful, Traditional

What She Does: Questions whether someone so small can truly lead

5 WRITING & REFLECTION

Short Essay Prompt

Scatter says:

"I used to hate the name *Scatter* because it reminded me of how everyone ran from me. But now? Now I wear it with pride."

✎ What does this tell us about self-esteem and personal growth?

SENTENCE STARTER:

This quote shows that Scatter has grown because...

Write 3–4 thoughtful sentences. You may also sketch something if it helps express your answer.

[_____]
[_____]
[_____]
[_____]
[_____]
[_____]
[_____]
[_____]

✏ OPTIONAL SKETCH:

[_____]

[_____]
[_____]
[_____]
[_____]
[_____]
[_____]

✎ Bonus Writing Prompt – Words That Change Us

Scatter says she used to hate her name. Now she wears it with pride.

Write about a name, word, or nickname that shaped how you feel about yourself—good or bad.

How do words shape who we are?

[_____]
[_____]
[_____]
[_____]
[_____]
[_____]
[_____]
[_____]

6 CREATIVE CORNER – *UNITY SYMBOL DESIGN*

Imagine a magical item like the Sacred Ring. What would it be?

Draw it here and describe what it would do to help unite a group.

✎ [Drawing space]

[_____]
[_____]
[_____]
[_____]
[_____]
[_____]

[_____]
[_____]
[_____]
[_____]
[_____]

DESIGN REFLECTION:

What is your unity item called?

What does it help people remember or feel?

✎ MY UNITY ITEM: _____

ITS POWER: _____

IT HELPS PEOPLE:

[_____]
[_____]

COLOR + EMOTION IDEAS:

- Silver = Harmony
- Yellow = Confidence
- Teal = Calm communication
- Indigo = Wisdom
- Red = Powerful truth

NAME OF YOUR ITEM: _____

ITS POWER: _____

7 BONUS: POETIC FLUENCY

Poem Title:
> *Tiny Feet on a Giant Path* – A Sonnet

READ THE SONNET ALOUD. HIGHLIGHT LINES THAT STAND OUT to you.

POETRY PACK

Chapter 4: Tiny Feet on a Giant Path
Poetry Style: Sonnet

SCATTER'S COURAGE

In Wakaduo's night, a small mouse stands tall,
Holding high a ring, ancient tales recall.
"If you think you're too small to change the flow,
Spend a night with the mosquito's echo."
  Brave Scatter speaks beneath the stars that light,
Her voice a whisper against the cool night.
Every creature listens, hope does swell,
In her tiny paws, a world's story she'll tell.
  "Though small, our might combined can shift fate's weight,
This ring, our guide to a future we create.
Let doubters hear, let skeptics see the sign,
In unity, our strength, together we align."
  From the smallest mouse to the tallest tree,
Every heart beats to the sound of unity.
Scatter's tale, a new legend we compose,
In her story, a giant's heart enclosed.

POETRY ACTIVITIES
ACTIVITY 1: Sonnet Structure Detective

– Count the lines: _____
– Find 2 rhyming line pairs:
1. _____ rhymes with _____
2. _____ rhymes with _____

ACTIVITY 2: SMALL BUT MIGHTY

The line: *"Spend a night with the mosquito's echo."*

– Have you ever seen a small thing or person make a big difference?

Write about it:

[_____]
[_____]
[_____]
[_____]
[_____]
[_____]

ACTIVITY 3: THEME TRACKER

Choose ONE theme:

A) Bravery can come from small places

B) Only strong creatures succeed

C) Legends are forgotten quickly

Copy a line from the poem that proves your answer:

[_____]
[_____]
[_____]
[_____]

ACTIVITY 4: PICTURE THE POEM

Draw or describe what comes to mind when you read:

"In her tiny paws, a world's story she'll tell."

✎ [Sketch area or space for writing]

[_____]

[_____]
[_____]
[_____]
[_____]
[_____]
[_____]

ACTIVITY 5: Write Your Own Line of Hope

Pretend you are Scatter inspiring the crowd.

Write one powerful sentence:

"My words to inspire:

[_____]
[_____]
[_____]

✅ You're a leader like Scatter!

Keep going—one brave word at a time.

JOURNAL 1: AFTER CHAPTER 4 – THE CROSSING BEGINS

Journal Reflection

Use this space to reflect on what you've read, how your thinking is changing, and how the story connects to your own life

Chapters 1–4 Summary: Characters are introduced. The journey begins. Students meet the forest world and face early challenges that test their cooperation and courage.

Page 1 – Reflect & Write
Prompt 1:

"I used to think… but now I think…"

➤ About what it means to be brave

[_____]
[_____]
[_____]
[_____]
[_____]
[_____]
[_____]
[_____]

Prompt 2:

What surprised you most about the first part of the journey? Why?

[_____]
[_____]
[_____]
[_____]
[_____]
[_____]

Prompt 3:

Who do you think you'd be friends with in the story so far? What makes you connect with them?

[_____]
[_____]
[_____]
[_____]

Page 2 – Create & Connect

• **Draw** a map of the journey so far — where have they gone?

• **Write** a short poem from the forest's point of view (What does it see or feel about the travelers?)

[_____]
[_____]
[_____]
[_____]
[_____]
[_____]
[_____]
[_____]
[_____]
[_____]
[_____]
[_____]
[_____]

THE GATHERING

N ame: _____
Date: _____

THE GATHERING

CHAPTER QUEST

CORE READING SKILL FOCUS

Skill: Making Inferences + Analyzing Tone

WHY IT MATTERS: BUILDS DEEPER READING BY TEACHING students to interpret what characters feel or decide even when it isn't directly stated. Tone analysis strengthens emotional literacy.

. . .

🔍 **Focus in This Chapter:** Students infer emotions from dialogue and group dynamics during a pivotal decision. Characters wrestle with risk, courage, and loyalty. Adira's tone contrasts with Polly's, and Scatter grows as a leader by listening, not commanding.

1 CHAPTER RECAP: WHAT HAPPENED?

As night falls on Wakaduo, the animals gather at the edge of the Desert of No Return. Adira tells the story of Kabora the Lion, warning them of the mirage-filled desert ahead. Tension fills the air. Scatter clutches the Sacred Ring, unsure of her next step. But at dawn, her friends—Tusker, Henry, and Ernie—stand by her side. Their unity sparks hope, and the animals choose to journey forward with faith and purpose.

2 VOCABULARY IN CONTEXT

Match the Word to Its Meaning:
- Threshold –
- Allegiance –
- Mirage –
- Seriousness –

A. Loyalty to a cause or leader

B. An illusion, especially in the desert

C. A starting point or doorway

D. Importance, not to be taken lightly

NOW USE EACH WORD IN A SENTENCE ABOUT THE CHAPTER:

1 Threshold:

[_____]
[_____]
[_____]

2 MIRAGE:

[_____]
[_____]
[_____]

3 ALLEGIANCE:

[_____]
[_____]
[_____]

4 SERIOUSNESS:

[_____]
[_____]
[_____]
[_____]

MORPHOLOGY BONUS

WORD: MIRAGE

Root: *mirare* (Latin: to wonder or look at)

Suffix: *-age* (forms a noun)

→ *Mirage*: Something that appears real but isn't, especially due to heat or light

Challenge Word: Allegiance

Prefix: *al-* (to, toward)

Root: *liege* (feudal lord, one you owe loyalty to)

→ *Allegiance*: A deep commitment or loyalty

Word Builder Challenge – Chapter 5
Match each word part to the word it helps form:

• **MIR-** = TO LOOK OR WONDER

→ _____

• **-AGE** = FORMS A NOUN (THING OR ACTION)

→ _____

• **LIEGE** = A LORD OR ONE OWED LOYALTY

→ _____

• **AL-** = TOWARD

→ _____

Now explain one word in your own words:

. . .

✎ My word: _____

✎ I think it means:

[_____]
[_____]

✎ Because:

[_____]
[_____]

🔍 ❸ COMPREHENSION CHECK

Multiple Choice:

1 WHAT MAKES THE DESERT OF NO RETURN DANGEROUS?
   A. It is filled with lions
   B. It's very cold
   C. It has illusions and is hard to cross
   D. No animals have ever seen it

2 WHY DOES ADIRA TELL THE STORY OF KABORA THE LION?
   A. To scare the animals away
   B. To teach a lesson about pride and risk
   C. To entertain the crowd
   D. To honor Kabora's bravery

SHORT ANSWER:
   1. What emotions does Scatter feel during the gathering?

[_____]
[_____]

[_____]
[_____]

2. How do the other animals influence Scatter's decision to move forward?

[_____]
[_____]
[_____]
[_____]
[_____]

Inferential Thinking:

Why is it more powerful that the animals choose to follow Scatter, rather than being forced?

[_____]
[_____]
[_____]
[_____]
[_____]
[_____]

CAUSE & EFFECT

Match each cause to its correct effect:

• **Adira warns of desert illusions.** → B. Others become hesitant and reflect seriously

• **Polly the Parrot questions the legends.** → A. Some animals begin to doubt the journey

• **Henry pledges his support.** → C. The animals begin to feel inspired and hopeful

• **Scatter questions her leadership.** → D. Her friends' support helps her believe again

🔢 5️⃣ SEQUENCE OF EVENTS

Place these in order (1–7):

___ Scatter holds the ring and feels unsure

___ Polly the Parrot expresses doubt

___ Adira tells the story of Kabora the Lion

___ Henry the Honey Badger declares his bravery

___ The group debates the journey

___ Ernie, Tusker, and Henry stand with Scatter

___ They decide to travel to the Tree of Life

👥 6️⃣ CHARACTER REFLECTION

Character: Adira

Trait: Wise

What they do: Tells the cautionary tale of Kabora to guide and prepare the group

Character: Scatter

Trait: Courageous

What they do: Holds the ring, wrestles with doubt, and eventually steps forward

Character: Henry

Trait: Loyal

What they do: Declares his support, inspiring others to follow Scatter

Character: Polly

Trait: Doubtful

What they do: Voices concerns about the legends and the risks of the journey

🎤 Tone Tracker (SoR: Inference + Expression)

Choose two characters and write how their tone sounded during the Gathering:

Adira's tone was: _____

Polly's tone was: _____
What this tells me about them:

[_____]
[_____]
[_____]
[_____]
[_____]
[_____]
[_____]
[_____]

✍ 7 SHORT WRITING: PERSONAL REFLECTION

Prompt: Scatter doubts herself but still steps forward. Think of a time when you had to make a hard decision or take a risk. What helped you move forward?

Sentence Starter:

One time I felt unsure but kept going was when...
Write 3–4 sentences about your experience:

[_____]
[_____]
[_____]
[_____]
[_____]
[_____]
[_____]

🖌 8 CREATIVE CORNER: DESIGN YOUR DESERT SURVIVAL KIT 🐫 🌵

If you were about to cross the Desert of No Return, what would you bring? Draw or list at least **5 items** and explain why.

List:

1.

[_____]
[_____]

. . .

2.

[_____]
[_____]

3.

[_____]
[_____]
[_____]

4.

[_____]
[_____]
[_____]

5.

[_____]
[_____]
[_____]

DRAW:

[_____]
[_____]
[_____]
[_____]
[_____]
[_____]
[_____]
[_____]
[_____]
[_____]
[_____]

[_____]

COLOR & EMOTION PALETTE IDEAS
- Sand Yellow = caution, clarity
- Rust Orange = heat, bravery
- Deep Blue = calm under pressure
- Bone White = mystery, ancient secrets

BONUS: POETRY IN MOTION

Read this quote aloud:

"If we do not stand together, we will not stand at all." – Adira

Try reading it three ways:
- Serious and calm
- Loud and inspiring
- Quiet and emotional

WHICH ONE FELT MOST POWERFUL TO YOU AND WHY?

[_____]
[_____]
[_____]
[_____]

CER WRITING (CLAIM–EVIDENCE–REASONING)

Title: Chapter 5 — *The Gathering*

Prompt: Why was it important that Scatter had the support of her friends before crossing the desert?

CLAIM

Starter:

I believe it was important that Scatter had her friends' support because...

[_____]
[_____]

. . .

📚 EVIDENCE
✎ Starters:
• In the story it says...
• One example is when...
• The author shows that...

[_____]
[_____]

REASONING
✎ Starters:
• This shows that...
• This proves that...
• This means...

[_____]
[_____]

✐ CER Bonus Prompt – Proverb Focus
Proverb: *"If we do not stand together, we will not stand at all."*

🐾 CLAIM
✎ I believe this proverb matters because...

[_____]
[_____]
[_____]

📚 EVIDENCE
✎ In the story, we see this when...

[_____]
[_____]
[_____]

. . .

REASONING
✎ This shows that...

[_____]
[_____]
[_____]

◉ QUICK CHECKLIST
☑ Clear claim?
☑ Strong evidence?
☑ Good explanation?

BONUS (OPTIONAL):

Design a **Symbol of Support** — a token Scatter could carry that represents the loyalty of her friends. What would it look like?

📷 ✎

[Drawing Space]

[_____]
[_____]
[_____]
[_____]
[_____]
[_____]
[_____]
[_____]
[_____]
[_____]
[_____]
[_____]

CHALLENGE PROMPT:

What shape or symbol would represent the strength of being supported by others?

[_____]
[_____]
[_____]

✅ YOU'RE READY TO FACE ANY DESERT—ESPECIALLY WHEN YOU stand together.

Onward, brave reader!

❧ 6 ❧

THE TREE OF LIFE

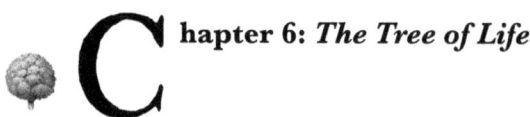 **C**hapter 6: *The Tree of Life*

NAME: _____

Date: _____

🧠 **CHAPTER PROVERB**
   "Wisdom is like a baobab tree—no one individual can embrace it alone."

CHAPTER QUEST

📖 CORE READING SKILL FOCUS

📖 **Skill:** Figurative Language + Theme Development

· · ·

◎ **WHY IT MATTERS:** TEACHES STUDENTS TO DECODE METAPHOR, allegory, and symbolism to understand deeper messages about growth, unity, and sacrifice.

◌ **FOCUS IN THIS CHAPTER:**

Students interpret the Tree of Life, offerings, and Queen Bee as symbols. They identify theme through characters' choices and metaphorical gifts. Scatter's pebble and Henry's struggle with honey reveal personal transformation and team unity.

⊔ CHAPTER SUMMARY

At the heart of Wakaduo stands the ancient Tree of Life. When Scatter and the other animals reach it, they expect answers. Instead, they are met with silence, carvings, and riddles hidden in the bark. There is no map, no clear direction—only a test of unity and character. To move forward, each hero must offer something personal. Together, their offerings awaken the tree's truth: wisdom isn't given to one, but earned by many—together.

▧ VOCABULARY PRACTICE & MORPHOLOGY

WORD LIST:
   • **Embrace** – To hold closely or accept willingly

- **Wisdom** – Knowledge and good judgment
- **Interwoven** – Woven together; deeply connected
- **Revelation** – A surprising or important discovery

MORPHOLOGY FOCUS:
- **Prefix: em-** = in, into → *embrace*
- **Prefix: re-** = again → *revelation*
- **Prefix: inter-** = between → *interwoven*

MATCH THE PREFIX TO ITS MEANING:
inter- = _____
em- = _____
re- = _____

BONUS CHALLENGE WORD:
- **Revelation** (re- = again, *velare* = to unveil in Latin)
→ What does *revelation* suggest about how truth is found?

[_____]
  [_____]
  [_____]

🔖 WORD PART DECODER – CHAPTER 6

🔠 INTERACTIVE MORPHOLOGY MATCHING

MATCH THE WORD PARTS TO THEIR FULL WORDS:

·   ·   ·

• **EM-** (IN, INTO) → _____

• **RE-** (AGAIN) + **VELARE** (TO UNVEIL)
  → _____

• **INTER-** (BETWEEN) + **WOVEN**
  → _____

CHOOSE ONE TO EXPLAIN:
  ✎ I chose: _____

✎ WHAT IT MEANS:
  [_____]
  [_____]

✎ THE WORD PARTS HELPED ME BECAUSE:
  [_____]
  [_____]

🔍 READING COMPREHENSION CHECK

1. What surprises the group about the Tree of Life?
  ✎
  [_____]
  [_____]
  [_____]

2. HOW DO THE ANIMALS BEGIN TO UNDERSTAND THE TREE'S RIDDLE?
  ✎

[_____]
[_____]
[_____]

3. WHY IS IT IMPORTANT THEY SOLVE IT *TOGETHER*?

[_____]
[_____]
[_____]

🌳 MEANING BEHIND THE OFFERING

Each animal gave something personal to the Tree of Life. These gifts were not just items—they were symbols of who they are and what they believe.

✎ Write about each character's offering:

1. SCATTER

Gift: _____

What it symbolizes:

[_____]

2. HENRY

Gift: _____

What it symbolizes:

[_____]

3. ADIRA (OR ANOTHER ANIMAL)

Gift: _____

What it symbolizes:

[_____]

● PREDICTION LADDER

1 What might happen if the animals can't agree on the riddle's meaning?

[_____]
[_____]

2 WHO MIGHT STEP UP NEXT TO HELP SOLVE THE MYSTERY?

[_____]
[_____]

3 WHAT DANGER COULD BE APPROACHING?

[_____]
[_____]

▤ FLUENCY & PROSODY PRACTICE

Read Aloud This Passage:

"The branches twisted above them like outstretched arms, heavy with silence and time. Scatter felt the hush, not as absence—but as invitation."

✔ I paused for effect
✔ I used tone to show mood
✔ I emphasized words like *silence* and *invitation*

PARTNER FEEDBACK:

"You sounded most powerful when you read:

[_____]
[_____]

🌐 REAL-WORLD REFLECTION

Proverb Connection:

"Wisdom is like a baobab tree—no one individual can embrace it alone."

Prompt:

Write about a time you needed help from others to understand something or solve a big problem. What did that experience teach you?

[_____]
[_____]
[_____]
[_____]
[_____]
[_____]

🌸 REFLECTION PROMPT: *COMMUNITY OF THOUGHT*

Scatter realizes the answer isn't just inside her—it's inside all of them.

Write about a time when *you* realized you didn't have to do something alone.

[_____]
[_____]
[_____]
[_____]
[_____]
[_____]
[_____]
[_____]
[_____]
[_____]

✍ CER WRITING: CLAIM–EVIDENCE–REASONING

Prompt: What lesson did Scatter and her friends learn from the Tree of Life?

🐿 CLAIM
I believe Scatter and her friends learned that...

[_____]
[_____]

📚 EVIDENCE
- In the story it says...
- One example is when...
- The author shows that...

[_____]
[_____]

REASONING
- This shows that...
- This proves that...
- This means...

[_____]
[_____]
[_____]
[_____]

☑ QUICK CHECKLIST:
✔ Did I make a clear claim?
✔ Did I support it with evidence?
✔ Did I explain my thinking?

DIFFERENTIATED CER WORKSHEET – CHAPTER 6

Prompt: What lesson did Scatter and her friends learn from the Tree of Life? (For developing writers or ELL learners)

CLAIM

I believe that Scatter and her friends learned that

[_____]
[_____]

BECAUSE

[_____]
[_____]

EVIDENCE

In the story it says,

[_____]
[_____]

WHICH SHOWS THAT

[_____]
[_____]
[_____]
[_____]

ANOTHER EXAMPLE IS WHEN

[_____]
[_____]

. . .

REASONING

This shows that

[_____]
[_____]

BECAUSE

[_____]
[_____]

IT MEANS THAT

[_____]
[_____]

✅ Quick Checklist

✔ I made a strong claim

✔ I used a real quote

✔ I explained my thinking

BONUS: DESIGN THE TREE OF LIFE

Draw the Tree glowing with light.

• Add the offerings from each hero

• Include bees, roots, or your own symbols of wisdom and unity

🖊 MY DRAWING:

[_____]
[_____]
[_____]
[_____]
[_____]
[_____]
[_____]
[_____]

[_____]
[_____]

My Tree Teaches:

[_____]
[_____]
[_____]

Second Differentiated Version - CER Worksheet

DIFFERENTIATED CER WORKSHEET

Prompt: *What lesson did Scatter and her friends learn from the Tree of Life?*

This version is scaffolded for emerging writers and ELL students, with sentence starters directly built into the response lines.

CLAIM (What do you believe?)

I believe that Scatter and her friends learned that

[_____]
[_____]
[_____]

BECAUSE

[_____]
[_____]
[_____]

EVIDENCE (What part of the story supports your answer?)

In the story it says,

[_____]
[_____]
[_____]

WHICH SHOWS THAT

[_____]
[_____]
[_____]
[_____]

ANOTHER EXAMPLE IS WHEN

[_____]
[_____]
[_____]
[_____]

REASONING (WHY DOES THAT PROVE YOUR ANSWER IS **true?**)

This shows that

[_____]
[_____]

BECAUSE

[_____]
[_____]
[_____]
[_____]

IT MEANS THAT

[_____]

[_____]
[_____]
[_____]

FINAL REFLECTION (WHAT CHANGED?)

Why do you think the Tree of Life stayed silent until **everyone gave something**?

[_____]
[_____]
[_____]
[_____]
[_____]
[_____]
[_____]

QUICK CHECKLIST:

✓ I made a strong **claim**.

✓ I found **evidence** from the story.

✓ I **explained** my thinking clearly.

BONUS ACTIVITY: DESIGN THE TREE OF LIFE

Draw the Tree glowing with magic.

• Add each hero's offering around the roots

• Include bees, leaves, or symbols of unity and growth

My drawing:

[_____]
[_____]
[_____]
[_____]
[_____]
[_____]

[_____]
[_____]
[_____]
[_____]

My Tree Teaches:

[_____]
[_____]
[_____]
[_____]
[_____]

✎ OPTIONAL CREATIVE WRITING EXTENSION

Prompt:

Imagine you're standing before the Tree of Life. It glows, waiting. You must offer something personal.

WRITE A SHORT PARAGRAPH DESCRIBING YOUR OFFERING AND WHAT it says about your past—and your future.

[_____]
[_____]
[_____]
[_____]
[_____]
[_____]
[_____]
[_____]
[_____]
[_____]
[_____]
[_____]

ROBERT G. WAUGH

[_____]
[_____]
[_____]
[_____]

ANCHOR CHART

What Makes a Gift Meaningful?

Character	What They Gave	Why It Mattered
Scatter	A small pebble	It reminded her she wasn't alone
Tusker	Shed skin	Showed she had grown and endured
Ernie	A note from a lost friend	Honored memory and connection
Henry	His favorite treat (eventually!)	Showed he could overcome temptation

✻ 7 ✻
THE DESERT OF NO RETURN

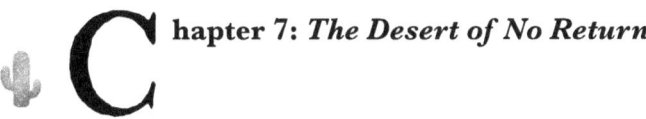 **C**hapter 7: *The Desert of No Return*

NAME: _____

   Date: _____

CHAPTER QUEST

📖 CORE READING SKILL FOCUS

📖 **Skill:** Symbolism + Cause and Effect

◎ **WHY IT MATTERS:** HELPS STUDENTS IDENTIFY DEEPER MEANINGS behind story elements and understand how character choices lead to major consequences.

. . .

🔍 **Focus in This Chapter:** STUDENTS ANALYZE THE MIRAGE AS A symbol of false hope and distraction. They track how choices (like Henry's) ripple through the group and deepen the theme of resilience. Through cause-and-effect mapping, students see how grief becomes a turning point in the team's unity and survival.

📖 CHAPTER SUMMARY

As the animals journey deeper into the treacherous desert, illusions blur their path. Heat waves, haunting silence, and shifting dunes test their unity. Tusker tells the tale of the Silent Caravan, and Henry, chasing a mirage, vanishes. Fear spreads, but Scatter leads the group with resolve. Together, they learn that survival in the "Desert of No Return" requires more than strength—it demands wisdom, team-work, and trust in one another.

The stark white sands of the Desert of No Return—silent, endless, and full of secrets.

🔤 VOCABULARY BUILDER & MORPHOLOGY

A. Match the Word to Its Meaning

WRITE THE CORRECT LETTER NEXT TO EACH WORD.

· · ·

Word Bank:

A. A false image, often water, seen in the heat

B. Dangerous and full of hidden risks

C. Very large, wide, and open

D. Silent guards or watchers

E. Disappeared completely and suddenly

• Mirage: _____

• Treacherous: _____

• Vast: _____

• Sentinels: _____

• Vanished: _____

B. Fill in the Blanks

Use these words: **mirage, treacherous, vast, sentinels, vanished**

1 Henry thought the water was real, but it was just a _____.

2 The _____ desert stretched before them, hot and empty.

3 The dead trees looked like _____ watching the travelers.

4 The sandstorm was _____, hiding dangers they could not see.

5 One minute Henry was there, and the next he _____.

Morphology Fix:

• **Mirage**: *Root:* mirare (to look/wonder) + *Suffix:* -age → "something that appears but isn't real."

• **Treacherous**: *Root:* trechier (to cheat, trick)

• **Vast**: Latin *vastus* (empty, enormous)

• **Sentinels**: *Root:* sentire (to feel/perceive)

• **Vanished**: *Prefix:* van- (to go) + *Suffix:* -ish (verb-forming) → "disappeared suddenly"

. . .

🝜 WORD PART DECODER: MORPHOLOGY MATCHING
Chapter Title: The Desert of No Return

SKILL FOCUS: MORPHOLOGY + VOCABULARY RECOGNITION

STUDENT INSTRUCTION: MATCH EACH WORD PART TO ITS MEANING, then decode the full word. Use clues from the story to figure out why the word matters in the desert journey.

MATCH THE WORD PARTS
Write the correct letter next to each word part.
Prefixes / Roots / Suffixes:
- mirare
- sentire
- van-
- -ish
- -age
- trech-
- vastus

DEFINITIONS:
- A. To disappear
- B. Related to size or emptiness
- C. A false appearance
- D. To cheat or trick
- E. To look or gaze
- F. To feel or perceive
- G. A verb ending (shows action)

. . .

✎ DECODE THE FULL WORD

Now use the word parts to define each vocabulary word in your own words.

1. MIRAGE

Word Parts: *mirare* + *-age*

🧠 Meaning in the story:

[_____]
[_____]

2. TREACHEROUS

Word Part: *trech-*

🧠 Meaning in the story:

[_____]
[_____]
[_____]

3. VAST

Word Part: *vastus*

🧠 Meaning in the story:

[_____]
[_____]
[_____]
[_____]

4. SENTINELS

Word Part: *sentire*

🧠 Meaning in the story:

[_____]
[_____]
[_____]
[_____]

· · ·

5. VANISHED

Word Parts: *van-* + *-ish*

🔖 Meaning in the story:

[_____]
[_____]
[_____]
[_____]

📖 READING COMPREHENSION

A. Multiple Choice

Choose the best answer.

1 What does the proverb **"The Sun is the King of Torches"** mean in the story?

☐ A) The sun is kind to travelers

☐ B) The sun is the leader of fire

☐ C) The sun lights the way but burns with power

☐ D) The sun helps them find water

2 WHY DOES TUSKER TELL THE STORY OF THE SILENT CARAVAN?

☐ A) To warn Scatter about ghosts

☐ B) To remind them not to sleep in the desert

☐ C) To pass the time

☐ D) To help them understand the dangers and mystery of the desert

3 WHAT HAPPENS TO HENRY IN THIS CHAPTER?

☐ A) He gets rescued by the group

☐ B) He finds a real oasis

☐ C) He runs toward a mirage and disappears

☐ D) He climbs a dune to look around

· · ·

4 WHAT DO THE **RED DUNES OF TIME** SYMBOLIZE IN THE STORY?

☐ A) A resting place

☐ B) The end of the desert

☐ C) A place where time and memory live

☐ D) A meeting place for all animals

B. SHORT ANSWER QUESTIONS

Answer in 1–2 full sentences.

1. WHY DOES SCATTER SAY, "WE WILL NOT BE NEXT"?

[_____]
[_____]
[_____]
[_____]
[_____]
[_____]

2. WHAT LESSON DOES THE GROUP LEARN ABOUT ILLUSIONS IN THE desert?

[_____]
[_____]
[_____]
[_____]

3 WHAT DOES TUSKER'S CHILDHOOD STORY TEACH THE OTHERS?

[_____]
[_____]
[_____]
[_____]

. . .

4 How does the group's unity help them through the journey?

[_____]
[_____]
[_____]
[_____]

CHARACTER REFLECTION

Scatter

- What is one trait Scatter shows in this chapter?
- How does she act like a leader during the desert test?

[_____]
[_____]
[_____]
[_____]
[_____]
[_____]
[_____]
[_____]

Tusker

- What wise action does Tusker take to help the group understand their danger?
- What does this show about his role in the journey?

[_____]
[_____]
[_____]
[_____]
[_____]
[_____]
[_____]

[_____]
[_____]

Henry

- Why does Henry chase the mirage?
- What does his mistake teach the others?

[_____]
[_____]
[_____]
[_____]
[_____]
[_____]
[_____]
[_____]
[_____]
[_____]

Ernie

- How does Ernie help from above?
- What makes his point of view valuable?

[_____]
[_____]
[_____]
[_____]
[_____]
[_____]
[_____]
[_____]
[_____]
[_____]

▮ CAUSE & EFFECT MATCHING

Draw lines to match the cause with its effect.

Cause:
- They sing while walking
- Henry runs toward a mirage
- They remember the Tree of Life
- Tusker shares a story

EFFECT:
- The group understands the desert better
- He vanishes
- They feel closer and stronger
- They find small oases

● PREDICTION PROMPT

What do you think will happen next at the **Red Dunes of Time**?

Will Henry return? Will the group stay strong?

✎ Write 4–5 sentences:

[_____]
[_____]
[_____]
[_____]
[_____]
[_____]
[_____]
[_____]
[_____]
[_____]
[_____]
[_____]

✎ VISUAL LEARNING

Choose one scene to draw:

- ✎ A. Henry running toward the mirage
- ✎ B. Tusker telling the story of the Silent Caravan
- ✎ C. The heroes reaching the Red Dunes at sunset
- ✎ Caption your drawing with a favorite line from the story:

[_____]
[_____]
[_____]
[_____]
[_____]
[_____]
[_____]
[_____]
[_____]
[_____]
[_____]
[_____]

✐ SCHEMA CONNECTION

Think of a time you believed something was real... but it wasn't.

- • What happened?
- • How did it make you feel?
- • What did you learn from it?
- ✎ Write a few sentences:

[_____]
[_____]
[_____]
[_____]
[_____]
[_____]
[_____]
[_____]

[_____]
[_____]
[_____]
[_____]

✍ CREATIVE WRITING PROMPT

Choose one:

A. Journal Entry from Scatter

"Dear Journal, I thought Henry was right behind me. But the desert… it doesn't forgive mistakes…"

B. Rewrite the Moment

What if Henry had stopped just in time? Rewrite how the moment might have changed.

C. Poem – "Whispers in the Sand"

Write a short poem about illusion, heat, bravery, or fear.

✍ Write your response:

[_____]
[_____]
[_____]
[_____]
[_____]
[_____]
[_____]
[_____]
[_____]
[_____]
[_____]
[_____]

✐ CER WRITING – CLAIM–EVIDENCE–REASONING

Title: The Desert of No Return

Prompt: What lesson did Scatter and her friends learn from their journey through the desert?

· · ·

CLAIM

I believe that Scatter and her friends learned that…

[_____]
[_____]

BECAUSE

[_____]
[_____]

EVIDENCE

In the story it says,

[_____]
[_____]

WHICH SHOWS THAT

[_____]
[_____]
[_____]

ANOTHER EXAMPLE IS WHEN

[_____]
[_____]
[_____]
[_____]
[_____]

REASONING

This shows that

[_____]
[_____]
[_____]

[_____]

BECAUSE

[_____]
[_____]
[_____]

IT MEANS THAT

[_____]
[_____]
[_____]
[_____]

BONUS DRAWING: THE MIRAGE

Draw what Henry thought he saw in the mirage. What was real? What wasn't?

[_____]
[_____]
[_____]
[_____]
[_____]
[_____]
[_____]
[_____]
[_____]

CAPTION:

[_____]
[_____]

▨ POETRY PACK: *THE DESERT'S TEST* (CINQUAIN SEQUENCE)

Poem Text:

⚊ Desert

Vast, harsh,
Whispering, shifting, testing,
Hides its deep secrets,
Expanse.

⚊ Sand dunes

Endless, red,
Rolling, towering, daunting,
Challenge the bravest hearts,
Silence.

⚊ Journey

Tough, long,
Walking, enduring, hoping,
Seeking paths never found,
Quest.

☻ Heroes

United, strong,
Supporting, believing, striving,
Facing fears together,
Band.

◎ POETRY ACTIVITIES

ACTIVITY 1: Cinquain Shape Detectives

Label each line of Cinquain 1:

1 _____ (noun)
2 _____ (2 adjectives)
3 _____ (3 verbs)
4 _____ (a phrase or sentence)
5 _____ (synonym or summary word)

. . .

ACTIVITY 2: PICTURE IT!

Choose one cinquain and draw what it describes. Add colors, shapes, feelings.

[_____]
[_____]
[_____]
[_____]
[_____]
[_____]
[_____]
[_____]

ACTIVITY 3: SECRET MESSAGE

What does Cinquain 4 ("Heroes") teach about bravery or teamwork?

[_____]
[_____]
[_____]
[_____]
[_____]

ACTIVITY 4: WRITE YOUR OWN DESERT CINQUAIN

1. NOUN:

2. ADJECTIVES:

3. VERBS:

.   .   .

4. PHRASE:

5. FINAL WORD:

ACTIVITY 5: WORD POWER!
Circle or list examples of:
• Movement words: _____
• Feeling words: _____
• Bravery words: _____

❧ FINAL REFLECTION – EXIT TICKET

1 One thing I learned about courage or leadership in this chapter:

[_____]
[_____]
[_____]

2 ONE QUESTION I STILL HAVE IS:

[_____]
[_____]
[_____]

☑ END OF STUDENT WORKBOOK – CHAPTER SEVEN
You've faced the desert, found the truth, and stayed strong—just like a real Wakaduo hero. Keep going!

8

MOUNTAINS OF THE MOON

C hapter 8: Mountains of the Moon
Name: _____
Date: _____

CHAPTER PROVERB
"However long the night, the dawn will break."

CHAPTER QUEST - CORE READING SKILL FOCUS

Skill: Inferring Theme Through Metaphor + Character Reflection

WHY IT MATTERS: STRENGTHENS COMPREHENSION BY TEACHING students to interpret dreams, settings, and symbolic moments to uncover character transformation and big-picture meaning.

. . .

🔍 **Focus in This Chapter:** Students infer how each dream trial reveals the heroes' inner strengths and identities. The mountain serves as a metaphor for growth. Through figurative language and dream analysis, students connect the characters' emotional journeys to their own lives and discover how reflection builds leadership.

📖 CHAPTER SUMMARY

After crossing the harsh desert, the group begins climbing the mysterious **Mountains of the Moon**. Every hero is tested—not by monsters, but by memory, fear, and longing. Scatter wonders if she's truly brave. Tusker questions the meaning of strength. Ernie finds power in creativity. Even Henry, far away, begins to dream of changing. When they reach the summit, their dreams reveal who they really are—and who they're becoming. With dawn breaking, they descend into a hidden paradise.

VOCABULARY & DECODING PRACTICE

Word List:

- **Majestic** – Grand or impressive
- **Enchantment** – Magical charm or feeling
- **Resilient** – Able to bounce back
- **Breathtaking** – So beautiful it takes your breath away

WORD STRUCTURE PRACTICE

Look at the word: **resilient**
- Prefix = _____
- Root = _____

What does the word mean in this chapter?

[_____]
[_____]

DECODING EXAMPLES:

- *majestic* → maj- (great) + -estic (having)
- *resilient* → re- + silient (jump, stand)

QUICK CHALLENGE:

Break the word "rugged" into two syllables and describe what it means in the chapter.

[_____]
[_____]
[_____]
[_____]
[_____]
[_____]
[_____]

WORD PART DECODER: MORPHOLOGY MATCHING

SKILL FOCUS: MORPHOLOGY + METAPHORICAL THINKING

. . .

STUDENT INSTRUCTION: BREAK APART THE VOCABULARY TO UNLOCK the hidden meaning inside. These words help describe what the characters face as they climb inward and upward.

MATCH THE WORD PARTS
Write the correct letter next to each part.
Prefixes / Roots / Suffixes:
- re-
- silient (from *salire*)
- maj-
- -estic
- en-
- chant (from *cantare*)
- breath-

DEFINITIONS:
A. Great or grand
B. To jump or leap
C. To put into
D. To sing or speak
E. To take in air
F. A suffix meaning "having the quality of"
G. Again or back

DECODE THE FULL WORD
Use the word parts to define the vocabulary in your own words.
1. Resilient
Word Parts: *re-* + *silient (salire)*
Meaning in the story:
[_____]
[_____]

. . .

2. Majestic

Word Parts: *maj-* + *-estic*

🧠 Meaning in the story:

[_____]
[_____]

3. Enchantment

Word Parts: *en-* + *chant*

🧠 Meaning in the story:

[_____]
[_____]
[_____]

4. Breathtaking

Word Part: *breath-*

🧠 Meaning in the story:

[_____]
[_____]
[_____]

📖 READING COMPREHENSION

Answer in complete sentences.

1. What emotions do the characters feel when they see the Mountains of the Moon?

[_____]
[_____]
[_____]

. . .

2. How do the dream trials help the animals understand themselves?

[_____]
[_____]
[_____]

3. What do the mountains symbolize in this chapter?

[_____]
[_____]
[_____]

⌁ PREDICTION LADDER

1. What do you think lies beyond the valley?

[_____]
[_____]
[_____]

2. Will Henry rejoin the group—and how might he have changed?

[_____]
[_____]
[_____]

3. What challenge might test what they've just learned?

[_____]
[_____]
[_____]

♫ FLUENCY & EXPRESSION PRACTICE

Read this aloud with drama and feeling:

"The mist curled around them like a blanket woven from stardust and time. In their dreams, they stood at the edge of who they were—and who they were becoming."

CHECKLIST:
- ☐ I paused at commas
- ☐ I used tone to show mystery and awe
- ☐ I emphasized poetic or emotional words

PARTNER FEEDBACK:

You made the moment feel _____ when you read

_____.

🌑 SCHEMA BUILDER: REAL-WORLD CONNECTION

Think of a personal challenge that helped you grow (even if it was scary or hard at first).

Write your "mountain moment" below:

[_____]
[_____]
[_____]
[_____]
[_____]
[_____]
[_____]
[_____]
[_____]

REFLECTION PROMPT: WHO ARE YOU BECOMING?

If you had a dream in the Mountains of the Moon, what would it show you about your strength or potential?

[_____]
[_____]
[_____]
[_____]
[_____]
[_____]

✍ CER WRITING — CLAIM, EVIDENCE, REASONING

Chapter 8: Dream Trials on the Mountain

Prompt: What lesson did the characters learn from their Dream Trials in the Mountains of the Moon?

🐾 CLAIM

I believe the characters learned

[_____]
[_____]

BECAUSE

[_____]
[_____]

📚 EVIDENCE

In the story, it says

[_____]
[_____]

. . .

AND ANOTHER EXAMPLE IS WHEN

[_____]
[_____]

REASONING
This shows that

[_____]
[_____]
[_____]

BECAUSE

[_____]
[_____]
[_____]

✅ CHECKLIST
☐ Clear claim
☐ Quote or example from the story
☐ Reasoning that explains your thinking

POETRY PACK

Chapter 8: *The Mountain's Challenge*

POETRY TYPE: ACROSTIC

MOUNTAINS
Majestic peaks touch the sky,
Offering challenges, high and dry.
Under stars, they whisper old tales,
Navigating through their rugged trails.
Trails that twist, turn, and ascend,
Above the world, they seem to suspend.

Inspiring those who dare to climb,
Nurturing dreams, transcending time.
Secrets held in their misty embrace,
beckoning the brave to chase.

☺ STUDENT POETRY ACTIVITIES

ACTIVITY 1: FIND THE HIDDEN WORD!

An acrostic spells a word down the side. What word is it?

Hidden Word: _____

ACTIVITY 2: POETRY DETECTIVE

Which line shows:

Adventure:

[_____]
[_____]
[_____]
[_____]
[_____]

NATURE OR BEAUTY:

[_____]
[_____]
[_____]
[_____]
[_____]

ACTIVITY 3: DRAW YOUR MOUNTAIN

Use words from the poem like **majestic**, **twist**, **ascend**, or **misty** to draw or describe the mountain in your imagination.

Sketch or description:

[_____]
[_____]
[_____]
[_____]
[_____]
[_____]
[_____]
[_____]
[_____]
[_____]
[_____]
[_____]

ACTIVITY 4: WRITE YOUR OWN ACROSTIC POEM

Choose a word like **COURAGE**, **CLIMBER**, or make your own.

Write a line for each letter:

C _____

O _____

U _____

R _____

A _____

G _____

E _____

ACTIVITY 5: WORD HUNT!

Circle or list examples of:

• Movement: _____

• Feeling: _____

• Nature: _____

☀ BONUS CLASS IDEA

Build a "Mountain of Words"

Each student, on a separate sheet of paper, writes one line describing their dream, hope, or challenge—then stack them into a class poem wall that grows as tall as the mountain they climbed!

☑ FINAL REFLECTION

Final Reflection Placement:

REFLECTION PROMPT: WHO ARE YOU BECOMING?

If you had a dream in the Mountains of the Moon, what would it show you about your strength or potential?

[_____]
[_____]
[_____]
[_____]
[_____]

☑ THEN AFTER POETRY ACTIVITIES, CLOSE WITH:
🎓 Final Reflection – Exit Ticket

ONE THING I LEARNED ABOUT MYSELF OR THE CHARACTERS IN THIS chapter:

[_____]
[_____]
[_____]
[_____]
[_____]
[_____]

. . .

2 ONE QUESTION I STILL HAVE IS:

[_____]
[_____]
[_____]

FINAL REFLECTION PLACEMENT:

REFLECTION PROMPT: WHO ARE YOU BECOMING?

If you had a dream in the Mountains of the Moon, what would it show you about your strength or potential?

[_____]
[_____]
[_____]
[_____]
[_____]
[_____]

BONUS IDEA:

Students **build a class "Mountain of Words".** Each person writes one line describing a mountain adventure, and you "stack" them on the wall into a giant paper mountain!

YOU CLIMBED TO THE STARS—AND LOOKED INWARD. YOU'RE growing into something great.

Ready for the next challenge? Let's go!

❊ 9 ❊

UGALLA

S tudent Workbook – Chapter 9: *Ugalla*
    Name: _____
    Date: _____

CHAPTER QUEST

CORE READING SKILL FOCUS

Skill: Character Motivation + Inferring Theme from Conflict

WHY IT MATTERS: ENCOURAGES STUDENTS TO ANALYZE WHY characters make difficult choices and how internal conflict can reveal broader themes like trust, loyalty, and leadership.

FOCUS IN THIS CHAPTER: STUDENTS EXPLORE THE EMOTIONAL weight of Ernie's betrayal and how characters respond to broken trust. Through dialogue and actions, they infer motivations and begin identifying thematic patterns around leadership, alliance, and forgiveness. Students practice using character decisions as windows into the story's deeper message.

CHAPTER SUMMARY

After their long journey, the heroes arrive at the mystical valley of Ugalla—lush, peaceful, and full of promise. They feel joy and relief, but a mysterious rustle in the trees reminds them that peace may still be fragile. Scatter feels different, changed by everything they've experienced. As they celebrate, they begin to understand that their greatest transformation has already begun.

VOCABULARY & MORPHOLOGY

A. Match Each Word to Its Meaning

(Match the word to the correct meaning by writing the letter.)

Words

1 Ugalla
2 Fortune
3 Whiskers
4 Valley
5 Shadow

Definitions

A. Sensitive hairs on an animal's face used to sense the environment

B. A mystical jungle valley representing new beginnings

C. Good luck or a reward earned after a hard journey

D. A dark shape caused by something blocking the light

E. A low area between hills or mountains, often lush and green

B. Fill in the Blank Using the Word Bank

Word Bank: fortune, shadow, whiskers, valley, Ugalla

1 The heroes stood at the edge of the _____, their new home.

2 Scatter's _____ twitched as she sensed something was near.

3 A strange _____ moved at the edge of the trees.

4 After all their hardships, they had found a land full of hope and _____.

5 The peaceful _____ stretched below them, quiet and green.

MATCH THE WORD PARTS

Match each word part to its meaning by writing the correct letter.

Prefixes / Roots / Suffixes:

- fort-
- vale-
- umbra-
- whisk-
- -une

Definitions:

A. To twitch or move lightly

B. Valley or hollow

C. Shadow or dark area

D. Luck or blessing

E. A noun ending meaning "result of" or "state"

DECODE THE FULL WORD

1. Fortune

Parts: *fort-* + *-une*

What it means in the story:

[_____]
[_____]

2. VALLEY

Root: *vale-*

What it means in the story:

[_____]
[_____]

3. SHADOW
Root: *umbra-*

What it means in the story:

[_____]
[_____]

4. WHISKERS
Root: *whisk-*

What it means in the story:

[_____]
[_____]

READING COMPREHENSION

Answer in complete sentences.

1 What is Ugalla, and why is it important in the story?

[_____]
[_____]

2 WHY DO YOU THINK SCATTER SAYS, "I FEEL DIFFERENT"?

[_____]
[_____]

3 HOW HAS THE GROUP CHANGED SINCE LEAVING WAKADUO? GIVE
one example.

[_____]
[_____]

4 WHY MIGHT THE HEROES STILL BE CAUTIOUS, EVEN AFTER reaching Ugalla?

[_____]
[_____]

SEQUENCING ACTIVITY

Put the events in the correct order by numbering them 1–5:

___ The heroes reflect on how much they've grown

___ They celebrate and shout, "Our new home!"

___ A shadow moves in the trees

___ They arrive at the Valley of Dreams

___ Ernie spreads his wings and breathes in the air

MAKING INFERENCES

Read this sentence:

"Scatter took a deep breath. The Valley of Dreams stretched out before them, peaceful, untouched. But something in the air felt... different."

Question: What can we infer about Scatter's feelings in this moment?

☐ She is totally relaxed and ready to go home

☐ She wants to build a house in the valley

☐ She plans to stay alone in the valley forever

☐ *She feels a little uneasy, as if there's something unknown ahead*

(Write your answer and explain why.)

[_____]
[_____]
[_____]

[_____]

CHARACTER REFLECTION

Fill in what you've learned about each character in this chapter:

Scatter

How They Feel: _____

What They Do or Say: "I feel different."

What This Shows:

[_____]
[_____]

TUSKER

How They Feel: _____

What They Do or Say: Dances, showers Scatter in dirt

What This Shows:

[_____]
[_____]

ERNIE

How They Feel: _____

What They Do or Say: Spreads wings and sighs, "We've come so far."

What This Shows:

[_____]
[_____]

REFLECTION PROMPT:

Which character changed the most from the beginning of the journey? Why?

[_____]
[_____]

ıl CAUSE AND EFFECT PRACTICE

Match the causes with their effects:
Causes
- The group climbs the Mountain of Dreams
- Tusker sees the new land
- Ernie notices something strange
- The group reflects on their journey

Effects
- They reach the peaceful valley of Ugalla
- She celebrates with joy and dancing
- He warns the group they may not be alone
- They realize how much they've changed

(WRITE THE MATCHING PAIRS CLEARLY IN A LIST OR DRAW LINES.)

[_____]
[_____]
[_____]
[_____]
[_____]
[_____]
[_____]
[_____]

PREDICTION & REFLECTION

What might happen next?

1 WILL THE VALLEY REMAIN SAFE? WHY OR WHY NOT?

[_____]
[_____]
[_____]

. . .

2 WHAT COULD THE SHADOW AT THE EDGE OF THE FOREST MEAN?

[_____]
[_____]
[_____]

3 WHAT WOULD YOU DO IF YOU WERE IN THE VALLEY WITH THE heroes?

[_____]
[_____]
[_____]

✍ CREATIVE CORNER

Choose one creative prompt to complete below:
  A. Journal Entry from Scatter:
  Write as Scatter, standing at the edge of Ugalla. What do you feel? What do you fear?
  B. Imagine If...
  You are one of the animals arriving in Ugalla. What would you do first—rest, explore, build something?
  C. Poem: "The Valley Below"
  Write a short poem describing the valley, how the air feels, and what emotions it brings.
  ✍ Write your response below:

[_____]
[_____]
[_____]
[_____]
[_____]
[_____]
[_____]
[_____]
[_____]

VISUAL LEARNING

Choose one moment to illustrate:

- Tusker dancing in the sun, showering Scatter in dirt
- The group seeing Ugalla for the first time
- The mysterious shadow in the trees
- Caption your drawing with one line from the story:

[_____]
[_____]
[_____]
[_____]
[_____]
[_____]
[_____]
[_____]
[_____]

PERSONAL CONNECTION

Think of a time when you worked really hard for something and finally reached your goal.

What did it feel like?

What did you learn from the experience?

Write 3–4 sentences:

[_____]
[_____]
[_____]
[_____]
[_____]
[_____]
[_____]
[_____]
[_____]

✍ CER WRITING – CLAIM, EVIDENCE, REASONING

Prompt: What did the heroes learn about *hope and caution* when they arrived in Ugalla?

📣 CLAIM

I BELIEVE THE HEROES LEARNED

[_____]
[_____]

BECAUSE

[_____]
[_____]

📚 EVIDENCE
In the story, it says

[_____]
[_____]

AND ANOTHER EXAMPLE IS WHEN

[_____]
[_____]

REASONING
This shows that

[_____]
[_____]

· · ·

BECAUSE

[_____]
[_____]

✅ CHECKLIST
- ☐ Clear claim
- ☐ Strong evidence from the story
- ☐ Solid explanation that connects back to the main idea

◎ FINAL REFLECTION – EXIT TICKET

1 One thing I learned about gratitude or discovery in this chapter:

[_____]
[_____]

2 ONE QUESTION I STILL HAVE IS:

[_____]
[_____]

YOU'VE FOUND THE VALLEY—BUT THE JOURNEY CONTINUES.

Let's keep climbing toward greatness—together.

✅ Standards Alignment

• **CCSS.ELA-LITERACY.RL.4.1**: Refer to details and examples when explaining what the text says and drawing inferences

• **CCSS.ELA-LITERACY.RL.4.2**: Summarize the text and determine its theme

• **CCSS.ELA-LITERACY.RL.4.3**: Describe in depth a character, setting, or event in a story

• **CCSS.ELA-LITERACY.RL.4.4**: Determine the meaning of words and phrases in context

◼ JOURNAL 2: AFTER CHAPTER 9 – THE GATHERING STORM

Chapters 5–9 Summary: The team faces internal doubts and meets new allies and enemies. Danger builds, and questions of loyalty arise.

Page 1 – Reflect & Write
Prompt 1:
"I used to think... but now I think..."

➤ About what makes someone a good friend or teammate

_____

_____

Prompt 2:
Has a character made a mistake in this arc? What can we learn from them?

_____

_____

Prompt 3:
When have you faced a difficult decision? What helped you decide?

_____

_____

Page 2 – Create & Connect

• **Draw** an emotional "weather report" for this section (e.g., stormy = fear, sunny = hope)

• **Write** a few lines Scatter might say to inspire her team in their hardest moment

[_____]
[_____]
[_____]
[_____]
[_____]
[_____]
[_____]
[_____]
[_____]
[_____]
[_____]
[_____]
[_____]
[_____]

GURR

Student Workbook – Chapter 10: *Gurr*
Name: _____
Date: _____

CHAPTER QUEST

CORE READING SKILL FOCUS

📖 **Skill:** Symbolism + Point of View

🎯 **Why it Matters:** Helps students interpret layered meaning behind imagery and understand how perspective shapes emotional impact and story tone.

🔍 **Focus in This Chapter:** Students examine how symbols like Gurr's scars, the quiet valley, and the proverb about the baobab tree represent wisdom, loss, and shared leadership. Through Scatter's and Gurr's perspectives, they analyze how different points of view influence interpretation of events and ethical dilemmas.

CHAPTER SUMMARY

In the lush valley of Ugalla, the heroes meet Gurr—a regal lion with wisdom and secrets. Gurr warns Scatter's group about Tau and the dangers of Ruaha, the jungle's corrupted side. But peace shatters when Scatter catches Ernie eating a mouse, shaking their trust. Gurr believes it's time to return to Wakaduo and unite against the growing threat—but not everyone may be ready. Trust, leadership, and betrayal take center stage.

VOCABULARY & MORPHOLOGY

WORD LIST:

- Sentinel – A guard or protector
- Alliance – A partnership for a shared goal
- Betrayal – The act of breaking someone's trust
- Tattered – Worn out, torn, or ragged
- Seers – Those who can see the future

YOUR TURN:

Pick **two** words from the list and write your own sentence for each.

1.
   [_____]
   [_____]

. . .

2.

[————————————————————————————]
[————————————————————————————]

🐾 CHAPTER 10 – WORD PART DECODER: MORPHOLOGY Matching

SKILL FOCUS: MORPHOLOGY + SYMBOLIC THINKING
Suggested Placement: Just after "Vocabulary & Morphology" and before "Reading Comprehension."

MATCH THE WORD PARTS
Match the word parts below with their meanings.

PREFIXES / ROOTS / SUFFIXES:
- sent-
- ali-
- tatter-
- -ance
- tray-

DEFINITIONS:
A. Tear or shred
B. A root meaning "to send" or "feel/watch"
C. Partnership or bond
D. Act of betraying or handing over
E. A noun-forming suffix meaning "state of" or "result of"

. . .

✎ Decode the Full Word

1. Sentinel

Root: *sent-*

🧠 What it means in the story:

[_____]
[_____]

2. Alliance

Root: *ali-* + suffix *-ance*

🧠 What it means in the story:

[_____]
[_____]

3. Tattered

Root: *tatter-*

🧠 What it means in the story:

[_____]
[_____]

4. Betrayal

Root: *tray-*

🧠 What it means in the story:

[_____]
[_____]

📖 READING COMPREHENSION

Answer in 1–2 complete sentences:

1 Who is Gurr, and how does he lead the animals of Ugalla?

☞

[_____]

[_____]

2 WHY DOES THE VALLEY FEEL STRANGELY QUIET?

[_____]
[_____]

3 WHAT CAUSES TENSION BETWEEN SCATTER AND ERNIE?

[_____]
[_____]

4 WHAT DOES GURR WARN ABOUT TAU AND RUAHA?

[_____]
[_____]

⬤ PREDICTION LADDER

Use clues from the chapter to make smart guesses:

1 What might happen when Scatter's group returns to Wakaduo?

[_____]
[_____]

2 WILL GURR'S PLAN WORK? WHY OR WHY NOT?

[_____]
[_____]

. . .

3 WILL SCATTER FORGIVE ERNIE? WHAT CLUES HELP YOU DECIDE?

[_____]
[_____]

FLUENCY & EXPRESSION PRACTICE

Reader's Theater

Practice reading Gurr and Scatter's dialogue with emotion and pacing.

Tips:
- Gurr's voice: slow, wise, strong
- Scatter's voice: hopeful, hurt, thoughtful

Checklist:
☐ Slow down for dramatic pauses
☐ Use emotion to show pain or wisdom
☐ Emphasize important words like "trust," "betrayal," and "return"

REAL-WORLD WISDOM CONNECTION

Proverb: "Wisdom is like a baobab tree; no one individual can embrace it."

1 What do you think this means in your own words?

[_____]
[_____]

2 THINK OF A TIME WHEN YOU NEEDED HELP TO SOLVE SOMETHING big or confusing. What did others help you see?

[_____]
[_____]

✎ REFLECTION PROMPT – ERNIE'S LETTER

Option A: Write from Ernie's point of view.

Imagine you're Ernie writing to Scatter after being caught breaking her trust. Share what you were feeling, and ask for forgiveness.

Dear Scatter,

[_____]
[_____]
[_____]
[_____]
[_____]
[_____]
[_____]
[_____]
[_____]
[_____]
[_____]
[_____]

SINCERELY,
Ernie

OPTION B: SCAFFOLDED VERSION

Use these sentence starters to help shape your thoughts.

DEAR SCATTER,
- I know I hurt you when I…
- I didn't mean to betray your trust, but I was feeling…
- If I could go back and change what happened, I would…
- I hope someday you can…

[_____]
[_____]

[_____]
[_____]
[_____]
[_____]
[_____]
[_____]
[_____]
[_____]
[_____]

SINCERELY,
   Ernie

DRAW ERNIE'S FACE

What do you imagine Ernie looks like as he writes the letter?
   Is he ashamed, hopeful, nervous, or something else?
   Draw:

[_____]
[_____]
[_____]
[_____]
[_____]
[_____]
[_____]
[_____]
[_____]
[_____]
[_____]
[_____]

CAPTION:
   "Ernie feels _____
   because _____."

NOTABLE QUOTES & RESPONSE

Quote 1:
"This valley should be teeming with life." – Tusker
Copy it here:

WHAT DO YOU THINK TUSKER MEANS?

[_____]
[_____]

QUOTE 2:
"We must be clever, brave, and outsmart Tau." – Gurr
Copy it here:

WHAT KIND OF LEADER IS GURR TRYING TO BE?
I think Gurr is a strong leader because...

[_____]
[_____]
[_____]
[_____]

QUOTE 3:
"How could you eat my parents and pretend to be my friend?" – Scatter
Copy it here:

WHAT IS SCATTER FEELING IN THIS MOMENT?
If I were Scatter, I would feel _____
because...

[_____]
[_____]

SCENE SKETCH

Choose one powerful scene to illustrate:

   Gurr beneath the baobab, his silver mane glowing in moonlight

   The secret predator meeting, hidden deep in the jungle

   Scatter discovering Ernie's betrayal—standing tall despite her tears

   My Drawing:

[_____]
[_____]
[_____]
[_____]
[_____]
[_____]
[_____]
[_____]
[_____]
[_____]
[_____]
[_____]

CAPTION:

"This moment matters because…"

[_____]
[_____]

CER WRITING – CLAIM, EVIDENCE, REASONING

Prompt: What lesson did the characters learn about trust in this chapter?

. . .

CLAIM

I believe the characters learned

[_____]
[_____]

because

[_____]
[_____]

EVIDENCE

In the story, it says

[_____]
[_____]

AND ANOTHER EXAMPLE IS WHEN

[_____]
[_____]

REASONING

This shows that

[_____]
[_____]

BECAUSE

[_____]
[_____]
[_____]
[_____]

CHECKLIST:

☐ Clear claim
☐ Evidence from the chapter
☐ Thoughtful reasoning

EXIT REFLECTION

1 One thing I learned about friendship or trust in this chapter:

[_____]
[_____]

2 ONE QUESTION I STILL HAVE IS:

[_____]
[_____]

END OF STUDENT WORKBOOK

Great work—your reading journey is getting deeper and stronger.

CHECKPOINT CHALLENGE: LET'S SEE HOW FAR YOU'VE COME!

"Your journey's halfway through! Let's pause and show what you've learned so far before we face what's next!"

DURING-TEST
READING PASSAGE: "Shadows in the Valley"
Adapted and condensed from Chapters 7–10

Shadows in the Valley

The heroes had finally reached Ugalla—a lush, green valley sparkling under the morning sun. For the first time in many days, Scatter, Tusker, and Ernie weren't running or hiding. They felt the soft grass under their feet and breathed in the cool mountain air.

But peace didn't last long. A rustle in the trees made Scatter's ears twitch. A shadow moved quickly, and Ernie fluffed his feathers. "We're not alone," he whispered.

Soon, they met Gurr, a wise lion with a silver mane and deep scars across his face. Gurr welcomed them kindly, but his eyes were heavy with memories. "This land was once filled with laughter," he said. "But disasters, sickness, and predators changed everything."

Later that night, as the others rested, Scatter heard a faint cry. Following the sound, she crept through the tall grass. There, she saw Ernie... crouched in the shadows, holding a lifeless mouse in his beak.

Her breath caught. "Ernie?" she whispered.

Ernie's eyes widened. "I—I didn't mean—Scatter, please!"

But Scatter turned and ran. Her heart felt like it had shattered. Was Ernie just like every other predator?

The next day, the group sat quietly around a crackling fire. Their friendship felt fragile, like a thread ready to snap.

Gurr spoke to the others in private. "We must return to Wakaduo," he said. "And we must outsmart Tau before it's too late."

Scatter stared at the horizon, her tail ring glowing. The journey wasn't over—but she was no longer the same.

DURING-TEST QUESTIONS
Part A: Vocabulary in Context (Multiple Choice – 4 pts)

1 What does the word **lush** most likely mean in the sentence:
"The heroes had finally reached Ugalla—a lush, green valley sparkling under the morning sun."
   ☐ Dry and empty
   ☐ Full and green
   ☐ Quiet and dusty
   ☐ Cold and snowy

2 The word **fragile** in "Their friendship felt fragile, like a thread ready to snap" means:
   ☐ Strong and steady
   ☐ Broken and lost
   ☐ Weak and delicate
   ☐ New and surprising

3 Which word best describes how **Gurr** speaks about the past?
   ☐ Cheerfully

☐ Gently

☐ Sadly

☐ Silently

4 What is the meaning of **outsmart** in the sentence:
"We must outsmart Tau before it's too late."

☐ Hide from

☐ Trick or defeat with clever thinking

☐ Fight directly

☐ Avoid completely

Part B: Reading Comprehension (Short Answer – 3 pts)

5 Why is Scatter so upset with Ernie?

_____

_____

6 What does Gurr mean when he says "this land was once filled with laughter"?

_____

_____

7 What might the glowing of Scatter's ring suggest at the end of the passage?

_____

_____

Part C: Morphology (1 Multiple Choice + 1 Constructed – 2 pts)

8 What does the word **lifeless** most likely mean?
□ Full of life and energy
□ Tired but still awake
□ Having no life or movement
□ Able to breathe deeply

9 Break apart the word **predators** into meaningful parts and explain:

Prefix/Root/Suffix: _____ + _____ + _____

Meaning:

_____

_____

Part D: Extended Writing (CER Format – 1 long response – 6 pts)

Prompt: What lesson do the characters learn about trust in this part of the story?

CLAIM

I believe the characters learned

_____

because

_____

EVIDENCE

In the story, it says

_____

and also when

_____

REASONING

This shows that

_____

because

_____

☑ Checklist:
    □ Clear claim
    □ At least two text-based details
    □ Explanation of why this matters

📖 STUDENT ANSWER SHEET
(Optional answer sheet)

Name: _____

Date: _____

PART A – Vocabulary (Circle your answer)

1. A B C D

2. A B C D

3. A B C D

4. A B C D

PART B – Short Answer
    5. _____
    _____
    6. _____
    _____
    7. _____
    _____

PART C – Morphology

8. A B C D

9. Prefix/Root/Suffix: _____ / _____ / _____

Meaning: _____

PART D – Writing:

❧ 11 ❧
THE RETURNING HEROES

 **tudent Workbook – Chapter 11: *The Returning Heroes***

NAME: _____

   Date: _____

PROVERB: *PATIENCE IS THE MOTHER OF A BEAUTIFUL CHILD.*

CHAPTER QUEST

⬤ **CHAPTER 11 – *The Returning Heroes***

📖 CORE READING SKILL FOCUS

📖 **Skill:** Character Change Through Conflict and Choice

. . .

☞ **WHY IT MATTERS:** THIS CHAPTER DEEPENS STUDENTS' understanding of character arcs by connecting internal growth with external decisions.

🔍 **FOCUS IN THIS CHAPTER:** STUDENTS EXPLORE HOW HENRY'S return, Scatter's decision to take the swamp path, and Ernie's redemption efforts illustrate complex emotional development. They practice tracing cause and effect in leadership decisions and recognizing how past actions inform future identity.

CHAPTER SUMMARY

As the heroes begin their return to Wakaduo, danger waits and the land is not the same. Tau the Mighty lurks nearby, planning an ambush. Guided by dreams and instincts, the group faces a crossroads. When Henry returns unexpectedly, they must choose between two paths: a safer route or a riskier journey through the mysterious Swamp of Mists. Loyalty, bravery, and the weight of leadership guide their decisions as they take their next step forward.

PROVERB: *PATIENCE IS THE MOTHER OF A BEAUTIFUL CHILD.*

WHAT DO YOU THINK THIS PROVERB MEANS IN YOUR OWN WORDS?

[_____]
[_____]

HOW DOES THIS APPLY TO HENRY'S RETURN OR SCATTER'S leadership?

[_____]
[_____]

🔤 VOCABULARY & WORD STRUCTURE

Words to Know:
- *Resonate* – To deeply connect or affect
- *Guile* – Cleverness, trickery
- *Stealth* – Moving quietly and unseen
- *Ambush* – A surprise attack
- *Resolve* – Determined purpose

WORD PARTS:
- *Resonate* → re- (again) + son (sound)
- *Guile* → from Old French, meaning "trick"
- *Stealth* → related to "steal" + suffix -th
- *Ambush* → am- (toward) + bush (hide)
- *Resolve* → re- (again) + solve (decide)

VOCABULARY CHALLENGE
A. Circle the word that best describes *Scatter* in this chapter.

B. Underline the word that best fits *Henry*.

Now write your own sentence using any two vocabulary words:

1.

[——————————————————————]
[——————————————————————]

2.

[——————————————————————]
[——————————————————————]

📖 MORPHOLOGY MATCH – WORD PARTS IN ACTION

Directions: Match the word part or root to the correct vocabulary word below. Then, choose one word and explain how knowing its parts helps you understand its meaning.

WORD PARTS AND WHAT THEY MEAN:
1 re- – again
2 son – sound
3 -th – turns a verb into a noun (a state or quality)
4 am- – toward
5 bush – hide
6 solve – decide

VOCABULARY WORDS TO USE:
- Resonate
- Guile
- Stealth
- Ambush
- Resolve

MATCH THE WORD PARTS:
1 re- → _____
2 son → _____
3 -th → _____
4 am- → _____
5 bush → _____
6 solve → _____

NOW TRY THIS!
Pick one word from above. What do its parts tell you about what it means?

✎ Word: _____

✎ What I learned from the word parts:

[_____]
[_____]

WORD BUILDING CHALLENGE (EMERGING READER VERSION)
Let's figure out what words are made of!

Each big word below has smaller parts called **prefixes** or **roots** that give clues about what it means.

WORD BUILDERS WITH SYMBOLS

Let the symbols help you figure out what each word means!

WORDS TO USE:
- Resonate
- Guile
- Stealth
- Ambush
- Resolve

PART 1: MATCH THE SYMBOLS TO THE WORD
Choose the word that fits each symbol and meaning.

1 🔄 **re-** means "again" → _____

2 🔊 **son** means "sound" → _____

3 🌀 **th** means "a thing or state" →

_____

4 🎯 **solve** means "to decide" →

_____

5   🏹   **am-**   means   "toward"   →

_____

6 🌿 **bush** means "hide" → _____

(🖈 *Tip: Some words go with more than one symbol! Try to find all the parts that make up the word.*)

◣ Part 2: Word Detective Sentence

Now choose one word and explain what the parts tell you.

My word is: _____

What I see in it:

I see the symbol: _____ (write the emoji or the word part)

That part means:

[_____]
[_____]

So I think this word means:

[_____]
[_____]

Example Response:

My word is: **Resonate**

I see the symbol: 🔄 (**re-**)

That part means: again

So I think this word means: to sound again or connect deeply.

⚆ Word Detective Bonus!

Curious about what "re-," "son," or "bush" really mean? Flip to the back of the book and try the **Word Builders Toolkit** to unlock the secrets inside big words.

⊔ READING COMPREHENSION

Answer in full sentences.

1 What is the "Dance of the Wild," and why is it important?

[_____]
[_____]
2 Why does Tau choose to wait instead of attack right away?

[_____]
[_____]

3 WHAT DIFFICULT CHOICE DOES SCATTER MAKE? WHY IS IT HARD for her?

[_____]
[_____]

4 HOW DOES HENRY SHOW THAT HE HAS GROWN AS A CHARACTER?

[_____]
[_____]

5. WHAT MIGHT THE SWAMP OF MISTS SYMBOLIZE?

[_____]
[_____]

6 WHAT DOES TAU'S SILENCE AND WATCHING SUGGEST ABOUT THE danger ahead?

[_____]
[_____]

⌁ PREDICTION LADDER

Use clues from the story to make smart predictions:

1 What do you think the Swamp of Mists will be like?

[_____]
[_____]

2 WHAT KIND OF CHALLENGES MIGHT THE GROUP FACE THERE?

[_____]
[_____]

3 HOW MIGHT THEIR FRIENDSHIP AND TRUST BE TESTED?

[_____]
[_____]

BONUS PROMPT: WHAT WOULD *YOU* PACK TO SURVIVE THE SWAMP OF Mists?

[_____]
[_____]

♫ FLUENCY & EXPRESSION PRACTICE

Read these lines aloud with drama and emotion:

• Tau: "Let them grow comfortable. A lion does not chase mice."

• Henry: "I followed the voice, and it led me right back to you!"

• Scatter: "It's a tougher path... but it might be our only way home."

Practice Tip: Switch between fear and hope as you read.

. . .

PARTNER FEEDBACK:

"You sounded most powerful when you said

[_____]
[_____]

✐ SCHEMA & REAL-LIFE CONNECTION

Think: Have you ever had to choose between two hard options? What helped you decide?

✐ Write or draw about it below:

[_____]
[_____]
[_____]
[_____]
[_____]
[_____]
[_____]

WHY IS PATIENCE IMPORTANT WHEN FACING DIFFICULT CHOICES?

[_____]
[_____]
[_____]
[_____]
[_____]
[_____]

▣ ✐ REFLECTION PROMPTS

Theme: Loyalty, Trust, and Choosing the Harder Path

Sentence Starters:

1 Henry came back even though

_____.

2 Taking the harder path is important because

_____.

3 False safety is dangerous because it can

_____.

4 The characters are changing because now they

_____.

✐ REFLECTION: HENRY'S JOURNAL

Prompt: Imagine you are *Henry*, writing in your journal the night you rejoined the group.

Write:

How did it feel to return? What did you fear? What gave you hope?

✎ Journal Entry:

[_____]
[_____]
[_____]
[_____]
[_____]
[_____]
[_____]
[_____]
[_____]

🐚 SCENE SKETCH: THE SWAMP OF MISTS

Draw: The moment the group steps into the foggy swamp.

Think About:
- What emotions are on their faces?
- How does the fog look?
- Are they holding hands? Staying close?

✎ CAPTION:

"We walked forward, even though

_____

_____

✏ [DRAWING SPACE]

[_____]
[_____]
[_____]
[_____]
[_____]
[_____]
[_____]
[_____]
[_____]
[_____]
[_____]
[_____]
[_____]

POETRY PACK

Chapter 11: "Echoes of the Wild"

POETRY ACTIVITY SHEET — *FREE VERSE POEM*

✏ **POEM TEXT:**
Free Verse Poem: Echoes of the Wild
Whispers on the wind,
Echoes of footsteps in the wild,
Heroes return, hearts bound,
With tales of courage, woven and compiled.
In the silence of their march,
A rhythm of resilience beats,
Under starry skies they arch,

Each step towards home, hope meets.
The earth speaks in soft murmurs,
A mother's lullaby to the weary,
They carry dreams, draped in fervor,
In their eyes, the light of query.
Their laughter weaves through the trees,
A tapestry rich with newfound ties,
They move with the grace of the evening breeze,
Under the watchful stars' guise.
Yet danger lurks, veiled in shadow,
Predators wait with bated breath,
The heroes' journey, far from shallow,
Tests their spirit, a dance with death.
Henry's return, a ripple in the calm,
His warning a thread in their woven fate,
Together they stand, a soothing balm,
United, they challenge the hands of fate.

☞ POETRY ACTIVITIES
ACTIVITY 1: Visualize the Poem

Draw a picture of the heroes on their journey. Label three things you include!

[_____]
[_____]
[_____]
[_____]
[_____]
[_____]
[_____]
[_____]
[_____]
[_____]
[_____]
[_____]

· · ·

ACTIVITY 2: FIND THE FEELING
- Beginning feeling: _____
- Middle feeling: _____
- Ending feeling: _____

ACTIVITY 3: WILD WORDS (SYMBOLISM)
Pick two strong images and explain what they mean:
- "Laughter weaves through the trees" →
  _____

- "A dance with death" →
  _____

ACTIVITY 4: ECHOES OF COURAGE
Write a short journal entry starting with:
"Today we crossed the wild once more..."

[_____]
[_____]
[_____]
[_____]
[_____]
[_____]
[_____]
[_____]
[_____]
[_____]
[_____]
[_____]

ACTIVITY 5: YOUR OWN FREE VERSE POEM
Write 4–6 lines about a brave moment in your life. No rhyming needed!

Starter: *"The world felt big / I felt small / But..."*

✍ Your Poem:

[_____]
[_____]
[_____]
[_____]
[_____]
[_____]

✍ CER WRITING – CLAIM, EVIDENCE, REASONING

Prompt: Why do you think Scatter chose the swamp over the safer path?

📢 CLAIM

I think Scatter chose the swamp because

[_____]
[_____]

📚 EVIDENCE

In the story it says,

[_____]
[_____]

WHICH SHOWS THAT

[_____]
[_____]

ANOTHER EXAMPLE IS WHEN

[_____]
[_____]

REASONING

This shows that

[_____]
[_____]

because

[_____]
[_____]

☑ CHECKLIST:
  ☐ Clear claim
  ☐ Strong evidence from the story
  ☐ Well-explained reasoning

☑ FINAL REFLECTION

Skill Tracker:
  Check the boxes for what you practiced today.
  ☐ Used vocabulary in context
  ☐ Made a prediction
  ☐ Practiced expressive reading
  ☐ Reflected on theme
  ☐ Completed a writing or drawing activity

YOU'RE BECOMING NOT JUST A READER—BUT A DEEP THINKER AND brave explorer. Keep walking the path, even through the fog.

❧ 12 ❧

THE WONDER HOLE

T he Wonder Hole:

PROVERB: *DO NOT STAND IN A PLACE OF DANGER TRUSTING IN miracles.*

Name: _____

Date: _____

CHAPTER QUEST

⬤ **CHAPTER 12 –** *The Wonder Hole*

📖 CORE READING SKILL FOCUS

📖 **Skill:** Theme Through Symbolism and Figurative Language

🎯 **Why it Matters:** Helps students interpret how mythical challenges (like Grootslang's riddle) reveal deeper truths about wisdom, power, and courage.

🔍 **Focus in This Chapter:** Students analyze how the Wonder Hole functions as a metaphor for inner testing and transformation. They unpack how the riddle and Scroll of Mists represent knowledge earned through cleverness rather than force. Figurative language and foreshadowing are central tools for comprehension and prediction.

CHAPTER SUMMARY

The heroes descend into a deep cavern known as *The Wonder Hole*, guarded by Grootslang—a legendary serpent from Wakaduo's oldest stories. Grootslang challenges them not with claws, but with a riddle. Scatter's wit saves the group, and Henry's bravery earns them the mystical *Scroll of Mists*. But the warning is clear: the swamp they're about to enter doesn't just test strength—it transforms those who enter it.

🔤 VOCABULARY & WORD STUDY

Vocabulary List
- *Ferocious* – Fierce or intense
- *Coiling* – Twisting into loops
- *Gleam* – A soft, glowing light
- *Tremor* – A slight vibration or shake
- *Lurk* – To hide and wait quietly

Word Roots & Structure Examples
- *Ferocious* → Root: **fer** (fierce) + Suffix: **-ious** (having)

- *Coiling* → Root: **coil** + Suffix: **-ing**
- *Tremor* → Root: **trem** (shake) + Suffix: **-or**
- *Lurk* → Root: **lur** + Suffix: **-ing**
- *Gleam* → (no affixes)

Task:

Choose **two** words and write original sentences that show you understand what they mean.

1.

[————————————————————————————]
[————————————————————————————]

2.

[————————————————————————————]
[————————————————————————————]

WORD PART DECODER – CHAPTER 12: *THE WONDER HOLE*

Match the root or affix to its meaning or function. Then decode the word's meaning.

1 **fer** → _____
2 **-ious** → _____
3 **trem** → _____
4 **-or** → _____
5 **coil** → _____

NOW DECODE TWO WORDS FROM THE STORY USING THE ROOT AND affix clues:

- **Ferocious** = fer () **+ -ious** ()

Meaning:

[————————————————————————————]
[————————————————————————————]

· · ·

- **TREMOR** = TREM () **+ -OR** ()
  ✎ Meaning:

  [_____]
  [_____]

BONUS CHALLENGE:

Grootslang is a mythological being. What root or affix might appear in words related to myths or hidden knowledge? (Hint: Think of words like *mystery* or *legend.*)

  [_____]
  [_____]

▣ SYMBOL-BASED LEARNING PROMPTS

Use the symbol to decode the meaning! Match the icon to its word.

▣ = REPEATING, BACK
  ↪ = **coiling, twisting**
   . = **gleam, light**
  ⚡ = **tremor, shake**
  ♨ = **ferocious, fierce**

MATCH THE SYMBOL WITH THE CORRECT VOCABULARY WORD:
  ▣   ↪   .   ⚡   ♨
  • Tremor → _____
  • Coiling → _____
  • Gleam → _____
  • Ferocious → _____

📖 READING COMPREHENSION

Answer in complete sentences.

1 Why do the heroes enter the Wonder Hole?

[_____]
[_____]

2 WHO IS GROOTSLANG, AND HOW DOES SHE TEST THEM?

[_____]
[_____]

3 HOW DO THEY EARN THE *SCROLL OF MISTS*?

[_____]
[_____]

4 WHY IS SCATTER'S ANSWER TO THE RIDDLE IMPORTANT?

[_____]
[_____]

REFLECTION PROMPTS

Theme: Wit, Courage, and Facing the Unseen

"Do not stand in a place of danger trusting in miracles."

1 GROOTSLANG CHALLENGES THE HEROES WITH A RIDDLE. WHAT does this teach us about clever thinking?

☞ Grootslang's riddle showed me that...

[_____]
[_____]

. . .

2 SCATTER REMEMBERS HER PAST TO SOLVE THE RIDDLE. WHEN HAS a memory helped you figure something out?

I think Scatter remembered the bottle because...

[_____]
[_____]

3 THE GROUP JOKES, EVEN IN FEAR. HOW CAN HUMOR HELP IN tough situations?

In tough moments, humor can help by...

[_____]
[_____]

4 WHAT IMPORTANT LESSON DID THE HEROES LEARN IN THE WONDER Hole?

One lesson the group learned is...

[_____]
[_____]

● PREDICTION LADDER

Grootslang warns: *"The swamp changes those who enter."*

1 I think the Swamp of Mists will be...

[_____]
[_____]

2 ONE CHALLENGE THE GROUP MIGHT FACE IS...

[_____]
[_____]

3 THEY MIGHT BE CHANGED BY...

[_____]
[_____]

4 THIS MAKES ME THINK THAT...

[_____]
[_____]

CRITICAL THINKING: RIDDLE MASTERY

Grootslang's riddle: *"What do you look in with one eye, but never with two?"*
     Scatter answered: *"A bottle."*

PROMPT:
     Why was this riddle meaningful for Scatter?

[_____]
[_____]

NOW, WRITE YOUR OWN RIDDLE INSPIRED BY SOMETHING FROM THE
story.
     Riddle:
     What am I?

[_____]
[_____]
[_____]
[_____]
[_____]
[_____]
[_____]
[_____]

FLUENCY & EXPRESSION PRACTICE

Reader's Theater
- **Narrator** – Calm and steady
- **Grootslang** – Deep and echoing
- **Scatter** – Nervous, then confident

Voice Tips:
- Pause after delivering the riddle
- Whisper *"A bottle..."*
- Boom with *"Clever... little one."*

SCHEMA CONNECTION

Have you ever read or heard a story with a riddle-solving hero?
(Example: Bilbo Baggins in *The Hobbit*)
Write your connection:

[_____]
[_____]

Reflection Prompt:

What does this chapter teach us about power and wisdom?
How did cleverness and teamwork help the group?

[_____]
[_____]

CER WRITING — CLAIM, EVIDENCE, REASONING

Prompt: Why was wisdom more powerful than force in the Wonder Hole?
CLAIM

I believe wisdom was more powerful than force in this chapter because...

[_____]
[_____]

📚 EVIDENCE

One example is when...

[_____]
[_____]

Another part that shows this is...

[_____]
[_____]

REASONING

This proves that...

[_____]
[_____]

IT MEANS THAT...

[_____]
[_____]

📖 CREATIVE WRITING PROMPT

Diary Entry from Grootslang's Point of View

Imagine you are Grootslang, writing in your journal after the heroes leave.

What did you think about Scatter?

Why did you give them the scroll?

What does the swamp mean to you?

WRITE YOUR ENTRY BELOW:

Dear Journal,

[_____]
[_____]

[_____]
[_____]
[_____]
[_____]
[_____]
[_____]
[_____]
[_____]
[_____]
[_____]

— GROOTSLANG

🐚 SCENE SKETCH: THE WONDER HOLE

Choose a moment to draw:

• GROOTSLANG RISING FROM THE SHADOWS

• SCATTER WHISPERING HER ANSWER

• HENRY REACHING FOR THE SCROLL
   ✎ Caption:
   "This moment stood out because..."

   [_____]
   [_____]

✏ [DRAWING SPACE]

   [_____]
   [_____]

[_____]
[_____]
[_____]
[_____]
[_____]
[_____]
[_____]
[_____]
[_____]
[_____]
[_____]
[_____]
[_____]
[_____]
[_____]

✅ FINAL SKILL TRACKER

☐ I practiced using new vocabulary

    ☐ I reflected on wisdom and teamwork

    ☐ I made predictions

    ☐ I explored poetic language

    ☐ I completed a creative or dramatic activity

You've faced the riddle of the Wonder Hole—and answered with courage.

Next stop: The Swamp of Mists. Stay sharp, stay brave. 🐾

❧ 13 ❧
THE SWAMP OF THE MISTS

 **S**tudent Workbook – Chapter 13: *The Swamp of the Mists*

PROVERB: *SHOW ME YOUR FRIENDS AND I WILL SHOW YOU YOUR character.*

Name: _____

Date: _____

CHAPTER QUEST

● **CHAPTER 13 – *The Swamp of Mists***

📖 CORE READING SKILL FOCUS

📖 **Skill:** Inference Through Emotional and Symbolic Cues

◎ **Why it Matters:** This chapter challenges students to infer feelings and character growth based on actions, dialogue, and symbolism rather than explicit narration.

🔍 **Focus in This Chapter:** Students interpret how fog, illusions, and forced choices reflect each character's inner truth. They examine how Ernie's confession and Scatter's reaction reveal layered emotional shifts—and consider how forgiveness, leadership, and self-awareness are connected through subtle details.

CHAPTER SUMMARY

The Swamp of Mists is no ordinary swamp—it sees inside your heart. Fog clouds the path, but it's the secrets, fears, and memories the heroes carry that cause the real trouble. The Swamp Guardians offer a chilling challenge: give up a truth or lose a memory. Henry admits his fear of not belonging. Ernie confesses a betrayal that shakes the group. When vultures descend, Harry the Water Mongoose leaps in to help. The heroes survive the swamp—but their friendship may not.

🔤 VOCABULARY PRACTICE

Word List
- *Murky* – Dark, foggy, unclear
- *Daunting* – Scary or difficult
- *Mistrust* – Doubt or lack of trust
- *Eerie* – Strange, spooky
- *Character* – The deep qualities that define a person

. . .

TASK 1: FILL IN THE BLANKS

1 The swamp looked so _____ the heroes could barely see ahead.

2 Henry's _____ made him brave enough to speak truth.

Task 2: Vocabulary Art

Choose **two** words and draw small scenes that show their meaning. Use a few labels to explain what's happening.

✏ Drawing Box 1

[_____]
[_____]
[_____]
[_____]
[_____]
[_____]
[_____]
[_____]
[_____]

WORD: _____

▭ Description:

[_____]
[_____]

✏ DRAWING BOX 2

[_____]
[_____]
[_____]
[_____]
[_____]
[_____]
[_____]
[_____]
[_____]

[_____]
[_____]
[_____]

WORD: _____
📓 Description:

[_____]
[_____]
[_____]
[_____]

🐌 WORD PART DECODER – CHAPTER 13: *THE SWAMP OF MISTS*

📍 MATCH THE WORD PART TO ITS MEANING OR FUNCTION:

1 murk → _____
2 -y → _____
3 mis- → _____
4 trust → _____
5 -ing → _____

NOW DECODE TWO WORDS FROM THE STORY USING WHAT YOU'VE learned:

• **Mistrust** = mis- () + **trust** ()

✏️ Meaning:

[_____]
[_____]

• **MURKY** = MURK () + **-Y** ()

✏️ Meaning:

[_____]
[_____]

· · ·

BONUS PROMPT:

The word *character* comes from a Greek word meaning "engraved mark." What does this suggest about how character is formed in this chapter?

✎ Your thoughts (Character means…..):

[_____]
[_____]
[_____]
[_____]
[_____]
[_____]

SYMBOL-BASED LEARNING PROMPTS

MATCH THE ICON TO THE VOCABULARY WORD. USE THE VISUAL clues to remember each word's meaning!

= MURKY
⊘ = mistrust
= character
◉ = daunting
= eerie

• THE SWAMP LOOKED SO _____ ( )
   • Henry's _____ ( ) helped him be brave
   • The fog made the path feel _____ (◉)
   • Ernie's secret created _____ (⊘)
   • The Guardians gave off an _____ vibe ( )

· · ·

DRAW IT CHALLENGE:

Pick one symbol and draw a scene that matches it.
Add a caption using the vocabulary word in a sentence!

[_____]
[_____]
[_____]
[_____]
[_____]
[_____]
[_____]
[_____]
[_____]
[_____]
[_____]
[_____]

📖 COMPREHENSION CHECK

Answer in complete sentences.

1. What challenge do the Guardians present to the heroes?

[_____]
[_____]

2.

What truth does Henry reveal?

[_____]
[_____]

3. WHAT DOES ERNIE CONFESS?

[_____]
[_____]

. . .

4. WHO COMES TO SAVE THE GROUP DURING THE ATTACK?

[_____]
[_____]

5. HOW DO THE HEROES FEEL AT THE END OF THE CHAPTER?

[_____]
[_____]

REFLECTION PROMPTS

Theme: Truth, Forgiveness, and Facing Inner Demons

"SHOW ME YOUR FRIENDS AND I WILL SHOW YOU YOUR character."

1. THE SWAMP TESTS THE HEROES WITH ILLUSIONS AND TRUTHS. What truth would be hardest for you to face?

The hardest truth I could face would be...

[_____]
[_____]
[_____]

2. DO YOU THINK SOME MISTAKES CAN NEVER BE FORGIVEN? WHY OR why not?

I think some mistakes can/can't be forgiven because...

[_____]
[_____]
[_____]

. . .

3. The Guardians say: *"Nothing in the swamp is given. Everything is borrowed."* What do you think this means?

☞ "Nothing in the swamp is given" means to me that...

[_____]
[_____]
[_____]

4. Scatter says the real path doesn't feel safe. Why is the right choice sometimes the scariest?

☞ The right choice is sometimes scary because...

[_____]
[_____]
[_____]

● PREDICTION LADDER

1 Will Scatter forgive Ernie?

☞ I think Scatter will / won't forgive Ernie because...

[_____]
[_____]

2 What does "no one comes out the same" mean?

☞ It might mean that...

[_____]
[_____]

3 Who might become the next leader?

☞ I predict that _____ will lead because...

[_____]
[_____]

♒ FLUENCY PRACTICE

Line Practice

Read this line aloud in three different tones: mysterious, threatening, calm.

Line: "Leave behind a truth… or lose a memory."

Choose the tone that felt strongest.

I think the _____ tone worked best because...

[_____]
[_____]

℘ SCHEMA CONNECTIONS

Have you ever been in a situation where you had to be honest, forgive someone, or rebuild trust?

Describe it:

[_____]
[_____]
[_____]
[_____]

CAN YOU THINK OF A SPOOKY PLACE IN A BOOK OR MOVIE WHERE the hero had to face their fears?

[_____]
[_____]
[_____]
[_____]

EXTENDED REFLECTION PROMPT

What does this chapter teach us about friendship and forgiveness?

Is honesty always the best choice—even when it hurts?

Write 3–4 thoughtful sentences:

[_____]
[_____]
[_____]
[_____]
[_____]
[_____]
[_____]
[_____]
[_____]
[_____]

✍ CER WRITING — CLAIM, EVIDENCE, REASONING

Prompt: Was it right for Ernie to tell the truth, even though it hurt Scatter?

📣 CLAIM

I believe it was / was not the right choice for Ernie to confess because...

[_____]
[_____]

📚 EVIDENCE

In the story, we see that...

[_____]
[_____]

ONE EXAMPLE IS WHEN...

[_____]

[_____]

REASONING

This shows that...

[_____]
[_____]

EVEN THOUGH IT HURT, IT MEANS...

[_____]
[_____]

☑ CHECKLIST

☐ Clear claim
☐ Text evidence
☐ Thoughtful reasoning

POETRY PACK

Chapter 13: "Whispers of the Swamp"

Poetry Style: Narrative Poem

Excerpt from the Poem:

In the heart of the forest, under moon's ghostly light,
Through twisted ironwood trees, past the edge of night,
Lies the Swamp of Mists, where secrets sleep tight,
And shadows dance with the fog's eerie sight.

☞ Poetry Activities

ACTIVITY 1: Mood Map

Match the poem's lines to their emotion.

• "Blue Orchid Moonflowers glow without a sound"
  Feeling: _____
• "Shadows dance with the fog's eerie sight"

☞ Feeling: _____
• "Friends show their truth, and their character appears"
☞ Feeling: _____

ACTIVITY 2: Sketch the Swamp

Draw a scene based on the poem:

🌫 What do you see?

🌳 What grows there?

🔦 What color is the light?

✏ [Blank space for drawing]

[_____]
[_____]
[_____]
[_____]
[_____]
[_____]
[_____]
[_____]
[_____]
[_____]

ACTIVITY 3: Fog Words

Write three "foggy" words—words that sound spooky, soft, or secretive.

1.

2.

3.

ACTIVITY 4: Story Starter

Begin this story in 2–3 sentences:

"Through the thick mist, I spotted a faint blue light..."

☞

[_____]

[_____]
[_____]
[_____]
[_____]
[_____]
[_____]

⏱ BONUS ACTIVITY: TRAIT TRACKER

Track a character's emotions across key events. Choose one character.

Event: Entering the swamp
Emotion: _____

Event: Meeting the Guardians
Emotion: _____

Event: After Henry's confession
Emotion: _____

Event: During the vulture attack
Emotion: _____

Event: After Ernie's confession
Emotion: _____

Event: Escaping the swamp
Emotion: _____

☑ SKILL TRACKER

☐ I used new vocabulary
  ☐ I made predictions
  ☐ I practiced expressive reading
  ☐ I connected ideas to friendship and forgiveness
  ☐ I reflected thoughtfully on truth and trust

You made it through the Swamp of Mists—not just with courage, but with insight. Keep going. The road ahead still waits... and so does Wakaduo.

14

TRAPPED AND TRICKED

Student Workbook – Chapter 14: *Trapped and Tricked*
Proverb: *No matter how many times you wash a goat, it still smells like a goat.*

Name: _____

Date: _____

CHAPTER QUEST

● **CHAPTER 14 –** *Trapped and Tricked*

▌ CORE READING SKILL FOCUS

▢ **Skill:** Analyzing Leadership Through Cause and Effect

◉ **WHY IT MATTERS:** GURR'S ACTIONS TEST THE IDEA OF NOBLE leadership versus self-serving cunning. Students deepen their understanding of ethical dilemmas, examining how strategy, sacrifice, and deception shape outcomes.

🔍 **Focus in This Chapter:** Readers analyze how Gurr's choices lead to immediate safety but long-term uncertainty. They track cause-and-effect moments and evaluate whether ends justify the means, using text evidence to form arguments about what makes someone a true leader.

CHAPTER SUMMARY

In the wild Congo jungle, Gurr leads his followers through vines, mud, and danger. When tiger fish strike, he survives. When quicksand threatens, he pushes forward. But when the Boulder of Passage blocks the way, Gurr doesn't fight—he tricks. Pretending to be someone he's not, he gets Adira to open Wakaduo. He declares himself king. Not with strength, but with deception. The animals are safe… for now. But Tau watches from the shadows.

🔤 VOCABULARY PRACTICE

WORD LIST
- *Goat* – Symbol of stubbornness
- *Deception* – The act of tricking
- *Quicksand* – Wet sand that pulls you down
- *Predator* – A hunter animal
- *Treacherous* – Full of hidden danger

· · ·

Task A: Fill-in-the-blank

Choose from the word bank above:

1 The _____ vines hid dangers beneath beauty.

2 Gurr used _____ to enter Wakaduo.

Task B: Vocabulary Art

Choose one word and draw a quick sketch showing its meaning. Label your illustration.

✏ Word: _____

✎ Description:

[_____]
[_____]
[_____]
[_____]
[_____]
[_____]
[_____]
[_____]

⬤ Word Part Decoder – Morphology Match

📍 Match the word parts to their meanings:

1 de- → _____

2 cept → _____

3 -ion → _____

4 pred → _____

5 -or → _____

Now decode:

• **Deception** = de- () + **cept** () + -ion (_____)

✎ Meaning:

[_____]
[_____]

. . .

- **PREDATOR** = PRED () **+ -OR** ()
  ✎ Meaning:

  [_____]
  [_____]

BONUS WORD:

- **Treacherous** = treach + -erous

What do you think "treach" might mean based on context?

✎ Treacherous means:

  [_____]
  [_____]

SYMBOL-BASED LEARNING PROMPT

Match each word with a visual symbol:

🐐 = Goat (symbol of stubbornness)

🃏 = Deception

⌇ = Quicksand

🐾 = Predator

! = Treacherous

WRITE THE MATCHING WORD NEXT TO EACH:

1 _____ = 🐐
2 _____ = 🃏
3 _____ = ⌇
4 _____ = 🐾
5 _____ = !

PROVERB REFLECTION

📜 Proverb: *"No matter how many times you wash a goat, it still smells like a goat."*

. . .

Prompt:

This proverb means that some people or things can't be changed just by appearance or effort. Their true nature remains.

✍ What does this proverb mean to you?

[_____]
[_____]
[_____]
[_____]
[_____]
[_____]

Gurr changes how he *looks*, but not who he is. How is this connected?

[_____]
[_____]
[_____]
[_____]

📖 COMPREHENSION CHECK

Answer in complete sentences.

1 What blocks Gurr's path on the way to Wakaduo?

[_____]
[_____]

2 **How does he survive the tiger fish attack?**

[_____]
[_____]

3 **Why does Gurr trick Adira?**

[_____]
[_____]

4 WHAT HAPPENS AFTER THE BOULDER OF PASSAGE OPENS?

[_____]
[_____]

5 WHY IS TAU STILL FEARED, EVEN THOUGH GURR BECOMES KING?

[_____]
[_____]

● PREDICTION LADDER

1 What might Tau do next?

[_____]
[_____]

2 WILL THE ANIMALS ACCEPT GURR AS KING? WHY OR WHY NOT?

[_____]
[_____]

3 WHAT COULD GO WRONG UNDER GURR'S RULE?

[_____]
[_____]

🎵 FLUENCY PRACTICE

Try reading these lines aloud with a partner using tone and feeling.
- Gurr (bold): *"I am Gurr. I am the new king."*
- Undarvu (afraid): *"Gurr... what are you doing? Tau will not stand for this!"*

◎ Try reading each line:
☐ Bold
☐ Angry
☐ Calm
☐ Disappointed
☐ Urgent

Discuss: Which tone felt strongest? Why?

✏ I chose _____ because it made the character sound _____.

🔗 SCHEMA CONNECTIONS

Have you ever experienced something like this? Choose one and write a short response:
- A time you were tricked or tricked someone else
- A pressured decision you had to make
- A time when being clever helped you succeed

✎ YOUR CONNECTION:

[_____]
[_____]
[_____]
[_____]

REFLECTION PROMPTS

Theme: Trickery, Power, and Leadership

1 Gurr takes Wakaduo by surprise. Is he a hero, a villain, or something in between?

✍ I think Gurr is a _____ because...

[_____]
[_____]

✍ Even though he helped his group, he also...

[_____]
[_____]

✍ This shows that leaders can be...

[_____]
[_____]

2 Tomba and Undarvu must choose between safety and sacrifice. When have you seen someone be brave for others?

✍ A time I saw someone be brave was when...

[_____]
[_____]

✍ They put others first by...

[_____]
[_____]

✍ That reminded me of how Tomba/Undarvu...

3 Gurr says: *"Together, we are strong."* Do you agree?

✍ I agree with Gurr because...

[_____]

[_____]

✎ ONE TIME A GROUP HELPED ME WAS WHEN...

[_____]
[_____]

✎ BEING PART OF A TEAM GAVE ME THE COURAGE TO...

[_____]
[_____]

4 THE BOULDER OF PASSAGE OPENS THROUGH A LIE. WHAT ARE THE dangers of pretending to be someone you're not?

✎ Pretending to be someone else can be dangerous because...

[_____]
[_____]

✎ GURR'S ACTIONS SHOW THAT LYING MIGHT LEAD TO...

[_____]
[_____]

✎ SOMETIMES IT'S BETTER TO TELL THE TRUTH BECAUSE...

[_____]
[_____]

✎ EXTENDED REFLECTION PROMPT

Gurr used deception to claim power.

Do you think his leadership will last?
• What kind of leader does Wakaduo truly need?
• Can someone who lies to lead be trusted?
✎ Write 3–4 thoughtful sentences below:

[_____]
[_____]
[_____]
[_____]
[_____]
[_____]
[_____]
[_____]
[_____]
[_____]

MINI CER WRITING PROMPT

Prompt: Was Gurr a true leader—or just a clever usurper?

CLAIM

I believe Gurr is a (true leader / trickster / something in between) because...

[_____]
[_____]

EVIDENCE

In the story, he...

[_____]
[_____]

ONE EXAMPLE IS WHEN...

[_____]
[_____]

. . .

REASONING

This shows that Gurr...

[_____]
[_____]

EVEN THOUGH HE USED DECEPTION, IT MEANS...

[_____]
[_____]

✅ CHECKLIST

☐ Clear claim
☐ Evidence from the text
☐ Good explanation of reasoning

📓 POETRY PACK

Chapter 14: "The Old Path Through the Congo"
Poetry Style: Narrative Poem

NARRATIVE POEM: THE OLD PATH THROUGH THE CONGO

Through the winding paths where wild vines creep,
Gurr's band pressed on, through jungle deep.
The trees stood watch, both friend and foe,
Where dangers lurked in the green below.

THE RIVER ROARED, A BEAST UNSEEN,
Its waters dark, its teeth so keen.
Quicksand whispered beneath the leaves,

A trap for those whom fate deceives.

SHADOWS SLITHERED, SILENT, FAST,
  The jungle hummed of dangers past.
  A hunter's snare, a stalker's gaze,
  Through tangled green, the fireflies blazed.

YET GURR, WITH EYES BOTH SHARP AND WISE,
  Saw through the jungle's clever guise.
  "This path deceives, but we'll outplay,
  Not by strength, but wits today."

THEY MOVED LIKE WHISPERS, SWIFT AND LOW,
  Through river's breath and tangled woe.
  To cross the tide, to test their fate,
  With cunning hearts, they'd shift their state.

☉ POETRY ACTIVITIES

ACTIVITY 1: DANGER DETECTIVES

THE JUNGLE IS FULL OF RISKS. UNDERLINE OR LIST ALL THE DANGERS you find in the poem.
  • River's roar
  • Quicksand
  • Stalker's gaze
  • Slippery stones
  • Tiger fish

. . .

WRITE TWO DANGERS YOU WOULD BE MOST AFRAID OF:

1. _____

2. _____

ACTIVITY 2: SOUND EXPLORER

List three sounds you imagine in this jungle:

1. _____

2. _____

3. _____

ACTIVITY 3: WHAT WOULD YOU DO?

You're stuck in the jungle. Quicksand is ahead! What do you do?
✎ Write your escape plan (2–3 sentences):

[_____]
[_____]
[_____]
[_____]
[_____]
[_____]
[_____]
[_____]

ACTIVITY 4: SECRET POEM TITLE

Make up your own secret title for this poem:
My title:

[_____]
[_____]

WHY DID YOU CHOOSE THIS TITLE?

[_____]
[_____]
[_____]
[_____]

BONUS: JOURNEY CHART

Track the group's journey by place, challenge, and outcome.

Place: Congo Jungle
• Challenge: _____
• Outcome: _____
Place: Ugalla River
• Challenge: _____
• Outcome: _____
Place: Wakaduo
• Challenge: _____
• Outcome: _____

FINAL REFLECTION – EXIT TICKET

1. One thing I learned about leadership or truth in this chapter:

[_____]
[_____]

2. One question I still have is:

[_____]
[_____]

✅ SKILL TRACKER

☐ Understood vocabulary
   ☐ Summarized the chapter
   ☐ Made predictions
   ☐ Explored character choices
   ☐ Connected poetry to theme
   ☐ Reflected on truth and leadership

YOU MADE IT THROUGH VINES, SHADOWS, AND SHARP TEETH. BUT **the greatest challenge may lie just ahead.**

JOURNAL 3: AFTER CHAPTER 14 – SECRETS AND SHADOWS

Chapters 10–14 Summary: Betrayals are revealed. Scatter begins showing leadership qualities. The tension in the forest rises.

Page 1 – Reflect & Write

Prompt 1:

"I used to think… but now I think…"

➤ About whether it's okay to hide the truth to protect others

_____

_____

Prompt 2:

Who changed the most in these chapters? What caused that change?

_____

_____

Prompt 3:

If you were Scatter, what would you do differently? Why?

_____

_____

Page 2 – Create & Connect

• **Draw** your own "trust scale" with characters placed from "most trustworthy" to "least"

• **Write** a forest law you think should be added to protect everyone.

[_____]
[_____]
[_____]
[_____]

🌸 15 🌸

LAKE EYASI

Name: _____
Date: _____

CHAPTER QUEST

● **CHAPTER 15 –** *Lake Eyasi*

📖 CORE READING SKILL FOCUS

📖 **Skill:** Interpreting Theme Through Setting and Symbolism

◎ **WHY IT MATTERS:** THIS CHAPTER TEACHES STUDENTS TO LOOK beyond surface descriptions and recognize how a setting can reflect emotional depth, hidden threats, and character growth.

🔍 **FOCUS IN THIS CHAPTER:** STUDENTS WILL ANALYZE HOW LAKE Eyasi is both serene and treacherous, connecting its beauty to risk. Through metaphor and mood shifts, they interpret how trust and danger coexist—and how strength is shown not just in survival, but in sending messages of hope.

CHAPTER SUMMARY

The heroes reach Lake Eyasi, a place of beauty and danger. Tusker is attacked by a crocodile but saved by a hippo. They meet **Lebron**, the Sacred Ibis, who agrees to carry a message back to Wakaduo—bringing hope to those resisting Gurr's rule. As they reflect on their journey, the group learns that beauty may hide danger—and that strength comes not only from force, but from trust, unity, and courage.

VOCABULARY PRACTICE

Word List:

- *CHALLENGES* – HARD SITUATIONS OR TESTS

- *SILVERTIP TREE* – A SILVER-LEAFED TREE FOUND NEAR THE LAKE

- *TREACHEROUS* – DANGEROUS OR DECEPTIVE

. . .

• *GRACE* – SMOOTH, ELEGANT MOVEMENT OR BEHAVIOR

🖐 WORD PART DECODER – MORPHOLOGY MATCH

🔎 **BREAK THESE WORDS INTO PARTS:**

1. Deceptive = de- + cept + -ive

✎ Means:

[_____]
[_____]
[_____]

2 REFLECTION = RE- + FLECT + -ION

✎ Means:

[_____]
[_____]
[_____]

3 NAVIGATE = NAV + -IGATE

✎ Means:

[_____]
[_____]
[_____]

MINI CHALLENGE:

What does the root **nav** suggest about movement or travel?

✎ Clue: It's also in "navy," "navigate," "navigation"...

[_____]
[_____]
[_____]

• • •

MATCH THE MEANING

Write the word next to its meaning.

1 _____: Something that seems nice but may be dangerous

2 _____: Beautiful movement or kind behavior

3 _____: Difficult tests or struggles

4 _____: A tree with shimmering silver leaves

SYMBOL-BASED VOCABULARY MATCHING

Use emojis to visually connect each word:

= Silvertip Tree

= Grace

= Reflection

= Treacherous

= Challenges

1 Silvertip Tree = _____

2 Grace = _____

3 Reflection = _____

4 Treacherous = _____

5 Challenges = _____

BONUS SKETCH TASK:

Draw one symbol and write a sentence using the word in context!

[Drawing Space]

[_____]
[_____]
[_____]
[_____]
[_____]
[_____]
[_____]

📖 COMPREHENSION CHECK

Answer in full sentences.

1 What danger surprises the group at Lake Eyasi?

[_____]
[_____]
[_____]

2 WHO RESCUES TUSKER DURING THE ATTACK?

[_____]
[_____]
[_____]

3 WHAT ROLE DOES LEBRON PLAY IN THIS CHAPTER?

[_____]
[_____]
[_____]

4 WHAT LESSON DOES THE LAKE SEEM TO TEACH THE GROUP?

[_____]
[_____]
[_____]

⬤ PREDICTION LADDER

1 What do you think Wakaduo will do after receiving Lebron's message?

[_____]

[_____]
[_____]

2 WILL THE HEROES STAY SAFE AT LAKE EYASI, OR WILL NEW
dangers appear?

[_____]
[_____]
[_____]

3 WHAT DO YOU THINK WILL TEST THE GROUP NEXT ON THEIR
journey?

[_____]
[_____]
[_____]

☘ FLUENCY & EXPRESSION PRACTICE

Read aloud with emotion:
- Tusker: *"Stick together, and we'll be fine."*
- Ernie: *"There are crocodiles below! Move now!"*
- Narrator: *"The lake, once calm, exploded into chaos."*
- ◎ Practice Tip: Try changing your tone:
- Calm → Panicked
- Steady → Urgent
- Hopeful → Scared

Partner Response:
☞ "You sounded most powerful when you read:

[_____]
[_____]

✐ SCHEMA CONNECTION

Think about your own experiences.

Have you ever seen or experienced something beautiful that turned out to be dangerous or surprising?

✎ Write a short reflection:

[_____]
[_____]
[_____]
[_____]

REFLECTION PROMPTS

Theme: Beauty, Danger, and Hidden Strength
   Proverb: *A beautiful thing is never perfect.*

1. WHAT DOES THIS PROVERB MEAN IN YOUR OWN WORDS?

[_____]
[_____]

2. HOW DOES LAKE EYASI SHOW BOTH BEAUTY AND DANGER?

[_____]
[_____]

3 CAN YOU THINK OF ANOTHER PLACE OR SITUATION THAT WAS BOTH lovely and risky?

[_____]
[_____]

🐚 PROVERB REFLECTION

🪨 Proverb: *"A beautiful thing is never perfect."*

Prompt 1: What does this mean in your own words?

[_____]
[_____]

PROMPT 2: HOW DOES THIS IDEA APPEAR IN THE CHAPTER?

☞ Lake Eyasi looks _____, but underneath it _____.

PROMPT 3: CAN BEAUTY AND DANGER EXIST IN PEOPLE TOO?

☞ One example of this is...

[_____]
[_____]

⚱ MINI CER WRITING PROMPT — CHAPTER 15

Prompt: How do Tusker and Lebron show leadership in different ways?

Who do you think is the stronger leader in this chapter?

📣 CLAIM

I believe that _____ is the stronger leader because...

[_____]
[_____]

📜 EVIDENCE

In the chapter, _____ shows leadership when...

[_____]
[_____]

ANOTHER EXAMPLE IS WHEN...

[_____]
[_____]

REASONING

This shows that _____ leads by...

[_____]
[_____]

IT ALSO PROVES THAT _____ HELPS OTHERS BY...

[_____]
[_____]

THEIR LEADERSHIP MATTERS BECAUSE...

[_____]
[_____]

✅ CHECKLIST
☐ Clear opinion
☐ At least one piece of evidence

□ Reasoning that explains leadership

POETRY PACK — *WHISPERS OF LAKE EYASI*

Poem Type: Lyric Poem
   Theme: Nature, Reflection, Hidden Dangers
   Proverb Connection: *"A beautiful thing is never perfect."*
   Excerpt:
In the early dawn's embrace,
Where whispers dress the morning's face,
Lake Eyasi reveals her grace,
Mirroring the sky's wide space.
Below her calm and shining glow,
Dark shapes drift in the depths below.
Her beauty hides what none can know—
A dance of danger, swift and slow.

POETRY ACTIVITIES
ACTIVITY 1: Hidden Dangers
Circle any words or phrases from the poem that hint at danger.
- Glimmering waters
- Crocodile shadows
- Shining glow
- Dark shapes
- Morning's face

ACTIVITY 2: NATURE'S MIRROR
The lake reflects more than just the sky. What else might it reflect?

It reflects:

[_____]
[_____]

. . .

(HINT: FEAR, TEAMWORK, LOSS, STRENGTH, MEMORY...)

ACTIVITY 3: WHISPER LINE

Imagine the lake is whispering something to you. Write your own poetic "whisper."

✎ My Whisper Line:

[_____]
[_____]

ACTIVITY 4: SKETCH THE SCENE

Draw Lake Eyasi with:
- One beautiful feature
- ! One hidden danger

✏ Label your drawing:

- Beautiful thing: _____
- Dangerous thing: _____

[_____]
[_____]
[_____]
[_____]
[_____]
[_____]
[_____]
[_____]
[_____]
[_____]
[_____]
[_____]

BONUS ACTIVITY – COMPARE BEAUTY & DANGER

Write two bullet points for each:
Peaceful Parts of Lake Eyasi:

-
-

DANGEROUS PARTS OF LAKE EYASI:

-
-

Optional: Create a mini Venn diagram comparing beauty and risk at the lake.

[_____]
[_____]
[_____]
[_____]
[_____]
[_____]
[_____]
[_____]

FINAL REFLECTION – EXIT TICKET

1 One thing I learned about nature or trust in this chapter:

[_____]
[_____]

2 ONE QUESTION I STILL HAVE IS:

[_____]
[_____]

☑ SKILL TRACKER

☐ Used vocabulary in context
   ☐ Summarized the story clearly
   ☐ Analyzed character leadership

☐ Connected poem to story theme
☐ Reflected on danger, beauty, and trust

You're moving forward with wisdom and courage. Keep your eyes open—the surface may shimmer, but danger swims below.

 Standards Connections:
- RL.4.1: Use evidence to support theme and mood
- RL.4.4: Understand figurative and sensory language
- W.4.3: Write with imagery and emotion

※

✅ Great work completing the workbook. Keep going!

❧ 16 ❧

PREDATOR'S BATTLE

PREDATOR'S BATTLE

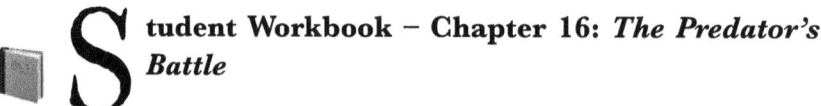

Student Workbook – Chapter 16: *The Predator's Battle*

NAME: _____

   Date: _____

PROVERB: *A BEING WHO USES FORCE IS AFRAID OF REASONING.*

CHAPTER QUEST

📖 CORE READING SKILL FOCUS

📖 **Skill:** Evaluating Leadership Through Dialogue and Motivation

◎ **WHY IT MATTERS:** THIS CHAPTER CENTERS ON POWER, persuasion, and the complexity of alliances. Students explore how tone, word choice, and hidden motives reveal different styles of leadership—and which are most effective.

🔍 **Focus in This Chapter:** Readers compare Liona's reasoned unity to Dirty Donald's sarcastic doubt, analyzing how dialogue and demeanor shape power. They infer motivations, evaluate loyalty, and consider how wisdom may (or may not) prevail over force.

CHAPTER SUMMARY

Under moonlight in the Ruaha savanna, predator factions battle for control. Growls echo, tensions rise—but then Liona, the lioness, steps forward. Her calm voice and sharp mind cut through the chaos. She reminds them: the true enemy is not each other, but the heroes of Wakaduo. A fragile alliance begins to form. Yet behind the uneasy peace, betrayal is already slinking in the shadows.

🔤 VOCABULARY PRACTICE

A. Key Words in Context

Write the meaning in your own words after reading:

• **Reasoning**:

[_____]
[_____]

· · ·

• **CONFRONTATION**:

[_____]
[_____]

• **CRUCIAL**:

[_____]
[_____]

B. MORPHOLOGY PRACTICE
Break each word into its parts:
• *Deception* = _____ + _____ + _____
• *Predator* = _____ + _____ + _____
• *Treacherous* = _____ + _____ + _____

CHAPTER 16 – *THE PREDATOR'S BATTLE*
Word Part Decoder – Morphology Match

MATCH THE WORD PARTS TO THEIR MEANING:
1 re- → _____
2 -ing → _____
3 con- → _____
4 front → _____
5 -ation → _____

DECODE EXAMPLES:
• **Reasoning** = re- () **+ son** () + -ing (_____)
Meaning:

[_____]
[_____]

. . .

- **CONFRONTATION** = CON- () **+ FRONT** () + -ATION (_____)
  ✎ Meaning:

  [_____]
  [_____]

SYMBOL-BASED VOCABULARY MAP

Match each term to its symbol:

- 🧠 = Reasoning
- ⚔ = Confrontation
- ❗ = Crucial
- 🗨 = Deception
- 🐺 = Predator

Write the matching word beside each icon:

1 🧠 → _____
2 ⚔ → _____
3 ❗ → _____
4 🗨 → _____
5 🐺 → _____

PROVERB REFLECTION PROMPT

"A being who uses force is afraid of reasoning."

1. WHAT DOES THIS MEAN IN YOUR OWN WORDS?

   [_____]
   [_____]

2. HOW IS THIS PROVERB REFLECTED IN LIONA'S LEADERSHIP STYLE?

   [_____]
   [_____]

· · ·

3. Do you agree that force often hides fear or weakness? Why or why not?

[_____]
[_____]

C. Vocabulary Synonym Match

Match the vocabulary word to its synonym by writing the correct letter.

Words:

1 Reasoning

2 Confrontation

3 Crucial

Synonyms:

A. Logical thinking

B. Face-off or argument

C. Very important

Your Answers:

1 → _____

2 → _____

3 → _____

READING COMPREHENSION CHECK

Multiple Choice

Choose the best answer for each question.

1 What was Liona's goal during the fight?

☐ A) Prove her strength

☐ B) Join Dirty Donald

☐ C) Stop the predators from fighting each other

☐ D) Defend her territory

. . .

2 WHY DO THE WILD DOGS WAIT NEAR THE EDGE OF THE BATTLE?
- ☐ A) They don't care
- ☐ B) They're scared of Tau
- ☐ C) They want to see who wins before choosing sides
- ☐ D) They're planning to attack last

3 WHAT IS THE MAJOR THEME OF THIS CHAPTER?
- ☐ A) Nature vs. civilization
- ☐ B) Magic vs. power
- ☐ C) Power struggles and alliances
- ☐ D) Revenge and fear

SHORT ANSWER

Answer in 1–2 complete sentences.

1. Why is the predators' alliance important?

[_____]
[_____]
[_____]
[_____]

2. WHAT DOES DIRTY DONALD'S BEHAVIOR REVEAL ABOUT HIS personality?

[_____]
[_____]
[_____]
[_____]

. . .

3. WHAT DOES THE PROVERB "A BEING WHO USES FORCE IS AFRAID OF reasoning" mean in this chapter?

[_____]
[_____]
[_____]
[_____]

PREDICTION LADDER

Answer using your best thinking and clues from the story.

1. Will the predators stay united? Why or why not?

[_____]
[_____]
[_____]
[_____]

2. WHO DO YOU THINK MIGHT BETRAY THE GROUP?

[_____]
[_____]
[_____]
[_____]

FLUENCY & EXPRESSION PRACTICE

Read aloud the following lines with emotion and pacing. Try three tones: serious, sarcastic, and tense.

• **Liona** (firm): "We're wasting our strength fighting among ourselves."

• **Dirty Donald** (skeptical): "You think a fancy speech makes us allies?"

• **Narrator** (tense): "In the shadows, the leopard said nothing— just watched."

☞ **Partner Feedback:**

You sounded most powerful when you read:

[_____]
[_____]

✐ SCHEMA CONNECTION

Think about a time a group you were in stopped arguing and began working together.

What helped them change?

✎ Write about it here:

[_____]
[_____]
[_____]
[_____]

✎ REFLECTION PROMPTS

Proverbs to Consider:

• *A being who uses force is afraid of reasoning.*
• *Knowledge without wisdom is like water in the sand.*

1 What do these proverbs mean in your own words?

[_____]
[_____]

2 How do they connect to the story and what happens in this chapter?

[_____]
[_____]

3 Can you think of a time someone led with wisdom instead of power?

· · ·

[_____]
[_____]

✍ CER WRITING – COMPARING LEADERS

Prompt: Who is the more effective leader in this chapter—Liona or Dirty Donald?

📣 CLAIM

I believe _____ is the more effective leader because...

[_____]
[_____]

📚 EVIDENCE

One moment that shows this is when...

[_____]
[_____]

ANOTHER EXAMPLE IS...

[_____]
[_____]

REASONING

This shows that _____ leads by...

[_____]
[_____]

It proves that...

[_____]
[_____]

POETRY PACK – *"WHISPER OF WAR"*

Poem Type: Free Verse

THEMES: POWER, REASONING, ALLIANCES, HIDDEN DANGER

Excerpt:

In the cool shadows of Ruaha,
where whispers weave through the leaves,
and the air shivers with the growls of the night,
the earth itself holds its breath...
Alliances shift like sand in a river,
and old grudges sharpen their claws.

POETRY ACTIVITIES
ACTIVITY 1: Mood & Tone Detectives

Circle or write down 2–3 words from the poem that show:
• Danger: _____
• Tension: _____
• Fear: _____

ACTIVITY 2: VIVID IMAGE DRAWING

Pick one line that creates a clear picture in your mind.
Favorite Line:

[_____]
[_____]

. . .

Now draw what you see:

[Sketch Space]

[_____]
[_____]
[_____]
[_____]
[_____]
[_____]
[_____]
[_____]
[_____]
[_____]

ACTIVITY 3: Sound Words

What sounds might you hear in this jungle scene?

Write 3 onomatopoeia (sound) words:

1.
2.
3.

ACTIVITY 4: Whisper from the Trees

Imagine you're a tree in the Ruaha jungle. You hear the predators planning.

Write one warning whisper to the heroes:

[_____]
[_____]
[_____]
[_____]

◎ BONUS ACTIVITIES (OPTIONAL)

• 🐾 Draw the predators' moonlit gathering

• 💬 REWRITE LIONA'S SPEECH TO MAKE IT EVEN MORE PERSUASIVE

• 📖 COMIC STRIP: DIRTY DONALD'S SECRET PLAN UNFOLDS IN FOUR panels

FINAL REFLECTION – EXIT TICKET

1. ONE THING I LEARNED ABOUT POWER OR PERSUASION IN THIS chapter:

[_____]
[_____]

2. ONE QUESTION I STILL HAVE IS:

[_____]
[_____]

☑ GREAT JOB COMPLETING CHAPTER 16!

The jungle is stirring, and alliances may break before they're built. Can words truly stop war—or will someone strike first?

➡ NEXT STOP: *CHAPTER 17 – TRAPPED.* KEEP YOUR REASONING sharp. 🐾🐾

❧ 17 ❧
TRAPPED

S tudent Workbook – Chapter 17: *Trapped*

NAME: _____

Date: _____

PROVERB: *TO RUN IS NOT NECESSARILY TO ARRIVE.*

CHAPTER QUEST

❧ CHAPTER 17 – *Trapped*

CORE READING SKILL FOCUS

Skill: Analyzing Character Motivation and Moral Complexity

· · ·

⊚ **WHY IT MATTERS:** STUDENTS ARE INVITED TO EXPLORE WHAT drives character choices under pressure—especially when instincts clash with loyalty. They consider how betrayal, regret, and redemption create emotional stakes that deepen character arcs.

⚲ **FOCUS IN THIS CHAPTER:** THROUGH TRICKER'S FEAR AND Henry's courageous instinct, readers examine the causes and consequences of difficult decisions. Students infer motivations, debate forgiveness, and reflect on how trust is broken—and how it might be rebuilt.

CHAPTER SUMMARY

Tricker finds himself caught between two sides—his past with the predators, and the heroes he's growing to care for. After being captured, he leads Tau's forces straight to the lake... but it's a trap. Henry summons a swarm of bees to scatter the enemy. Though the heroes escape, trust is shaken. Tricker must now face what it means to be both a betrayer—and someone seeking redemption.

[Image: *A swarm of bees chasing hyenas and predators through the tall grass*]

VOCABULARY BUILDER

MATCH THE WORD TO ITS MEANING

1 Predicament → _____

2 Treachery → _____

3 Deceived → _____

A. Tricked or misled into believing something false

B. Betrayal of trust; deceptive action or nature

C. A difficult, unpleasant, or embarrassing situation

USE THE WORDS IN A SENTENCE

• **Predicament:**

[_____]
[_____]

• **TREACHERY:**

[_____]
[_____]

• **DECEIVED:**

[_____]
[_____]

VOCABULARY EXTENSION

Use each word in a new sentence that shows its meaning:

• **Redemption** (making something right again):

[_____]
[_____]

. . .

• **INSTINCT** (NATURAL REACTION, NOT THOUGHT THROUGH):

[_____]
[_____]

CHAPTER 17 – *TRAPPED*
Morphology Match – Word Part Decoder
Break each word into its components and define:
• **Deceived** = de- () **+ ceive** () + -ed (_____)
• **Redemption** = re- () **+ dempt** () + -ion (_____)
• **Instinct** = in- () **+ stinct** ()

ONE THING THESE WORD PARTS TELL ME ABOUT "REDEMPTION" is...

[_____]
[_____]

SYMBOL-BASED WORD MATCHING
Symbol match for key ideas:
ⓢ = Predicament
↳ = Treachery
🐾 = Deception
 = Redemption
🔥 = Instinct

Match each icon to the word:

1 ⓢ → _____
2 ↳ → _____
3 🐾 → _____
4 → _____
5 🔥 → _____

. . .

OPTIONAL DRAWING PROMPT:

Draw one icon and illustrate a moment from the chapter where this symbol fits.

[_____]
[_____]
[_____]
[_____]
[_____]
[_____]
[_____]
[_____]
[_____]
[_____]

PROVERB REFLECTION

"To run is not necessarily to arrive."

1. What does this mean to you?

[_____]
[_____]

2. HOW DOES IT CONNECT TO TRICKER'S FEAR AND DECISION?

[_____]
[_____]

3. WHEN MIGHT "RUNNING" (OR AVOIDING SOMETHING) CAUSE MORE trouble than facing it?

[_____]
[_____]

📚 READING FOR MEANING

Multiple Choice

1. WHY DOES TRICKER BETRAY THE GROUP?
   - ☐ Ignorance
   - ☐ Self-preservation
   - ☐ Revenge
   - ☐ Envy

2. HOW DOES HENRY SAVE THE DAY?
   - ☐ Attacks the predators
   - ☐ Runs for safety
   - ☐ Summons the bees
   - ☐ Distracts the predators with yelling

SHORT ANSWER

- What mistake do the predators make?

[_____]
[_____]

- WHAT EMOTIONS DOES TRICKER FEEL AT THE END OF THE chapter?

[_____]
[_____]

🔄 CAUSE & EFFECT

Match the cause to its effect by writing a short explanation.

• • •

- **TRICKER LEADS PREDATORS TO LAKE** →

  [_____]
  [_____]

- **HENRY CALLS THE BEES** →

  [_____]
  [_____]

- **TRICKER IS CAPTURED** →

  [_____]
  [_____]

⏳ SEQUENCING THE EVENTS

Place the events in the correct order (1–5):

    ___ Tricker is captured
    ___ Henry calls the bees
    ___ Heroes cross the lake
    ___ Tricker offers betrayal
    ___ Predators are tricked

⬤ CHARACTER ANALYSIS

Write the character trait shown by the quote.

    • **Tricker** → "He offered to lead them to the heroes…"
Trait: _____

    • **Tau** → "For your treachery, you will know our wrath."
Trait: _____

    • **Henry** → "Henry called the bees to protect the camp."
Trait: _____

✍ CREATIVE WRITING: TRICKER'S JOURNAL

Write from Tricker's point of view.

Begin with:

Dear Journal, today I did something I never thought I would...

✍ [_____]
[_____]
[_____]
[_____]
[_____]
[_____]
[_____]
[_____]

❀ THEME TRACKER

Main Idea: ☑ *Betrayal can lead to survival—but at a cost.*

Proverb Connection:

What does *"To run is not necessarily to arrive"* mean in this chapter?

[_____]
[_____]
[_____]
[_____]

FIGURATIVE LANGUAGE DETECTIVE

"Like warriors of the wind..."

What does this metaphor tell you about the bees?

[_____]
[_____]

VISUAL LEARNING

Draw one of these scenes:
- Tricker's capture
- The bee swarm attack
- The heroes escaping across the lake

[_____]
[_____]
[_____]
[_____]
[_____]
[_____]
[_____]
[_____]
[_____]
[_____]

CAPTION:

"This moment matters because…"

[_____]
[_____]

REFLECTION QUESTIONS

Would you have done what Tricker did?

☐ Yes ☐ No — *Explain why:*

[_____]
[_____]

SHOULD TRICKER BE FORGIVEN?

☐ Yes ☐ No — *Explain why or why not:*

[_____]
[_____]

Most courageous character in this chapter?

☐ Henry ☐ Scatter ☐ Tau ☐ Charlese — *Explain:*

[_____]
[_____]

✏ CER WRITING – CHAPTER 17

Prompt: Why was Tricker's choice so difficult when he was trapped?

Claim

I believe Tricker's choice was difficult because...

[_____]
[_____]

Evidence

In the story it says...

[_____]
[_____]

One example is when...

[_____]
[_____]

Reasoning

This shows that...

[_____]

[_____]
[_____]

It means that...

[_____]
[_____]

Checklist:
☐ Clear claim
☐ Strong evidence from the text
☐ Clear reasoning

POST-READING PREDICTION TRACKER

Tricker has made a difficult choice. What happens next?
   1. What Tricker Did: He led the predators to the lake.
   How others might react:

[_____]
[_____]

What Tricker might do next:

[_____]
[_____]

2. What Tricker Did: He was saved by Henry and the bees.
   How others might react:

[_____]
[_____]

What Tricker might do next:

[_____]
[_____]

3. WHAT TRICKER DID: HE RETURNED TO THE GROUP, FULL OF guilt.

How others might react:

[_____]
[_____]

What Tricker might do next:

[_____]
[_____]

DISCUSSION STARTERS

• What would *you* have done in Tricker's place?

• WHAT'S HARDER—*EARNING FORGIVENESS* OR *FORGIVING SOMEONE else?*

• DOES THE GROUP *NEED* TO FORGIVE HIM TO MOVE ON? WHY OR why not?

POETRY PACK – CHAPTER 18 SNEAK PEEK:

The Welcome of Shadows and Light (For use next chapter)

This sonnet contrasts return, memory, and transformation. Use this to prepare for the emotional return to Wakaduo.

🌀 CHALLENGE EXTENSION

Write a Letter to Tricker:

What would you say to him if you were a fellow hero?

[_____]
[_____]
[_____]
[_____]
[_____]
[_____]
[_____]
[_____]
[_____]
[_____]

FINAL REFLECTION – EXIT TICKET

1. One insight I gained about fear or redemption:

[_____]
[_____]

2. ONE QUESTION I STILL WONDER ABOUT TRICKER OR THE GROUP'S next step:

[_____]
[_____]

✅ END OF CHAPTER 17

Your understanding of truth, fear, and redemption just deepened.

Keep asking hard questions—and keep turning the page. 🦋

A HERO'S WELCOME

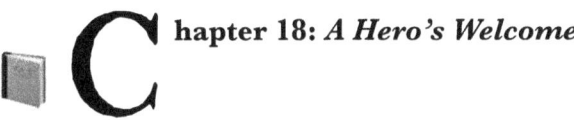

Chapter 18: *A Hero's Welcome*

NAME: _____

Date: _____

PROVERB: *CLOUDS COME FLOATING INTO MY LIFE, NO LONGER USHER storm or carry destruction, but add color to my sunset sky.*

CHAPTER QUEST

◼ **CHAPTER 18 –** *A Hero's Welcome*

▮ CORE READING SKILL FOCUS

📖 **Skill:** Tracking Mood Shifts and Theme Through Setting and Tone

. . .

☞ **WHY IT MATTERS:** IN THIS EMOTIONAL HOMECOMING, STUDENTS learn to "read between the lines" of celebration and suspicion. Tone, setting, and figurative language create tension as joy turns to confrontation.

🔍 **FOCUS IN THIS CHAPTER:** READERS INTERPRET HOW LANGUAGE and imagery foreshadow danger beneath the surface of Wakaduo's welcome. They analyze the symbolic power of forgiveness and reconciliation, while evaluating leadership in times of emotional upheaval.

📖 CHAPTER SUMMARY

The heroes return to Wakaduo. Though the land is familiar, everything has changed. Tricker apologizes for his betrayal. Some forgive him, others hesitate. As the villagers whisper, Gurr arrives and declares the heroes prisoners. A standoff begins—but so does a test of forgiveness, trust, and calm leadership.

🔤 VOCABULARY BUILDER

Word Match

Match each word to its correct meaning:

Orchestrated → _____

Betrayal → _____

Standoff → _____

Definitions:

A. A situation where two sides face each other and neither moves first

B. Carefully planned or arranged to reach a goal

C. A disloyal action that feels especially heartless or uncaring

. . .

USE IN A SENTENCE
- Orchestrated:

[_____]
[_____]
[_____]

- BETRAYAL:

[_____]
[_____]
[_____]

- STANDOFF:

[_____]
[_____]

☑ SYMBOL + MORPHOLOGY ENHANCEMENTS
For Chapter 18: *A Hero's Welcome*

🥢 MORPHOLOGY + WORD PART PRACTICE (VELLUM-FRIENDLY text)

Break the words below into their parts and define their meanings:

- **ORCHESTRATED** = PREFIX: *(NONE)* + ROOT: *ORCHESTR* (TO organize) + suffix: *-ated* (past participle)

- **BETRAYAL** = ROOT: *BETRAY* (TO DECEIVE) + SUFFIX: *-AL* (ACT OR result of)

. . .

• **FORGIVENESS** = ROOT: *FORGIVE* + SUFFIX: *-NESS* (STATE OF BEING)

PROMPT:

Which of these words best represents Tricker's growth in this chapter? Why?

[_____]
[_____]
[_____]

🎴 SYMBOL-BASED LEARNING

🎴 FORGIVENESS
– Choosing understanding over punishment
– Tricker hopes his apology restores trust

🪨 BETRAYAL
– Breaking trust or turning against your group
– Gurr's claim and past actions remind us betrayal has long shadows

🔗 STANDOFF
– Two sides face each other with no movement
– The moment before action, heavy with tension

🎼 ORCHESTRATED
– Carefully arranged or planned
– Gurr's appearance seems too perfect to be random

. . .

ACTIVITY: MATCH THE WORD TO THE SYMBOL

Write the word that best matches each symbol below:

1 🔧 → _____

2 🔨 → _____

3 🔍 → _____

4 🎼 → _____

DESIGN YOUR OWN SYMBOL

Create a symbol for **truth** or **calm leadership**.

What shape or object would represent that idea?

✏️ Sketch Space

[_____]
[_____]
[_____]
[_____]
[_____]
[_____]
[_____]
[_____]

🪶 MY SYMBOL NAME: _____

🪶 WHAT IT REPRESENTS:

[_____]
[_____]

🔍 READING FOR MEANING

Short Answer

• What is Tricker feeling when he apologizes?

[_____]
[_____]

. . .

- WHAT DOES THE PHRASE *"GRAIN IN A BAG WITH A HOLE"* MEAN?

  [_____]
  [_____]

- WHAT HAPPENS AFTER THE HEROES RETURN?

  [_____]
  [_____]

- WHY DOES GURR CALL THEM "PRISONERS"?

  [_____]
  [_____]
  [_____]
  [_____]

CAUSE & EFFECT

- Tricker feels regret → Apologizes
  - Gurr appears → Standoff begins
  - Scatter stays calm → Heroes prepare

SEQUENCING EVENTS

Place the events in order (1–5):

___ Tricker apologizes
___ Heroes return
___ Elders whisper
___ Gurr appears
___ Scatter prepares

CHARACTER DEEP DIVE

Scatter
- Traits: Calm, wise
- Quote: *"We'll stand our ground."*

TRICKER
- Traits: Honest, scared
- Quote: *"I almost betrayed you..."*

GURR
- Traits: Calculating
- Quote: *"Prisoners of your own fate."*

CREATIVE WRITING: *TRICKER'S REDEMPTION*

Write a journal entry from Tricker's point of view:

DEAR JOURNAL,
Today I told the truth. I was scared to say it, but...

[_____]
[_____]
[_____]
[_____]
[_____]
[_____]

VISUAL LEARNING: SCENE SKETCH

Choose and draw one moment:
- The heroes' return to Wakaduo
- Tricker's apology

- Gurr's dark reveal

[_____]
[_____]
[_____]
[_____]
[_____]
[_____]
[_____]
[_____]
[_____]
[_____]

MOOD METER (CIRCLE ONE):
- Arrival – Joyful
- Apology – Hopeful
- Gurr's entrance – Tense

⬛ THEME TRACKER

Theme: *Forgiveness helps restore peace*
Explain how this theme plays out in the chapter:

[_____]
[_____]
[_____]
[_____]
[_____]
[_____]

● REFLECTION QUESTIONS

- What lesson does Tricker learn?

[_____]
[_____]

. . .

- WHY DOES SCATTER FORGIVE HIM?

  [_____]
  [_____]

- HOW DOES GURR'S ENTRANCE SHIFT THE TONE?

  [_____]
  [_____]

- WHAT SHOULD THE HEROES DO NOW?

  [_____]
  [_____]

CER WRITING — OPTIONAL EXTENSION

Prompt: Why was forgiveness important for Tricker and the heroes?

CLAIM

I believe that...

[_____]
[_____]

EVIDENCE

In the story it says...

[_____]

[_____]
[_____]
[_____]

One example is when...

[_____]
[_____]

REASONING

This shows that...

[_____]
[_____]

It proves that...

[_____]
[_____]

Quick Checklist

☐ Clear answer
☐ Strong evidence
☐ Good explanation

CER Peer Review Checklist (Optional)

☑ Partner Checklist:

Clear claim about forgiveness

Specific text evidence

Good explanation

Focused on the question

. . .

WARM FEEDBACK:
"You did a great job explaining..."

SUGGESTION:
"Next time, maybe add more about..."

PREDICTION TRACKER

Tricker
- What is he feeling now?
- What might he do next?

[_____]
[_____]

SCATTER
- How is she responding as a leader?

[_____]
[_____]

Gurr
- What is his next move?
- What clues support your idea?

[_____]
[_____]

POETRY PACK – CHAPTER 18

Poem Title: *The Welcome of Shadows and Light*
  Poem Type: Sonnet
  Proverb Tie-In: "Clouds come floating into my life…"

· · ·

READ THE POEM:

Upon our return to fields once so bright,
The shadows stretch out, taking the light.
Our hearts full with tales of lands far and wide,
Find home transformed, with dusk where dawn once lied.
Marula whispers, children's laughter sings,
Yet beneath this joy, tension tightly clings.
Faces of old, with worry lines marked deep,
Stirring doubts that creep in, disrupting our sleep.
Yet here we stand, where roots and dreams entwine,
Wakaduo's soil, with destiny's design.
Gurr stands, his challenge dark against the sky,
Our welcome warm now a cold battle cry.
But heroes we are, through trials forged and tried,
Together we stand, with truth as our guide.

☞ STUDENT POETRY ACTIVITIES

ACTIVITY 1: FIND THE CONTRAST

Underline words in the poem that relate to:
• Light / Hope
• Darkness / Fear

ACTIVITY 2: WHAT CHANGED?

How is Wakaduo different now than when the heroes left?

[_____]
[_____]
[_____]
[_____]
[_____]
[_____]

. . .

ACTIVITY 3: Sound & Rhythm

Clap out this line: *"Upon our return to fields once so bright."*

Now write your own 5-beat line about Wakaduo:

✎

[_____]
[_____]
[_____]
[_____]
[_____]
[_____]

ACTIVITY 4: Your Own "Welcome" Line

Write a single poetic line imagining you return home after a long journey.

✎

[_____]
[_____]
[_____]
[_____]
[_____]
[_____]

☑ **End of Student Workbook – Chapter 18**

You've reached a turning point in the story—and in the heart. Keep going... the final trials await.

❧ 19 ❧
INTERLUDE - WHISPERS
BEFORE THE STORM

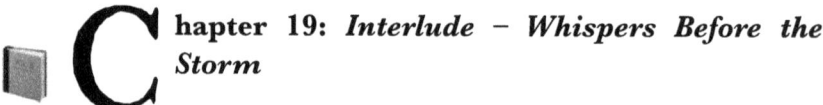

Chapter 19: *Interlude – Whispers Before the Storm*

NAME: _____

  Date: _____

PROVERB: *"NOT EVERY BATTLE IS FOUGHT WITH SWORDS. SOME BEGIN in silence."*

CHAPTER QUEST

CORE READING SKILL FOCUS

Skill: Synthesizing Meaning Across Chapters and Time

. . .

☉ **WHY IT MATTERS:** THIS INTERLUDE ASKS STUDENTS TO STEP back and see the *whole* story—how past choices echo into present tensions and future possibilities. It invites them to find connections between different characters, timelines, and truths.

🔍 **FOCUS IN THIS CHAPTER:** READERS GATHER THREADS FROM earlier chapters and preview those to come. They practice inference and synthesis, making sense of how stories, symbols, and history prepare both characters and readers for the turning point ahead.

📜 CHAPTER SUMMARY

Before the final storm arrives, the heroes take a breath. This interlude offers a pause in the action—a moment of quiet reflection. We learn how Wakaduo and Ruaha were once allies, and how fear, lies, and pride divided them. We are also introduced to three upcoming stories:
- Adira and Tau's shared past
- The predators' secret plan
- Alice's discovery of the Stone Bracelet

These glimpses remind us that strength isn't just about action—it's also about memory, legacy, and the choices we carry forward.

🔤 VOCABULARY BUILDER

Word List & Meanings

- **INTERLUDE** – A QUIET PAUSE BETWEEN MAJOR EVENTS
  - **Unity** – the state of being joined or working together
  - **Misinformation** – false or misleading information
  - **Reflection** – careful thought about something important
  - **Legacy** – what you leave behind for the future

. . .

Use in a Sentence
• Interlude:

[_____]
[_____]

• Misinformation:

[_____]
[_____]

• Legacy:

[_____]
[_____]

✅ SYMBOL + MORPHOLOGY ENHANCEMENTS
For Chapter 19: *Whispers Before the Storm*

This interlude is beautifully meditative. We'll add some visual + morphology support for key abstract concepts.

🪓 Morphology Word Builder
Decompose and define:

• **Interlude** = PREFIX: *INTER-* (BETWEEN) + ROOT: *LUDE* (PLAY)

• **Reflection** = ROOT: *REFLECT* (TO THINK OR BOUNCE BACK) + suffix: *-ion* (state or act of)

• **Misinformation** = PREFIX: *MIS-* (WRONG) + ROOT: *INFORM* + suffix: *-ation*

· · ·

DISCUSSION PROMPT:

Why might the author choose a word like *interlude* here? How does its root meaning connect to the chapter's purpose?

[_____]
[_____]
[_____]
[_____]

(THE INTERLUDE IS A GIFT. NOT OF ACTION, BUT OF AWARENESS. What do you carry into battle—truth, memory, unity? These are the real weapons.)

SYMBOL-BASED LEARNING

REFLECTION

– Looking inward; thinking deeply

– The interlude gives space to pause and understand what's been learned

LEGACY

– What we pass down to others

– The heroes begin to realize what they stand for and what they'll leave behind

MISINFORMATION

– Confusing or false information

– We learn how fear and false stories divided Wakaduo and Ruaha

. . .

UNITY
   – Togetherness, peace, and shared purpose
   – Once broken, the hope is that it can be restored

ACTIVITY: MATCH THE WORD TO THE SYMBOL
   1   → _____
   2   → _____
   3   → _____
   4   → _____

DESIGN YOUR OWN WHISPER SYMBOL
Imagine a symbol that shows **quiet strength** or **hidden wisdom**.

Sketch Space

[_____]
[_____]
[_____]
[_____]
[_____]
[_____]
[_____]

MY SYMBOL NAME: _____

WHAT IT REPRESENTS: _____

READING FOR MEANING

Answer each question in 1–2 thoughtful sentences.

. . .

1 WHY DO YOU THINK THE AUTHOR PAUSED THE ACTION HERE WITH an interlude?

[_____]
[_____]
[_____]

2 WHAT DO YOU THINK THE STONE BRACELET MIGHT REPRESENT IN the story?

[_____]
[_____]
[_____]

3 WHAT DOES ADIRA'S QUIET LEADERSHIP TEACH US ABOUT TRUE power?

[_____]
[_____]
[_____]

4 HOW DID THE PREDATORS NEARLY DIVIDE WAKADUO?

[_____]
[_____]
[_____]

⊙ SEQUENCING THE INTERLUDE CHAPTERS

Put these future-focused chapters in the correct order (1–3):

_____ *The Predator's Plot*
_____ *Alice and the Stone Bracelet*
_____ *Adira, the Tortoise, and Tau, the Lion*

. . .

HOW DO THESE THREE STORIES CONNECT TO THE BIGGER STORY OF
Wakaduo?

[_____]
[_____]
[_____]
[_____]
[_____]
[_____]

THEME TRACKER

Check off all themes that appear in this interlude. Then explain
how you saw them.

- ☐ Reflection
- ☐ Unity
- ☐ Leadership
- ☐ History
- ☐ Legacy

HOW DO THESE THEMES SHOW UP IN THE INTERLUDE?

[_____]
[_____]
[_____]
[_____]
[_____]
[_____]

WRITING REFLECTION

Prompt: The Interlude asks, *"What is your greatness—and how will you
unleash it?"*

. . .

WRITE A SHORT PARAGRAPH ABOUT A STRENGTH, GIFT, OR VALUE YOU want to carry forward in your own life—just like Scatter, Henry, or Adira does in the story.

[_____]
[_____]
[_____]
[_____]
[_____]
[_____]
[_____]
[_____]
[_____]

CREATIVE ACTIVITY: WHISPER SYMBOL

Design your own "whisper symbol"—a small shape, object, or symbol that represents quiet strength, hidden wisdom, or reflection.

Think of something simple but powerful. Give it a name and a short meaning.

Sketch your symbol here:

[_____]
[_____]
[_____]
[_____]
[_____]
[_____]
[_____]

NAME OF SYMBOL: _____

What it represents: _____

Examples:
- A spiral for deep thought
- A candle for truth

• A feather for quiet courage

⟳ OPTIONAL EXTENSION: THINK & DISCUSS

Choose one or more questions below and respond with your ideas.

1 What did Wakaduo and Ruaha once share that made them strong?

[_____]
[_____]
[_____]

2 HOW DOES KNOWING SOMEONE'S PAST OR HISTORY CHANGE HOW we see them?

[_____]
[_____]
[_____]

3 WHICH OF THE THREE FINAL CHAPTERS ARE YOU MOST CURIOUS about—and why?

[_____]
[_____]
[_____]

✔ END OF CHAPTER 19 WORKBOOK

This quiet moment reminds us: not all heroes roar. Some speak softly and still change the world.

Turn the page—the final truths await.

▌ JOURNAL 4: AFTER CHAPTER 19 – BEFORE THE FIRE

Chapters 15–19 Summary: Plans are made. Tensions peak. The group prepares for confrontation. Nature begins to mirror the characters' inner conflicts.

Page 1 – Reflect & Write
Prompt 1:
"I used to think… but now I think…"

➤ About whether kindness can be powerful in dangerous situations

_____
_____

Prompt 2:
What does leadership look like in hard times?

_____
_____

Prompt 3:
Describe a time when _you_ had to stay calm during something difficult.

_____
_____

Page 2 – Create & Connect

• **Draw** a symbol that shows courage in the face of fear

• **Write** a journal entry from the point of view of an animal watching the group pass by

[_____]

[_____]

[_____]

[_____]

[_____]

[_____]

[_____]

[_____]

[_____]

[_____]

[_____]

[_____]

[_____]

[_____]

[_____]

❧ 20 ❧

ADIRA THE TORTOISE AND
TAU THE LION

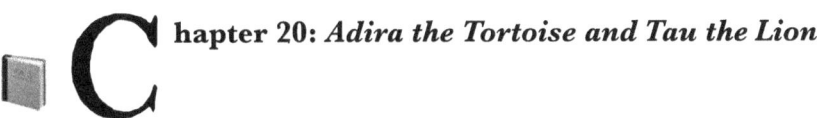

Chapter 20: *Adira the Tortoise and Tau the Lion*

NAME: _____

    Date: _____

PROVERB: *"WHEN THE MUSIC CHANGES, SO DOES THE DANCE."*

CHAPTER QUEST

🦁 **CHAPTER 20 –** *Adira the Tortoise and Tau the Lion*

📖 CORE READING SKILL FOCUS

📖 **Skill:** Analyzing Dialogue, Symbolism, and Leadership Contrast

· · ·

◉ **Why it Matters:** This chapter brings abstract themes—like tradition, power, and diplomacy—into a vivid moment of choice. Students compare leadership styles, analyze symbolism (like the boulder and storm), and consider how tone and language reflect internal conflict.

🔍 **Focus in This Chapter:** By examining Tau's refusal and Adira's hope, students explore how leaders' choices shape their people's futures. They practice using dialogue and metaphor as tools for understanding character psychology and moral tension.

📖 CHAPTER SUMMARY

Adira travels to the edge of Wakaduo to meet Tau, hoping to prevent war between Wakaduo and Ruaha. Calm and wise, she pleads for unity—but Tau, proud and cautious, refuses. He believes predators and prey will always be divided. As Adira returns home, clouds gather overhead—both in the sky and in the hearts of the animals waiting below. Adira is disappointed and thoughtful. Some animals feel relieved. Others wonder: is isolation really the safest path?

VOCABULARY BUILDER

MATCH THE WORD TO ITS MEANING

1 Haven → _____

2 Reluctance → _____

3 Sanctity → _____

Choose from:

A. Sacredness or importance

B. A safe, peaceful place

C. Hesitation or unwillingness

ADD-ON VOCABULARY

4. REFUGE – A PLACE OF SHELTER OR SAFETY

✎ Sentence Prompt: Wakaduo was a peaceful refuge from the dangers outside the boulder.

5. TREACHEROUS – FULL OF HIDDEN DANGERS OR BETRAYAL

✎ Sentence Prompt: The stormy skies made the meeting feel tense and treacherous.

CHALLENGE: USE BOTH WORDS IN YOUR OWN SENTENCE OR SHORT paragraph about Adira's journey.

✎ [_____]
  [_____]

✎ [_____]
  [_____]

· · ·

"LET'S CRACK THE CODE OF MEANING! USE THESE SIMPLE SYMBOLS to unlock word parts before you try the Word Part Decoder on your own."

Symbol-Based Learning Toolkit

ADIRA – THE VOICE OF PEACE

– Symbolizes diplomacy, wisdom, and quiet persistence

– Uses gentle reasoning and metaphor to reach across conflict

TAU – THE PROTECTOR OF PRIDE

– Represents strength, fear of vulnerability, and loyalty to tradition

– His body language and refusal reflect inner conflict

THE BOULDER

– Symbol of division and weight of history

– Stands between the two leaders as a physical and emotional obstacle

THE STORM CLOUDS

– Symbol of conflict rising, and emotional tension

– Mirrors the danger of unresolved disagreement

"WHEN THE MUSIC CHANGES…"

– Symbolic proverb: when circumstances shift, wise leaders must adapt

– A call for flexible, responsive leadership

ACTIVITY: SYMBOL MATCH-UP

Match each idea to its symbol. Write your answers below:

1 __ A leader who resists change
2 __ A symbol of division and history
3 __ A leader who speaks with calm and hope
4 __ A metaphor for approaching conflict
5 __ A saying that means: "Adapt or fall behind."

OPTIONAL DESIGN TASK

Create your own symbol for *unity*.

Draw a simple shape or object that represents coming together.

[_____]
[_____]
[_____]
[_____]
[_____]
[_____]

SYMBOL NAME: _____

WHAT IT REPRESENTS: _____

"NOW THAT YOU'VE EXPLORED OUR SYMBOL CLUES, TRY BUILDING your own words by finding roots, prefixes, and suffixes!"

WORD PART DECODER: CHAPTER 20 – *ADIRA THE TORTOISE and Tau the Lion*

FOCUS: UNDERSTANDING CHARACTER MOTIVATION THROUGH WORD structure

. . .

BREAK DOWN EACH WORD INTO **PREFIX**, **ROOT**, AND **SUFFIX** IF possible.

Write what each part means.

1. RELUCTANCE
- Prefix: re– (again/back)
- Root: luct (Latin: to struggle)
- Suffix: –ance (state of being)

✍ Meaning: A state of struggling against something; hesitation

2. SANCTITY
- Root: sanct (holy)
- Suffix: –ity (quality or state)

✍ Meaning: The quality of being sacred or important

3. REFUGE
- Root: fug (to flee)
- ✍ Meaning: A place where one flees for safety

🔄 MATCH THE MEANING

WRITE THE WORD THAT FITS EACH DEFINITION:

1 A place where you are protected: _____

2 Feeling of sacred importance: _____

3 Struggling to act: _____

🧠 Think & Reflect

How does the meaning of "reluctance" help us understand Tau?

[_____]
[_____]

· · ·

How does "sanctity" help explain Adira's vision for peace?

[_____]
[_____]

≋ READING FOR MEANING

Multiple Choice – Choose the best answer for each question:

1 Why does Adira visit Tau?
- ☐ A. To stop him from attacking Wakaduo
- ☐ B. To warn him about the storm
- ☐ C. To unite the two lands
- ☐ D. To find the Stone Bracelet

2 What is Tau afraid of?
- ☐ A. That he will lose power
- ☐ B. That peace will make predators weak
- ☐ C. That Wakaduo will trick him
- ☐ D. That Adira will betray him

3 What do the dark clouds symbolize?
- ☐ A. That a real storm is coming
- ☐ B. That night is falling
- ☐ C. Trouble or conflict ahead
- ☐ D. The death of an elder

Short Answer

4 What does Adira say to try convincing Tau?

[_____]

[_____]
[_____]
[_____]

5 WHY DOES TAU SAY NO?

[_____]
[_____]
[_____]

🔍 CHARACTER REFLECTION

Directions: For each character below, think about what they do, how they act, and what they want.

ADIRA

- One Action: _____
- One Trait: _____
- What She Wants: _____

TAU

- One Action: _____
- One Trait: _____
- What He Wants: _____

ADVICE PROMPT:

If you could give Tau one piece of advice, what would it be?

[_____]
[_____]

✎ VISUALIZING THE SCENE

Draw a moment from their meeting:
- The boulder between them
- Dark clouds gathering
- Adira's calm face, Tau's proud posture
- ✎ Caption: How do they feel during this moment?

[_____]
[_____]
[_____]
[_____]
[_____]
[_____]

✎ CAUSE & EFFECT PRACTICE

Match the cause to the correct effect:
- Adira sees the storm → _____
- Tau fears loss → _____
- Adira returns → _____

Match with:
A. Says no
B. Animals feel unsure
C. Asks Tau to unite

THINKING PROMPT

What might happen if the storm hits both lands while they remain divided?

✎

[_____]
[_____]
[_____]
[_____]

✍ WRITING PROMPT

Proverb Focus: *"When the music changes, so does the dance."*
What does this mean in the story? How does it apply to real life?

✍

[_____]
[_____]
[_____]
[_____]
[_____]
[_____]

✻ CHALLENGE ACTIVITY

Option A: *Letter to Tau (as Adira)*
Write a persuasive letter asking Tau to reconsider peace.

✍

[_____]
[_____]
[_____]
[_____]
[_____]
[_____]
[_____]
[_____]

OPTION B: *ALTERNATE ENDING*
What if Tau said yes? What would happen next?

✍

[_____]
[_____]
[_____]
[_____]

✍ CER WRITING EXTENSION

Title: Chapter 20 – *Adira the Tortoise and Tau the Lion*

PROMPT: WHAT LESSON ABOUT LEADERSHIP DID ADIRA TRY TO teach Tau?

🐾 CLAIM

✍ I believe that...

[_____]
[_____]

📚 EVIDENCE

✍ In the story it says...
✍ One example is when...
✍ The author shows that...

[_____]
[_____]
[_____]

REASONING

✍ This shows that...
✍ This proves that...
✍ This means...

[_____]
[_____]
[_____]

✅ CHECKLIST

☐ Clear idea?
☐ Strong example?

☐ Good explanation?

🪶 BONUS: DRAW ADIRA AND TAU AT THE BOULDER. HOW DO THEY look as they speak?

[_____]
[_____]
[_____]
[_____]
[_____]
[_____]

📜 POETRY PACK – CHAPTER 20

Poem Title: *The Ballad of Two Realms*
Poem Type: Ballad

✏️ FULL POEM TEXT:

In lands apart yet bound by fate,
Two leaders stood at destiny's gate.
One shell-bound slow, one lion bold,
Both weighed the future yet untold.
The boulder sat, their silent judge,
Its shadow deep, its edges grudge.
The tortoise spoke of peace and rain,
The lion roared of pride and pain.
Storms brewed above, the clouds grew thick,
Each word exchanged a warning quick.
A paw of might, a voice of grace—
They met as rivals, face to face.
One turned to leave, her hope grown dim,
One held his ground, the light gone grim.
But still the wind, it whispered low,
That change begins when one lets go.

. . .

☞ POETRY ACTIVITIES

ACTIVITY 1: CHARACTER TRAITS

Circle the names of the two leaders:

☑ Adira

☑ Tau

Then describe:

• Adira: _____

• Tau: _____

ACTIVITY 2: PREDICT THE FUTURE

What do you think happens next?

✎

[_____]
[_____]
[_____]
[_____]

ACTIVITY 3: RHYME HUNT ♫

Highlight or list 3 rhyming word pairs from the poem.

1 _____ / _____
2 _____ / _____
3 _____ / _____

ACTIVITY 4: TWO LEADERS POEM

Write 2–4 lines imagining two very different animals trying to lead together:

✎

[_____]
[_____]
[_____]
[_____]

[_____]
[_____]

🎙 Bonus: Act out their conversation with a partner!

▥ Poetry Pack Enhancement – Chapter 20
Poem: *The Ballad of Two Realms*

◉ Sound & Rhythm Activity
Underline any repeated sounds (alliteration, assonance):
Examples:
• "shell-bound slow"
• "paw of might"
Now write your own line using repetition or rhyme:
✎

[_____]
[_____]

🖌 Imagery Builder
Draw what the line below makes you visualize:
"The boulder sat, their silent judge…"
✎ Caption your drawing with a feeling or mood that fits the image.

[_____]
[_____]
[_____]
[_____]
[_____]
[_____]
[_____]
[_____]

. . .

METAPHOR MATCH-UP

Which line uses metaphor most clearly?

A. "The tortoise spoke of peace and rain"

B. "Each word exchanged a warning quick"

C. "They met as rivals, face to face"

Explain your answer:

[_____]
[_____]
[_____]
[_____]

EXIT TICKET

Do you think Tau made the right choice? Why or why not?

[_____]
[_____]
[_____]
[_____]

EXCELLENT THINKING, READER. LIKE ADIRA, YOU ANSWERS ARE wise. The final challenges are just ahead...

STANDARDS CONNECTION

RL.4.1 – Find evidence to support ideas

RL.4.3 – Describe characters/events

RL.4.4 – Use context to define words

RL.4.6 – Compare points of view

❧ 21 ❧

THE PREDATORS' PLOT

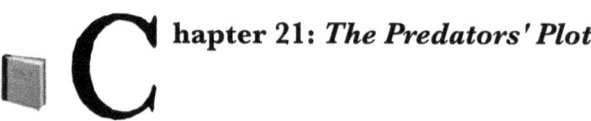

Chapter 21: *The Predators' Plot*

NAME: _____

Date: _____

PROVERB: *"DO NOT LOOK WHERE YOU FELL, BUT WHERE YOU SLIPPED."*

CHAPTER QUEST

Focus Skills: Vocabulary • Reading Comprehension • Cause & Effect • Character Analysis • Ethics

❧ CHAPTER 21 – *THE PREDATORS' PLOT*

📖 CORE READING SKILL FOCUS

📖 **Skill:** Identifying Cause & Effect and Evaluating Leadership Choices

🎯 **WHY IT MATTERS:** THIS CHAPTER EXPLORES HOW LEADERS AND groups use fear to gain power. Students track the ripple effects of one bold decision—and analyze whether the end justifies the means.

🔍 **FOCUS IN THIS CHAPTER:** READERS FOLLOW HOW HUGGER'S choices create a chain reaction—from Crusher's roar to the prey's panic. They weigh whether fear-based leadership can ever lead to real unity, and what the proverb means about noticing *where the mistake began*, not just where it ended.

📖 CHAPTER SUMMARY

In the shadows beneath the great Baobab tree, the predators of Ruaha meet. They plan not to fight—but to frighten. Using Crusher the Crocodile and the Voice of Doom, they aim to scatter Wakaduo's animals with fear. But cracks form: Kael the Leopard feels doubt. And far away, Mount Tanganyika begins to rumble. The storm is coming.

🔤 VOCABULARY PRACTICE

Match the word to its meaning:

1 Concoct → _____
2 Amplify → _____
3 Treachery → _____
4 Deceive → _____

Options:

A. A sneaky or dishonest action
B. To invent or create a plan
C. To make louder or more powerful
D. To trick or mislead

BONUS SENTENCE STARTER:
Amplify: Crusher's roar _____.

✎ TRY YOUR OWN SENTENCE USING ONE VOCABULARY WORD:

[_____]
[_____]

"LET'S CRACK THE CODE OF MEANING! USE THESE SIMPLE SYMBOLS to unlock word parts before you try the Word Part Decoder on your own."

🔣 Symbol-Based Learning Toolkit

🐍 HUGGER THE PYTHON

– Symbol of cunning, manipulation, and cold logic
– Uses planning and fear rather than force

🪨 THE VOICE OF DOOM CAVE

– Represents amplified fear and false alarms

– A literal echo chamber: turns whispers into roars

🐊 CRUSHER THE CROCODILE
– Symbol of raw power used as a tool of fear
– Roars not to attack, but to trigger panic

🐆 KAEL THE LEOPARD
– Represents moral tension and doubt
– Begins to question the group's actions and ethics

🌋 MOUNT TANGANYIKA (ERUPTION)
– Symbol of nature's power and looming consequence
– Echoes the idea that some forces are beyond control

ACTIVITY: SYMBOL MATCH-UP
Match each character or object to what it symbolizes:
1 __ Doubt and possible rebellion
2 __ Cold planning with hidden motives
3 __ A weaponized natural sound
4 __ The power of fear over truth
5 __ A warning that real danger may come

✏️ OPTIONAL DESIGN TASK
Design a symbol for *truth vs fear*.
Is it a crack of light in a cave? A scale tipping? A quiet eye watching?

[_____]
[_____]
[_____]
[_____]
[_____]

[_____]
[_____]
[_____]

⟡ SYMBOL NAME: _____
   ⟡ What It Represents: _____

"NOW THAT YOU'VE EXPLORED OUR SYMBOL CLUES, TRY BUILDING your own words by finding roots, prefixes, and suffixes!"

⬛ WORD PART DECODER: CHAPTER 21 – *THE PREDATORS' PLOT*
Focus: Manipulation, fear, and emotional language
Break down each word into meaningful parts:

1. CONCOCT
- ° Root: coct (Latin: to cook/prepare)
- ° Prefix: con– (together)
- ⟋ Meaning: To prepare or put together an idea or plan

2. AMPLIFY
- ° Root: ampl (large, big)
- ° Suffix: –ify (to make)
- ⟋ Meaning: To make something larger or louder

3. DECEIVE
- ° Prefix: de– (away)
- ° Root: ceive (to take or receive)
- ⟋ Meaning: To take away truth; to mislead

· · ·

⊚ APPLY THE ROOTS
Which word...

1 Means "to make something grow louder"?

[_____]
[_____]

2 IS RELATED TO TRICKING SOMEONE BY TAKING AWAY TRUTH?

[_____]
[_____]

3 REFERS TO A PLAN OR IDEA COOKED UP SECRETLY?

[_____]
[_____]

⊛ DISCUSSION PROMPT
How does understanding the root "ampl" help us think about Crusher's role in this chapter?

[_____]
[_____]
[_____]

WHAT DOES THE ROOT "CEIVE" TELL YOU ABOUT HOW DECEPTION works?

[_____]
[_____]
[_____]

🔍 READING FOR DETAIL

Multiple Choice – Choose the best answer:

1 WHAT IS THE GOAL OF THE PREDATORS' PLAN?
- ☐ A. To steal food from Wakaduo
- ☐ B. To scare prey into fleeing
- ☐ C. To unite Ruaha and Wakaduo
- ☐ D. To stop the volcano eruption

2 WHAT IS THE "VOICE OF DOOM"?
- ☐ A. A warning from Hugger
- ☐ B. A vulture's call
- ☐ C. A cave that makes sounds louder
- ☐ D. The name of Tau's old battle cry

3 WHICH PREDATOR SHOWS SIGNS OF GUILT?
- ☐ A. Hugger
- ☐ B. Dirty Donald
- ☐ C. Kael
- ☐ D. Crusher

4 WHAT NATURAL DISASTER IS APPROACHING?
- ☐ A. A great flood
- ☐ B. An earthquake
- ☐ C. Mount Tanganyika eruption
- ☐ D. A fire from the Baobab

🐚 CHARACTER REFLECTION

Directions: Read each character description. Think about what they say, do, and feel.

Hugger the Python
- One word to describe: _____
- What motivates her?

[_____]
[_____]

Kael the Leopard
- One word to describe: _____
- What is he starting to question?

[_____]
[_____]

Dirty Donald
- One word to describe: _____
- What does he seem to enjoy most?

[_____]
[_____]
[_____]

CAUSE & EFFECT

Fill in the blank with the correct effect:
- Cause: Predators envy Wakaduo's peace
- → Effect: _____
- Cause: Crusher roars inside the cave
- → Effect: _____
- Cause: Skylar warns of eruption
- → Effect: _____
- Cause: Hugger gathers predators
- → Effect: _____

🏷 INFERENCE

Read this line from the chapter:

"Kael stepped back, his tail twitching…"

What can we infer about Kael's feelings in this moment?

☐ A. He is excited

☐ B. He wants to fight

☐ C. He is nervous and unsure

☐ D. He is sleepy

✎ CREATIVE WRITING PROMPT: *KAEL'S JOURNAL ENTRY*

Imagine you are Kael. What are you thinking as the predators plot?

[_____]
[_____]

✎ "I DIDN'T SIGN UP FOR THIS KIND OF FEAR. CRUSHER'S ROAR still echoes in my head..."

Continue the journal:

[_____]
[_____]
[_____]
[_____]

◎ CRITICAL THINKING QUESTIONS

1 Why might the predators use fear instead of fighting?

✎

[_____]
[_____]

2 WHAT MIGHT THE VOLCANO'S ERUPTION CHANGE?

✎ [_____]

[_____]
[_____]
[_____]

3 WHAT DOES THE PROVERB MEAN: *"DO NOT LOOK WHERE YOU FELL, but where you slipped"?*

✎ [_____]
[_____]
[_____]
[_____]

❧ VISUAL RESPONSE

Choose one to illustrate:

    A. The predator council at the Baobab tree

    B. Crusher roaring inside the echoing cave

    C. A map of Ruaha: Baobab Tree, Voice of Doom, Wakaduo

    ✎ Caption: "This moment shows…"

[_____]
[_____]
[_____]
[_____]
[_____]
[_____]

✎ CER WRITING EXTENSION

Prompt: Why did the predators choose fear instead of fighting in their plan against Wakaduo?

📢 CLAIM

    ✎ I believe that...

[_____]
[_____]

. . .

📚 EVIDENCE

✎ One example is when...

✎ The author shows that...

[_____]
[_____]

REASONING

✎ This shows that...

✎ This means...

[_____]
[_____]

✅ CHECKLIST

☐ Clear claim

☐ Strong evidence

☐ Thoughtful reasoning

🖌 **Bonus:** Draw Crusher roaring into the Voice of Doom cave.

[_____]
[_____]
[_____]
[_____]
[_____]
[_____]
[_____]
[_____]

📜 POETRY PACK – CHAPTER 21

Poem Title: *Whispers Under the Baobab Tree*

Type: Narrative Poem

. . .

✎ POEM TEXT:

Under the moon, by the Baobab's knee,
Predators plot with glee,
Hugger the Python, with her scale so sly,
Concocts a plan, "They will run or they'll die."
The night is still, the air is tight,
Dirty Donald laughs at their plight,
"Imagine the feast, oh, the glorious sight,
When the prey flees in the dead of the night."
But Kael, young and unsure,
Whispers, "Is this plan pure?
Tau has said, 'Let them be,'
Should we ignore him, set our greed free?"
Voices rise, a storm's brew,
In Ruaha, dark plans stew,
They speak of a cave, a voice of doom,
To chase the prey and seal their tomb.
Together they haul, with ropes they strive,
Crusher the croc, brought to life,
His roar so deep, through the cave it rings,
A false alarm of terrible things.
"Run for your lives," the echo lies,
In Wakaduo, fear multiplies,
As predators watch with hidden eyes,
Their hearts alight with the prize.

◎ POETRY ACTIVITIES

ACTIVITY 1: MOOD DETECTIVE

Circle the mood of the poem:
☐ Happy ☐ Excited ☐ Sad ☑ Dark and Secretive
✎ Why? "The poem feels _____ because _____."

. . .

ACTIVITY 2: CHARACTER CHECK-IN

List 2–3 characters from the poem:

- _____
- _____
- _____

✎   Who   doubts   the   plan   the   most?

[_____]

   [_____]

ACTIVITY 3: RHYME CATCHER ♪

Highlight or list 2 rhyming word pairs:

1 _____ / _____
2 _____ / _____

✎ WRITE YOUR OWN RHYMING LINE:

   [_____]
   [_____]

ACTIVITY 4: SECRET MEETING POEM

Write 2–4 lines imagining animals meeting in secret—for a good reason.

✎

   [_____]
   [_____]
   [_____]
   [_____]
   [_____]
   [_____]

♫ BONUS: ACT OUT A SHORT CONVERSATION BETWEEN HUGGER AND Kael.

· · ·

🏛 POETRY PACK ENHANCEMENT – CHAPTER 21
Poem: *Whispers Under the Baobab Tree*

🌀 SENSORY POEM RESPONSE
List one sound, one image, and one emotion from the poem:
- 👂 Sound: _____
- 👁 Image: _____
- 💚 Feeling: _____

🪶 POINT OF VIEW PRACTICE
Rewrite one stanza from **Kael's** point of view. Use first person
("I") to show his doubt.
📝 "I watched the ropes pull Crusher close..."
[_____]
[_____]

📠 OPTIONAL PARTNER SKIT
Act out a whispering scene between Kael and Hugger where
Kael expresses concern.

💬 EXIT TICKET

Leadership Lesson:
Fear is powerful, but it often hides guilt or weakness.

FINAL QUESTION:
Will Kael stay loyal—or find the courage to resist?
📝 I think Kael will...

✅ YOU'RE DOING DEEP THINKING NOW—LIKE KAEL, YOU'RE
learning what real strength means. Let's keep going!

❧ 22 ❧

ALICE AND THE STONE BRACELET

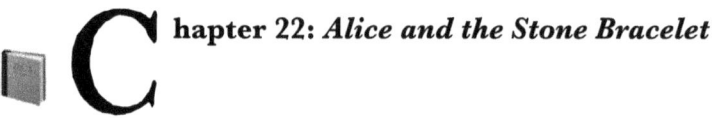

Chapter 22: *Alice and the Stone Bracelet*

NAME: _____

 Date: _____

PROVERB: *"TO GET LOST IS TO LEARN THE WAY."*

✦ CHAPTER QUEST

Focus Skills: Vocabulary • Comprehension • Cause & Effect • Prediction • Character Analysis • Creative Writing

🐆 CHAPTER 22 – *ALICE AND THE STONE BRACELET*

▌ CORE READING SKILL FOCUS

📖 **Skill:** Analyzing Symbolism and Character Motivation

◎ **WHY IT MATTERS:** SYMBOLS CARRY MEANING ACROSS CULTURES and stories. This chapter helps students explore how a small object —the bracelet—can test loyalty, build trust, or mask deception. They also evaluate each character's *true intentions*, sharpening their skills in inference.

🔍 **FOCUS IN THIS CHAPTER:** READERS EXAMINE HOW SCATTER, Beyboy, and Chimper each *interpret* the same object differently. This builds a deeper understanding of figurative language, moral complexity, and the emotional weight of choice.

📖 CHAPTER SUMMARY

In the dense and mysterious Rangu Forest, a surprising friendship begins to form. Alice, the cunning feline, appears to threaten the group. But when Beyboy escapes her trap and gives Scatter the stone bracelet, a chain of trust begins. Scatter chooses to give the bracelet to Chimper—a test, a risk, and perhaps a gesture of hope. The forest is dark, but a new path is forming.

🔤 VOCABULARY PRACTICE

MATCH THE WORD TO ITS DEFINITION

DIRECTIONS: DRAW A LINE OR WRITE THE LETTER THAT MATCHES each word to its meaning.

1 Daunting → _____
2 Mischief → _____
3 Stealthy → _____
4 Token → _____
5 Gesture → _____

Definitions:

a. Sneaky movement
b. Movement showing a feeling
c. Hard or scary
d. Small gift with meaning
e. Playful trouble

WORD SPOTLIGHT

Choose one word and use it in a sentence:

• Symbolic
• Instinct
• Deception
• Trinket

✏ My sentence:

[_____]
[_____]

FILL IN THE BLANKS

Directions: Use each vocabulary word once.

1. Beyboy held out the bracelet with a trembling paw, a simple _____ of surrender.

. . .

2. CHIMPER'S EYES SPARKLED WITH _____ AS HE SWUNG FROM tree to tree.

3. THE THICK VINES MADE THE PATH SEEM _____.

4. SCATTER GAVE CHIMPER THE BRACELET AS A _____ OF trust.

5. ALICE MOVED IN A _____ WAY, BARELY MAKING A SOUND.

🪨 CHAPTER 22 – WORD PART DECODER
Interactive Morphology Matching

BREAK THE WORDS TO UNLOCK THEIR MEANING

Match the word part to the full word. Then decode what it means.

Word Parts:
- 🔒 *mis-* →
- 🔤 *gest* →
- 🔍 *sym* →
- 🐛 *ceive* →
- 🎁 *token* →

FULL WORDS TO MATCH:
- A. Gesture
- B. Symbolic
- C. Token
- D. Mischief
- E. Deception

. . .

Your Match & Meaning:

1 mis- → _____ → "_____"

2 gest → _____ → "_____"

3 sym- → _____ → "_____"

4 ceive → _____ → "_____"

5 token → _____ → "_____"

Challenge: Add a new word you know that starts with **mis-** or **sym-**!

[_____]

[_____]

⊞ CHAPTER 22 – SYMBOL-BASED LEARNING TOOLKIT

Use these icons to help remember the meanings behind tricky word parts:

- 🔒 **mis-** = something gone wrong or mistaken (like "mischief")
- 〰 **gest** = a movement, like "gesture" (comes from Latin *gerere*, to carry)
- ❋ **sym-** = together or same (like "symbol" or "sympathy")
- ◉ **ceive** = to take or grasp (like "deceive" or "perceive")
- 🛡 **token** = a small object that represents something big (like trust)

Tip: Draw or copy these symbols in your notes next to the words—they'll help your brain remember faster!

⊔ READING COMPREHENSION

A. Multiple Choice

CHOOSE THE CORRECT ANSWER FOR EACH QUESTION:

1. Who is Chimper?

☐ A. Leopard

☐ B. Lion Cub

☐ C. Chimpanzee

☐ D. Turtle

. . .

2. WHY IS BEYBOY IMPORTANT IN THIS CHAPTER?
- ☐ A. He saves them from a flood
- ☐ B. He overhears Chimper's secret and warns the others
- ☐ C. He fights Alice
- ☐ D. He gets lost and doesn't return

3 WHAT DOES ALICE DO AFTER BEYBOY GIVES HER THE BRACELET?
- ☐ A. Laughs and runs
- ☐ B. Eats it
- ☐ C. Falls asleep
- ☐ D. Gives him directions

4 WHAT DOES SCATTER DO WITH THE BRACELET LATER?
- ☐ A. Buries it
- ☐ B. Gives it to Henry
- ☐ C. Puts it on Chimper
- ☐ D. Throws it away

B. SHORT ANSWER

Answer in one or two sentences:

5 Why is Henry suspicious of Chimper?

[_____]
[_____]

6 WHAT DOES THE BRACELET SYMBOLIZE?

[_____]
[_____]

. . .

7 WHY DO THE MONKEYS WORK TOGETHER TO HELP BEYBOY?

[_____]
[_____]

8 WHAT DOES THE PROVERB "TO GET LOST IS TO LEARN THE WAY" mean in this chapter?

[_____]
[_____]

DISCUSSION PROMPTS

Discuss or write about these questions:
- Is Scatter testing Chimper's loyalty?
- Would you trust Chimper in a place like Rangu Forest?
- What does the bracelet now mean to Chimper?

CREATIVE THINKING

A. Journal Entry

Write from the perspective of **Chimper** or **Beyboy** using this sentence starter:

"Tonight something happened I never expected..."

My Journal:

[_____]
[_____]
[_____]
[_____]
[_____]
[_____]
[_____]
[_____]

· · ·

B. BRACELET DESIGN

Design a symbolic bracelet that shows loyalty, courage, or forgiveness.
- What is it made of? (vine, bark, feathers, stones?)
- What does each part represent?

✎ Label your bracelet parts below or describe them in words:

[_____]
[_____]
[_____]
[_____]
[_____]
[_____]
[_____]
[_____]

✿ SEQUENCING ACTIVITY

Number these events in order (1–5):

____ Beyboy hears the secret

____ Alice captures him

____ Scatter gives the bracelet to Chimper

____ Chimper offers to guide

____ He gives the bracelet to Scatter

▮ CAUSE & EFFECT

Match each cause to its effect:
- Beyboy overhears the plan →

[_____]
[_____]

- ALICE IS DISTRACTED →

[_____]
[_____]

. . .

- SCATTER GIVES CHIMPER THE BRACELET →

  [_____]
  [_____]

- CHIMPER'S STRANGE BEHAVIOR →

  [_____]
  [_____]

PREDICTION CORNER

Do you think Chimper will betray the heroes—or redeem himself?

I believe Chimper will...

  [_____]
  [_____]
  [_____]

VISUAL LITERACY

Look closely at Alice in the image. How does her posture and expression make you feel?

  ☐ Curious   ☐ Nervous   ☐ Confused   ☐ Suspicious

  Why?

  [_____]
  [_____]

CER WRITING – CHAPTER 22

Prompt: *How did Scatter's kindness with the bracelet change what happened in Rangu Forest?*

CLAIM

I believe that...

  [_____]
  [_____]

. . .

📚 EVIDENCE

✎ One example is when...

[_____]
[_____]

✎ THE AUTHOR SHOWS THAT...

[_____]
[_____]

REASONING

✎ THIS SHOWS THAT...

[_____]
[_____]

✎ THIS PROVES THAT...

[_____]
[_____]

✎ THIS MEANS...

[_____]
[_____]

☑ CHECKLIST:

☐ Clear claim
☐ Strong evidence
☐ Good explanation
🔘 Bonus: Draw Chimper holding the bracelet—or Scatter

placing it in his hand.

[_____]
[_____]
[_____]
[_____]
[_____]
[_____]
[_____]
[_____]

▌ POETRY PACK – CHAPTER 22

Poem Title: *To Get Lost Is to Learn the Way*
  Theme: Curiosity • Mistrust • Bravery • Guidance
  Poem Activities
  ACTIVITY 1: Setting Detective
  The forest feels _____ because _____.
  ☑ Circle: towering trees   whispering breeze   earthy peat
  Bonus: Add your own word! _____

ACTIVITY 2: Character Clues
  Who is trustworthy? _____
  Who is suspicious? _____
  ✎ "_____ seems suspicious because _____
  _____."

ACTIVITY 3: Mood Meter
  Circle one:
  ☐ Adventurous   ☐ Mysterious   ☐ Happy   ☐ Scary
  Draw a matching emoji: 😕 😨 😊 😕

ACTIVITY 4: Forest Sound Poem
  Write 2–3 lines about sounds in Rangu Forest:

[_____]
[_____]
[_____]
[_____]

🍂 BONUS: READ IT IN A SOFT "FOREST WHISPER" VOICE TO A partner.

🖼 **Poetry Prompt (Extension)**

🍂 **Write Your Own Riddle Poem** about the **stone bracelet**.

Use clues and mystery to describe the object without naming it directly.

Example starter:

"I am small but not weak,

I carry more than you think..."

[_____]
[_____]
[_____]
[_____]

🍃 MIND MAP: RANGU FOREST – A PLACE OF CHANGE

Think about this chapter's setting and what happens in it. Write or sketch notes under each idea:

- Characters: _____
- Decisions: _____
- Emotions: _____
- Lessons: _____

YOU'RE DEEP IN THE FOREST NOW—AND EVERY STEP MATTERS. THE bracelet is more than a gift... it's a choice. Keep going! 🌿

❦ 23 ❦
NEXT DAY

Chapter 23: *Next Day*
Name: _____
Date: _____

PROVERB: *"A GOOD FRIEND IS LIKE A FOUR-LEAF CLOVER—HARD TO find and lucky to have."*

CHAPTER QUEST

Focus Skills: Vocabulary • Comprehension • Cause & Effect • Character Analysis • Prediction • Creative Writing • Theme Exploration

CHAPTER 23 – *NEXT DAY*

📖 CORE READING SKILL FOCUS

📖 **Skill:** Analyzing Cause & Effect and Symbolism in Action

🎯 **WHY IT MATTERS:** THIS CHAPTER CENTERS ON HOW SMALL strategic choices ripple into major turning points. Readers explore how a *bracelet*, a *trumpet call*, and a *look of trust* can shift power without direct confrontation.

🔍 **FOCUS IN THIS CHAPTER:** STUDENTS TRACE HOW *SCATTER'S quiet strategy* and *Beyboy's loyalty* flip the power dynamic on Chimper. They also discuss the **emotional weight of symbols** and ask: Can kindness *be* a weapon?

📖 CHAPTER SUMMARY

As dawn breaks, the heroes continue their journey through Rangu Forest. Doubt, deception, and danger swirl around them. Scatter gives Chimper the bracelet—but was it a symbol of trust, or a trap to reveal the truth? Elephants protect the group, Alice makes her move, and Beyboy delivers a warning. Trust is tested. Loyalties shift. Every step matters now.

VOCABULARY DEVELOPMENT

MATCH THE WORD TO ITS DEFINITION

Directions: Match each word to its correct definition by writing the letter next to the number.

1 Strategy → _____
2 Alert → _____
3 Maze → _____
4 Betrayal → _____
5 Expression → _____

Definitions:

A. A facial look that shows feeling
B. A twisty, confusing path
C. When trust is broken or someone is tricked
D. A smart plan to reach a goal
E. Ready and paying close attention

FILL IN THE BLANKS

Directions: Use the vocabulary words from above to complete each sentence.

1 Scatter kept her face calm, but her _____ showed she was thinking carefully.

2 The heroes moved through a thick _____ of tangled trees and vines.

3 Henry stayed _____, always scanning for danger.

4 Chimper's _____ hurt the team and made them question his loyalty.

5 Beyboy and the monkeys had a clever _____ to outsmart Alice.

CHAPTER 23 – WORD PART DECODER
Break the Words and Reveal the Strategy

. . .

WORD PARTS TO DECODE:

- ✂ *betray* →
- ☁ *strate-* →
- ⊚ *maze* →
- ◉ *spect* →
- ! *alert* →

Match the Full Words:

A. Strategy

B. Expression

C. Alert

D. Betrayal

E. Maze

YOUR MATCH & MEANING:

1 betray → _____ → "_____"

2 strate- → _____ → "_____"

3 maze → _____ → "_____"

4 spect → _____ → "_____"

5 alert → _____ → "_____"

⟳ *EXTRA TASK:* WHAT OTHER WORDS USE **SPECT** (LIKE "INSPECT" OR "respect")? Write one here: _____

▦ CHAPTER 23 – SYMBOL-BASED LEARNING TOOLKIT

Quick visual codes to help break down complex words:

- ✂ **betray** = to break trust (from Old French *traïr*)
- ☁ **strate** = plan or design (from Greek *strategos*, a general)
- ⊚ **maze** = twisty path or confusing situation
- ◉ **spect** = to see or watch (like "inspect" or "spectator")
- ! **alert** = watchful and ready

☁ *Mnemonic Idea:* "◉spect" means "to see" — you **inspect** when you look closely!

READING COMPREHENSION

Multiple Choice
Directions: Circle or check the best answer for each question.

1 WHAT WARNING DOES BEYBOY GIVE THE GROUP?
- ☐ A. Alice is coming with Tau
- ☐ B. Chimper has run away
- ☐ C. Chimper may be working with Tau
- ☐ D. The Lion's Tooth has been lost

2 WHAT DOES SCATTER SECRETLY GIVE TO CHIMPER?
- ☐ A. A necklace
- ☐ B. A bracelet
- ☐ C. A map
- ☐ D. A letter

3 HOW DO THE ELEPHANTS HELP THE HEROES?
- ☐ A. They stomp the ground to scare Alice
- ☐ B. They trumpet loudly to create a distraction
- ☐ C. They form a circle to guard Scatter
- ☐ D. They carry everyone to safety

4 WHAT DOES ALICE DO TO CHIMPER?
- ☐ A. She disappears
- ☐ B. She gives him a gift
- ☐ C. She pins him and drags him away
- ☐ D. She asks him questions

5 WHAT DOES THE LION'S TOOTH REPRESENT?
- ☐ A. A treasure to be buried

☐ B. A magical seed
☐ C. A weapon against predators
☐ D. Courage and leadership

SHORT ANSWER

Directions: Answer each question in 1–2 complete sentences.

6 Why was Scatter's gift of the bracelet to Chimper actually part of a strategy?

[_____]
[_____]

7 WHAT DO THE ELEPHANTS' TRUMPET CALLS SHOW ABOUT teamwork?

[_____]
[_____]

8 HOW DOES ALICE KNOW CHIMPER HAS SOMETHING TO DO WITH the missing prey?

[_____]
[_____]

9 WHAT DOES BEYBOY GIVE SCATTER AT THE END, AND WHAT DOES it symbolize?

[_____]
[_____]

· · ·

10 WHAT LESSON ABOUT FRIENDSHIP AND TRUST DOES THIS CHAPTER teach?

[_____]
[_____]

CHARACTER ANALYSIS

Character Chart

Directions: Use clues from the story to complete each row.

CHARACTER: SCATTER

What They Say: _____

What They Do: _____

What They Feel: _____

Motivation: _____

CHARACTER: CHIMPER

What They Say: _____

What They Do: _____

What They Feel: _____

Motivation: _____

CHARACTER: ALICE

What They Say: _____

What They Do: _____

What They Feel: _____

Motivation: _____

CHARACTER: BEYBOY

What They Say: _____

What They Do: _____

What They Feel: _____

Motivation: _____

✐ CREATIVE WRITING

Journal Entry

Prompt: Imagine you are Chimper, right after Alice drags you away. What are you thinking and feeling?

Use this starter if you'd like:

"Everything changed today in the forest. I thought I had a plan, but..."

✐ Journal:

[_____]
[_____]
[_____]
[_____]
[_____]
[_____]
[_____]
[_____]

◈ VISUAL REPRESENTATION

Prompt: Draw the moment when Scatter places the bracelet on Chimper's wrist.

Under your sketch, reflect on:

• Why does this moment matter?
• What does the bracelet mean?
• How might this affect the story later?

[_____]
[_____]
[_____]
[_____]
[_____]
[_____]

𝒫 CAUSE AND EFFECT

Directions: Match each cause to its correct effect by writing the matching letter.

1 Alice sees the bracelet on Chimper → _____
2 Beyboy warns the group → _____
3 The elephants trumpet loudly → _____
4 Scatter gives Chimper the bracelet → _____

Effects:

A. The group is able to escape
B. Chimper feels he may be trusted again
C. Alice becomes suspicious and attacks
D. The group becomes wary of Chimper

● PREDICTION CORNER

Prompt: Use 3–4 sentences to answer:

• What do you think will happen now that Alice has taken Chimper?

• Will the Lion's Tooth become more important?

• What might Scatter be planning next?

✎ My Prediction:

[_____]
[_____]
[_____]
[_____]
[_____]
[_____]

THEME REFLECTION

Proverb: *"A good friend is like a four-leaf clover—hard to find and lucky to have."*

. . .

Prompt: Choose one character who shows they are a good friend.

Write a paragraph explaining:
• What they did that showed loyalty
• How they helped others
• Why they were important to the group

✎ My Response:

[_____]
[_____]
[_____]
[_____]
[_____]
[_____]
[_____]
[_____]

📖 BONUS VOCABULARY CHALLENGE

Directions: Use each word below in a complete sentence. Show its meaning through your sentence.
• Stealth
• Strategy
• Betrayal
• Trust
• Predator
• Alliance
• Tremble
• Deceive

✎ My Sentences:

[_____]
[_____]
[_____]
[_____]
[_____]
[_____]
[_____]

[_____]
[_____]
[_____]
[_____]
[_____]

POETRY PACK – CHAPTER 23

Poem Title: *Journey of the Brave*
  Poem Type: Narrative Poem
  Poem Text:
  In the heart of the Rangu's embrace,
  Our heroes tread a hidden trace.
  Forests thick with secrets deep,
  Paths that twist and turns that leap.
  Henry, with a cautious voice,
  Reminds his friends they have a choice:
  To find new ways through lands unknown,
  And by these trials, they have grown.
  Beyboy waits with news to share,
  Of treachery lurking in the air.
  Chimper's plots weave dark and wide,
  In shadows where dangers bide.
  The heroes must, with cunning stride,
  Navigate the forest's tide.
  A journey not just of the feet,
  But of the heart, their fears to meet.

STUDENT POETRY ACTIVITIES

ACTIVITY 1: Adventure Map Drawing
  • Draw a simple map of the heroes' journey.
  • Mark key areas like:
  • Hidden Secrets
  • Twisting Paths
  • Danger Zones

[_____]
[_____]
[_____]
[_____]
[_____]
[_____]
[_____]
[_____]

ACTIVITY 2: CHARACTER DECISION TREE

Henry says, "We must choose our path."

Make a Choice Tree:

• If they go Left, they might find...
• If they go Right, they might face...

[_____]
[_____]
[_____]
[_____]
[_____]
[_____]
[_____]
[_____]

BONUS: WHAT WOULD YOU CHOOSE?

[_____]
[_____]

ACTIVITY 3: WORD BUILDER

Pick 3 power words from the poem (like: brave, cunning, treachery).

For each:

• Write a sentence
• Draw a doodle or symbol that represents the word

[_____]
[_____]
[_____]
[_____]
[_____]
[_____]
[_____]
[_____]

ACTIVITY 4: COURAGE QUOTE

Write an inspirational line a hero might say in Rangu Forest.
Courage is:

[_____]
[_____]

CHAPTER 23 POETRY EXTENSION

EMOTION ECHO POEM

Write a short free-verse poem where each line reflects a **feeling**
changing in Rangu Forest.
Structure:
• Line 1: A sound you hear
• Line 2: A feeling it brings
• Line 3: A color you imagine
• Line 4: A quiet thought someone has
Example:
A low trumpet in the trees
Makes the ground feel nervous
The green turns grey
And Scatter says nothing, but wonders everything

[_____]
[_____]
[_____]

[_____]
[_____]
[_____]
[_____]
[_____]

CER WRITING

Title: *Chapter 23 — Next Day*

Prompt: Why was trust so important for the heroes' survival in Rangu Forest?

CLAIM

I believe that...

[_____]
[_____]

EVIDENCE

One example is when...

In the story it says...

[_____]
[_____]

REASONING

This shows that...

This proves that...

This means...

[_____]
[_____]
[_____]
[_____]

. . .

☑ CHECKLIST:
- ☐ Clear claim
- ☐ Strong evidence
- ☐ Logical reasoning

YOU'RE ALMOST THROUGH THE FOREST—BUT THE TRUTH IS STILL hiding in the shadows. Trust wisely. Choose carefully. Keep moving forward. 🌲

❧ 24 ❦

TESTED BY FIRE

Chapter 24: *Tested by Fire*

NAME: _____

Date: _____

PROVERB: *"IN THE MOMENT OF CRISIS, THE WISE BUILD BRIDGES AND the foolish build dams."*

CHAPTER QUEST

Focus Skills: Vocabulary • Comprehension • Character Study • Cause & Effect • Theme Reflection • Creative Writing • Visual Literacy

▲ **CHAPTER 24 – *TESTED BY FIRE***

📖 CORE READING SKILL FOCUS

📖 **Skill:** Interpreting Symbolism and Character Transformation

🎯 WHY IT MATTERS: THE VOLCANO BECOMES BOTH A LITERAL **obstacle** and a **metaphor for inner growth**. Students track how facing danger forces characters to evolve—and how leadership rooted in unity overcomes brute force.

🔍 FOCUS IN THIS CHAPTER: READERS EXPLORE HOW NATURAL **symbols**—lava, embers, fire—represent the characters' emotions and decisions. Scatter's courage is contrasted with Tau's rigidity, sparking deep discussion about the **true meaning of power.**

📖 CHAPTER SUMMARY

The group reaches Mount Tanganyika—only to find the volcano awakening. As embers rain and ash clouds rise, the heroes must cross dangerous lava fields. Scatter leads with courage, Ernie scouts ahead, and Tusker calms the group. But in the shadows, Tau lurks, ready to strike. The fire reveals who is bold, who is afraid—and who is changed forever.

🔤 VOCABULARY DEVELOPMENT

MATCH THE WORD TO THE DEFINITION

DIRECTIONS: MATCH EACH VOCABULARY WORD TO THE CORRECT meaning by writing the letter next to the number.

1 Resolve → _____

2 Embers → _____

3 Daunting → _____

4 Treacherous → _____

5 Volcano → _____

Definitions (Jumbled):

A. A fiery mountain that can erupt with lava

B. Hot glowing pieces left after a fire

C. Dangerous and unpredictable

D. Scary or difficult to face

E. Strong determination or decision

BONUS DRAWING PROMPT

Prompt: Draw a close-up of embers glowing with meaning.

Use color, shapes, or symbols to show what they might represent in this chapter (hope, danger, power, transformation).

[_____]
[_____]
[_____]
[_____]
[_____]
[_____]
[_____]
[_____]

🎲 SYMBOL-BASED LEARNING TOOLKIT – CHAPTER 24: *Tested by Fire*

Help students visually and conceptually link complex vocabulary to meaning.

- 🔥 **volcano** – a fiery mountain (from Latin *vulcanus*, god of fire)
- 🔥 **resolve** – strong inner strength; to decide firmly
- 🔥 **embers** – glowing remains of fire (from Old English *æmerge*)
- ❗ **daunt** – to intimidate or make afraid
- 🌿 **treachery** – betrayal or hidden danger

🗡 Tip: Draw the symbol beside each word on flashcards or in your notes. For example, draw a tiny flame beside *resolve* to show determination under pressure.

🗡 WORD PART DECODER – CHAPTER 24
Break the Words to Reveal Their Power

MATCH THE **WORD PARTS** TO THEIR FULL VOCABULARY WORDS. THEN define or explain their deeper meaning.

WORD PARTS:

🔥 *volc-* →
🔥 *-ember-* →
❗ *daunt-* →
🌿 *treach-* →
🔥 *solve / resolv-* →

FULL WORDS TO MATCH:

A. Resolve
B. Treacherous
C. Embers
D. Volcano
E. Daunting

Your Match + Meaning:

1 volc- → _____ → "_____"
2 ember → _____ → "_____"
3 daunt → _____ → "_____"
4 treach → _____ → "_____"
5 resolve → _____ → "_____"

✎ Challenge: Add your own word that uses *solve* or *volc-* and define it!

[_____]
[_____]

📖 READING COMPREHENSION

Multiple Choice

Directions: Choose the best answer for each question.

1 WHAT LANDMARK SHOWS THE GROUP THEY'RE NEAR WAKADUO?
   ☐ A. A tall tree
   ☐ B. Mount Tanganyika
   ☐ C. A river of light
   ☐ D. The Tree of Life

2 WHAT ROLE DOES ERNIE PLAY IN THE VOLCANO SCENE?
   ☐ A. He scouts the path and warns the group
   ☐ B. He gets stuck in ash
   ☐ C. He chases Tau
   ☐ D. He leads them up the mountain

3 WHAT IS TAU'S PLAN?
   ☐ A. To warn the group
   ☐ B. To ambush them
   ☐ C. To surrender
   ☐ D. To steal the Lion's Tooth

. . .

SHORT ANSWER

Directions: Write 1–2 complete sentences for each response.

4 WHAT CLUES SHOW THAT THE VOLCANO IS ACTIVE AND dangerous?

[_____]
[_____]

5 WHY IS THIS PART OF THE JOURNEY IMPORTANT FOR THE HEROES?

[_____]
[_____]

6 HOW DOES THE PROVERB CONNECT TO WHAT SCATTER AND TAU are doing?

[_____]
[_____]

CHARACTER STUDY

Directions: Describe what each character's action reveals about their traits or values.

CHARACTER: SCATTER
- **Action:** Leads through lava fields
- **What It Shows About Them:**

[_____]
[_____]

. . .

CHARACTER: ERNIE
- **Action:** Scouts the path ahead
- **What It Shows About Them:**

[_____]
[_____]

CHARACTER: TUSKER
- **Action:** Keeps everyone calm and moving
- **What It Shows About Them:**

[_____]
[_____]

CHARACTER: TAU
- **Action:** Waits in hiding to attack
- **What It Shows About Them:**

[_____]
[_____]

✎ CAUSE AND EFFECT

Directions: Match each cause to its effect by writing the correct letter.

1 The volcano becomes active → _____
2 Ernie scouts ahead → _____
3 Tau hides behind rocks → _____
4 Scatter leads with bravery → _____

Effects (Jumbled):

A. The group feels inspired to continue

B. The planned route must change

C. The group receives warnings of danger

D. An ambush is set in motion

🌑 PREDICTIVE THINKING

Prompt: Based on what's happened so far, answer in 3–5 sentences
.

- What do you think will happen in the next chapter?
- Who might surprise us by helping—or betraying—the group?
- What role will the volcano play in the final showdown?

🔺 My Prediction:

[_____]
[_____]
[_____]

THEME REFLECTION

Theme: *Fire = Transformation*

Prompt: Think of a moment in your life when you were challenged or pushed beyond your limits.

Write about:

- What the moment was
- How it tested or changed you
- How you came through it stronger

🔺 My "Fire Moment":

[_____]
[_____]
[_____]
[_____]
[_____]
[_____]
[_____]
[_____]
[_____]

🔺 CREATIVE WRITING

Choose one prompt below and respond with a paragraph or a full page.

A. Journal Entry

Imagine you're crossing the fire trail. What do you see, feel, smell? What are you thinking?

B. Poem – "The Fire Inside"

Write about courage, pressure, and personal growth.

C. Sensory Scene

Describe the scene using all five senses:

• What do you see?
• What do you hear?
• What do you feel?
• What do you smell?
• What do you taste?

[_____]
[_____]
[_____]
[_____]
[_____]
[_____]
[_____]
[_____]
[_____]
[_____]
[_____]
[_____]
[_____]
[_____]

▓ VISUAL MAP ACTIVITY

Prompt: Create a map showing the heroes' path in this chapter.

Label key locations:

• Mount Tanganyika
• The lava flow
• The ambush site
• The entrance to Wakaduo

Use arrows to show movement, danger, and choices.

[_____]
[_____]
[_____]
[_____]
[_____]
[_____]
[_____]

CER WRITING

Title: *Chapter 24 — Tested by Fire*

Prompt: How did Scatter and the heroes show true bravery when facing Mount Tanganyika?

CLAIM

I believe that...

[_____]
[_____]

EVIDENCE

One example is when...

In the story it says...

[_____]
[_____]

REASONING

This shows that...

This proves that...

This means...

[_____]
[_____]

CHECKLIST:

□ Clear claim

☐ Strong evidence
☐ Good explanation
  BONUS Drawing Prompt:

DRAW THE HEROES CHARGING ACROSS THE VOLCANO—FLAMES, ASH, lava, courage!

[_____]
[_____]
[_____]
[_____]
[_____]
[_____]
[_____]

POETRY PACK – CHAPTER 24: *TESTED BY FIRE*

Poetry Type: Narrative Poem
  Theme: Perseverance • Courage • Unity

POEM TEXT:
Tested by Fire
Before the mighty Tanganyika's fire,
Heroes stand, their spirits soaring higher.
Golden dawn breaks, skies alight with flame,
Each step they take, they pronounce their name.
Earth trembles beneath their weary feet,
Volcano's breath, sulfur's bitter greet.
Mountains of challenge, vast savannas wide,
Where shadows of fierce predators may hide.
"Press on!" cries Scatter, with fervor so bold,
"Not mountains nor foes our spirits will hold.
We're children of Wakaduo, brave and true,
Together, there's nothing we cannot do."
Ernie soars high, eyes sharp as the day,

Scouting the dangers that may block their way.
"The path is clear," he calls to his band,
"We must be swift to cross this heated land."
With courage that rivals the fire's fierce glow,
Through smoking ash and ember's flow,
They face each trial on this treacherous road,
United as one, bearing destiny's load.
Tusker, wise giant, feels the land's raw power,
"Our hearts must be strong in this fiery hour.
As beasts of the wild, we'll claim our fate,
Beyond this trial, Wakaduo's gate."

◎ **POETRY ACTIVITIES**
ACTIVITY 1: Fire and Courage Comic Strip 🖐💀
Draw a 4-panel comic strip:
• Panel 1 – "Press on, brave ones!"
• Panel 2 – "Look, the path clears!"
• Panel 3 – "We're almost there!"
• Panel 4 – "Together, we made it!"

[_____]
[_____]
[_____]
[_____]
[_____]
[_____]
[_____]
[_____]
[_____]
[_____]

ACTIVITY 2: SENSORY IMAGERY BUILDER 🍃
If you stood beside Mount Tanganyika, what would you:
See: _____
Hear: _____

Smell: _____

Feel: _____

ACTIVITY 3: BUILD A TEAM CHANT ✏️🏆

Write a 2–4 line chant for the heroes as they cross the lava fields.
Example:
"We march through fire, we rise with might,
Together as one, we claim our light!"
✍️ My Team Chant:

[_____]
[_____]
[_____]
[_____]
[_____]
[_____]
[_____]

ACTIVITY 4: THEME REFLECTION

What does the poem teach about perseverance or unity?
✍️ My Reflection:

[_____]
[_____]
[_____]
[_____]

POETRY EXTENSION – CHAPTER 24
🔥 "The Fire Inside" Poem Prompt

Write a short poem about facing fear or challenge. Use fire
imagery to describe:
• An inner struggle
• A moment of growth
• A decision to lead or change
Structure: 3–5 lines, free verse

Example starter:
I walked into the fire,
Not to burn,
But to become something new.

[_____]
[_____]
[_____]
[_____]
[_____]
[_____]

🔥 YOU'RE ALMOST AT THE FINAL GATES. THE FIRE HAS TESTED YOU —and lit the way forward. Keep going!

BONUS (OPTIONAL):

🎨 **Draw It!**

Draw the heroes racing across the volcano or facing the erupting mountain!

[_____]
[_____]
[_____]
[_____]
[_____]
[_____]
[_____]
[_____]
[_____]
[_____]
[_____]
[_____]

JOURNAL 5: AFTER CHAPTER 24 – TESTED BY FIRE

Chapters 20–24 Summary: The group survives the volcano. Leadership is tested. The climax is near, and unity becomes the key to survival.

Page 1 – Reflect & Write

Prompt 1:

"I used to think… but now I think…"

➤ About what it means to be a true leader

_____
_____
_____

Prompt 2:

How has Scatter grown since the beginning of the story?

_____
_____

Prompt 3:

What would _your_ "test by fire" be in real life?

_____
_____

Page 2 – Create & Connect

• **Draw** a moment when someone helped someone else in these chapters

• **Write** a "team chant" the heroes might say as they face the volcano

[_____]
[_____]
[_____]
[_____]
[_____]
[_____]
[_____]
[_____]
[_____]
[_____]
[_____]
[_____]
[_____]
[_____]

$\mathscr{L}$ *25* $\mathscr{R}$

THE CIRCLE OF UNITY

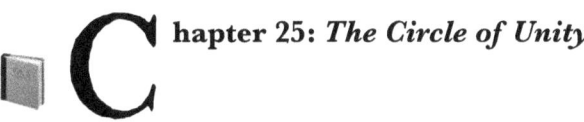

Chapter 25: *The Circle of Unity*

NAME: _____

Date: _____

PROVERB: *"YOU CANNOT EVER LEAVE AFRICA. IT IS ALWAYS WITH YOU, there, inside your head."*

CHAPTER QUEST

Focus Skills: Vocabulary • Comprehension • Character Analysis • Sequencing • Theme Reflection • Visual Learning • Creative Writing

💀 **CHAPTER 25 –** *THE CIRCLE OF UNITY*

📖 CORE READING SKILL FOCUS

📖 **Skill:** Analyzing Theme Through Character Choices and Symbolism

🎯 **WHY IT MATTERS:** THIS CHAPTER REVEALS THAT TRUE leadership isn't about power—it's about compassion, wisdom, and shared responsibility. Students explore how actions like **claiming proxy**, **refusing the crown**, and **uniting rivals** build a theme of **unity over domination**.

🔍 **FOCUS IN THIS CHAPTER:** THROUGH CLOSE READING AND discussion, students connect symbolic elements (river, volcano, pit, wind) with moral choices. Scatter's refusal to rule alone becomes a lens for exploring power, humility, and transformation.

📖 CHAPTER SUMMARY

As the journey ends, Scatter and the heroes stand in the sacred Circle of Unity. A final challenge is set. Scatter invokes the Right of Proxy—choosing courage, not conquest. Gurr demands control but stumbles. Scatter offers shared leadership, and peace returns to Wakaduo. The circle closes… but unity begins.

🔤 VOCABULARY DEVELOPMENT

MATCH THE WORD TO THE DEFINITION

DIRECTIONS: WRITE THE LETTER OF THE CORRECT DEFINITION NEXT to the word.

Words:

1 Resolve → _____
2 Solemn → _____
3 Proverb → _____
4 Unity → _____
5 Proxy → _____

DEFINITIONS (JUMBLED):

A. Deeply serious or thoughtful in tone
B. A wise saying that teaches a life lesson
C. Acting on someone else's behalf
D. A shared sense of purpose or togetherness
E. A strong decision or sense of determination

🔣 SYMBOL-BASED LEARNING TOOLKIT – CHAPTER 25: *THE Circle of Unity*

- 🌼 **proxy** – acting on someone else's behalf (Latin *pro* = for, *agere* = to act)
- 🍂 **resolve** – to decide with strength
- ☁ **unity** – being joined or working together
- ▓ **proverb** – a wise saying or lesson (Latin *pro* = for, *verbum* = word)
- 😐 **solemn** – serious, respectful in tone

MEMORY TIP:
- Draw a 🌀 to represent *unity* (everything connected)

- A handshake for *proxy*
- A scroll for *proverb*

🪨 WORD PART DECODER – CHAPTER 25
Decode the Leadership Language
Word Parts:

🪨 *uni-* →

🏛 *verb* →

🪨 *solve / resolv-* →

👥 *prox-* →

😀 *solemn* →

FULL WORDS TO MATCH:

A. Unity
B. Resolve
C. Proverb
D. Proxy
E. Solemn

MATCH & MEANING:

1 uni- → _____ → "_____"
2 verb → _____ → "_____"
3 resolve → _____ → "_____"
4 prox- → _____ → "_____"
5 solemn → _____ → "_____"

🪨 EXTRA CHALLENGE: CREATE A SENTENCE USING *UNITY* OR *PROXY* that connects to the story's theme.

[_____]
[_____]

⊔ READING COMPREHENSION

Directions: Use your memory and reading skills to answer in complete sentences.

1. What does Scatter's "Right of Proxy" mean in the trials?

[_____]
[_____]

2. WHY DOES GURR FALL, AND SCATTER SUCCEED?

[_____]
[_____]

3. How does Scatter's way of sharing power create real victory?

[_____]
[_____]

4. What does the whispering wind at the end symbolize?

[_____]
[_____]

⊜ SEQUENCING EVENTS

Directions: Number the events (1–7) in the order they happened.

___ Scatter claims proxy
___ Shared leadership declared
___ Adira suggests trials
___ Reach Wakaduo
___ Unity is born
___ River crossing
___ Gurr falls

👥 CHARACTER COMPARISON

Directions: Complete the chart for each key character in the final chapter.

👥 CHARACTER REFLECTIONS: LEARNING FROM THE JOURNEY
Character: Scatter

💀 What is one word to describe Scatter in this chapter?

☞ *Example: Brave, Wise, Calm*

✍ **My Word:** _____

◡ What did Scatter learn?

✍ **My Answer:**

[_____]
[_____]

CHARACTER: TAU

💀 What is one word to describe Tau in this chapter?

☞ *Example: Proud, Changed, Thoughtful*

✍ **My Word:** _____

◡ What did Tau learn?

✍ **My Answer:**

[_____]
[_____]

CHARACTER: GURR

💀 What is one word to describe Gurr in this chapter?

☞ *Example: Controlling, Proud, Stubborn*

✍ **My Word:** _____

◡ What did Gurr learn (or fail to learn)?

✍ **My Answer:**

[_____]
[_____]

· · ·

CHARACTER: ADIRA

What is one word to describe Adira in this chapter?

Example: Wise, Gentle, Caring

My Word: _____

What did Adira show or teach others?

My Answer:

[_____]
[_____]

THEME EXPLORATION: *UNITY*

Prompt: The chapter ends with the words *"We are one."*

What makes unity real—not just a word, but a truth? How can you build unity in your school, family, or community?

[_____]
[_____]
[_____]
[_____]

[_____]
[_____]

CREATE A UNITY POSTER

Art Prompt: Design a mini-poster with the theme *We Are One.*

Include symbols, colors, and words that represent unity. You may:

- Use quotes from the book
- Include characters or settings
- Create your own motto or symbol for peace

✎ CREATIVE WRITING

Choose one prompt below and respond in 1–2 paragraphs.

A. What if Gurr had won?
How would Wakaduo change? What kind of leader would he be?
B. Advice to a Leader
Write a letter to Scatter. Congratulate her and offer encouragement as she begins her journey as a leader.

✎ My Response:

[_____]
[_____]
[_____]
[_____]
[_____]
[_____]
[_____]
[_____]
[_____]
[_____]

✐ CER WRITING

Title: *Chapter 25 — The Circle of Unity*

Prompt: How did Scatter prove that true leadership is about unity, not power?

📣 CLAIM
✎ I believe that...

[_____]
[_____]

· · ·

✎ EVIDENCE

✎ In the story it says...
✎ One example is when...

[_____]
[_____]
[_____]
[_____]

REASONING

✎ This shows that...
✎ This proves that...
✎ This means...

[_____]
[_____]
[_____]
[_____]
[_____]
[_____]

✅ CHECKLIST:

☐ Clear claim
☐ Strong evidence
☐ Thoughtful reasoning

Bonus Drawing Prompt:

Draw Scatter standing in the Circle of Unity as the animals gather around her.

[_____]
[_____]
[_____]
[_____]
[_____]
[_____]
[_____]
[_____]

POETRY ACTIVITY SHEET – LYRICAL POEM (UNITY, WISDOM, AND COURAGE)

Poem: *The Circle of Unity*

In the heart of Africa, where the sun kisses the earth,
Lies a tale of valor, of untold worth.
Under skies wide and a horizon deep,
The heroes of Wakaduo their vigil keep.
Across the savanna, under Mount Tanganyika's gaze,
Through trials by fire, through the smoke and haze,
They've walked paths where lesser spirits would falter,
By strength and by wisdom, they refuse to alter.
"Unity," whispers the wind through the grass,
"A bond forged in trials, none can surpass."
The lions roar, the elephants trumpet call,
In unity, they stand, in unity, they fall.
Gurr and Tau, the lions, their might contested,
In the challenge of wills, their spirits tested.
Yet, when the earth shook and the fires did rage,
Together they turned, a new page.
For the wise build bridges, the foolish, dams,
In the circle of unity, the true power stands.
As Scatter and Tau, side by side,
Prove that together, wide is their stride.
In the Circle of Unity, under Africa's sun,
The journey of heroes, never truly done.
For each step on this land, each challenge met,
Is a beat of the heart, a further path set.
In every whisper of the wind, in every challenge they face,
Is the spirit of Africa, their enduring grace.
For you never leave Africa, nor does it you,
In the circle of unity, forever true.

POETRY ACTIVITIES – STUDENT VERSION

. . .

ACTIVITY 1: UNITY SYMBOLS 🌐

Draw a symbol that shows Unity.

Examples:

• A circle of paw prints
• A tree surrounded by animals
• Interlocking hands or tails

[_____]
[_____]
[_____]
[_____]
[_____]
[_____]

WHAT DOES YOUR SYMBOL MEAN?

Write one sentence below.

[_____]
[_____]

ACTIVITY 2: POETRY PAIR LINES

Pick 2 lines from the poem that go together.
Write the lines here:

LINE 1: _____

LINE 2: _____

WHY DO THEY BELONG TOGETHER?

[_____]
[_____]

[———————————————————————————]

ACTIVITY 3: CREATE A UNITY CHANT 📢

Imagine Scatter and Tau leading the group.

Write a chant they might shout to inspire everyone.

Start with:

"One heart, one land…"

Now you try:

[———————————————————————————]
[———————————————————————————]
[———————————————————————————]
[———————————————————————————]

ACTIVITY 4: CIRCLE OF LIFE REFLECTION 🌳

The poem says: *"You never leave Africa, nor does it you."*

Write a short reflection:

What place, memory, or person will you always carry in your heart?

[———————————————————————————]
[———————————————————————————]
[———————————————————————————]
[———————————————————————————]

JOURNAL PROMPT:

"What does it mean to carry a place in your heart?"

[———————————————————————————]
[———————————————————————————]
[———————————————————————————]
[———————————————————————————]

ACTIVITY 5: POETRY ILLUSTRATION PROJECT 🖌️

Choose 4–6 lines from the poem.

Design a **"Circle of Unity"** using those lines.

You can:

• Draw in a circle

• Make a banner

• Use scroll shapes or animals

Label your picture with the poem lines and your message of unity.

POETRY PROMPT – CHAPTER 25: "ONE CIRCLE, ONE VOICE"

Write a free verse or rhyming poem about:

• What it means to lead with humility

• How different animals (or people) can unite

• The lasting power of shared truth

Optional first line:

"In the circle of unity, we saw not one, but all."

[_____]
[_____]
[_____]
[_____]
[_____]
[_____]
[_____]

BONUS CHALLENGE: GROUP PERFORMANCE!

In a small group, each person reads one line from the final stanza:

In every whisper of the wind, in every challenge they face,

Is the spirit of Africa, their enduring grace.

For you never leave Africa, nor does it you,

In the circle of unity, forever true.

Tip: Read with pride and rhythm. Let each voice carry the spirit of the story!

FINAL THOUGHT

Scatter's final act wasn't just courage—it was a **choice to share power**.

Unity isn't easy. It takes bravery, trust, and heart.

But when we build bridges—instead of walls—we rise together.

You are part of that circle now.

Keep writing. Keep leading.

You are not alone.

My Poem

Poetry Prompt: *"Select one of the Titles below and write your own poem"*

Theme: Courage • Change • Unity • The Spirit of Africa

Title Options:

• *The Fire Inside*

• *One Circle, One Voice*

• *Africa Remembers*

✏ **Write your poem using:**

• **Nature images** (fire, water, wind, dust, stars)

• **Emotions** (hope, fear, peace, transformation)

• **Your voice** — be proud, reflective, brave

✍ My Poem:

[_____]
[_____]
[_____]
[_____]
[_____]
[_____]
[_____]
[_____]
[_____]
[_____]
[_____]
[_____]

[_____]
[_____]
[_____]
[_____]

Mapping the Final Trial

Prompt: Draw a map of the *Circle of Unity* trials.

Label key places:
• River Crossing
• Trial Locations
• The Final Speech Rock
• Gurr's Fall / Scatter's Stand

Use small symbols to show challenges, choices, and lessons learned.

[_____]
[_____]
[_____]
[_____]
[_____]
[_____]
[_____]
[_____]
[_____]
[_____]

Exit Reflection

Final Questions for You:

1 What did you carry away from this story—about friendship, leadership, or courage?

[_____]
[_____]
[_____]
[_____]

. . .

2 IF YOU COULD GIVE SCATTER ONE PIECE OF ADVICE AS SHE becomes a leader, what would it be?

[_____]
[_____]
[_____]
[_____]

CONGRATULATIONS—YOU'VE REACHED THE END OF THE JOURNEY through *Wakaduo*. Your wisdom, creativity, and voice matter. Now take what you've learned and keep building your own circle of unity. 🌐

BONUS (OPTIONAL):
🐚 Draw It!

Draw the heroes racing across the volcano or facing the erupting mountain!

[_____]
[_____]
[_____]
[_____]
[_____]
[_____]
[_____]
[_____]
[_____]
[_____]
[_____]
[_____]

✻ 26 ✻
FROM SHADOWS TO LIGHT

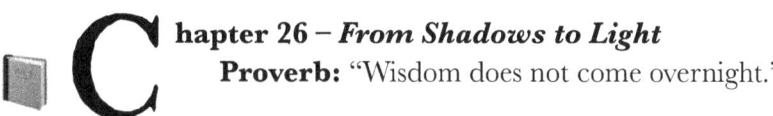

Chapter 26 – *From Shadows to Light*
Proverb: "Wisdom does not come overnight."

CHAPTER QUEST

📖 CORE READING SKILL FOCUS

📖 **Skill:** Connecting Symbolism and Real-World Application

◎ **WHY IT MATTERS:** THE RETURN TO THE REAL WORLD CEMENTS Wakaduo's message: leadership, courage, and unity are not just storybook lessons—they are **lifelong tools**. The **eclipse, animal forms**, and **tokens** all symbolize different parts of transformation.

🔍 **FOCUS IN THIS CHAPTER:** STUDENTS IDENTIFY HOW **MYTH blends into reality**, using evidence to show how the children's journey shapes their actions back home. They reflect on how unity and resilience break darkness—both in fiction and real life.

■ CHAPTER 26 SUMMARY – FROM SHADOWS TO LIGHT

During a big eclipse, the park becomes dark and quiet. Maya, Jalen, Zara, and Malik turn into their magical animal forms and place their glowing tokens—courage, wisdom, compassion, and unity—around the old oak tree. As they chant the word "Wakaduo," the light from the tokens pushes back the darkness and brings the whole neighborhood together. People start to remember, feel hope, and stand up for peace.

The gang tries to take over, but the light is too strong. In the end, the heroes help their community find a new beginning. Everyone starts working together again—through music, sports, learning, and helping others. The heroes' bravery helps turn fear into something powerful: **hope, change, and unity.**

VOCABULARY DEVELOPMENT

Match the Word to Its Meaning

Directions: Match each word with the correct definition by writing the letter next to the number.

Words:

1 Transformation

2 Eclipse

3 Illuminate

4 Resilience

5 Reconciliation

Definitions (Jumbled):

A. To light up or make clear

B. Becoming something new or different

C. The act of making peace after conflict

D. Strength to recover from difficulty

E. A darkening or blocking of light

WRITE YOUR OWN SENTENCES

Pick any two words from the list above. Write your own sentence for each to show you understand what it means.

1.

[_____]
[_____]

2.

[_____]
[_____]

SEQUENCING EVENTS

Number the events below (1–6) in the order they happen in this chapter.

☐ The chant rises from the crowd

☐ Cedric has a transformation

☐ Children return to human form

☐ The eclipse begins to spread

☐ The magical tokens begin to glow

☐ Cedric tries to stop the heroes

. . .

🔲 Symbol-Based Learning Toolkit – Chapter 26: *From Shadows to Light*

This chapter's vocabulary is deeply symbolic—each word reflects both outer events and inner transformation.

- ⬤ **Eclipse** – darkness hiding light (symbol of fear, change, or ignorance

- **Illuminate** – to light up (symbol of clarity, truth, hope)

- **Transformation** – change into something new (symbol of growth)

- **Resilience** – inner strength to recover (symbol of courage and persistence)

- **Reconciliation** – restoring peace (symbol of healing relationships)

Try This: Next to each word, draw a quick visual.
   Examples:

- *Eclipse* → moon covering sun

- *Resilience* → plant sprouting through concrete

- *Reconciliation* → two hands reaching out to meet

. . .

🪣 WORD PART DECODER – CHAPTER 26
Uncover the Power Inside the Words

MATCH THE **WORD PARTS** TO THE FULL VOCABULARY WORDS AND explain what they suggest.

WORD PARTS:
🌑 *e-* / *ex-* (out/from) + *-clipse* (hide) →

lumen / *lumin-* (light) →

🌀 *trans-* (across/change) + *form* (shape) →

re- (again) + *-sil-* (leap/jump) →

re- (again) + *concili-* (make friendly) →

FULL VOCABULARY WORDS:
A. Eclipse
B. Illuminate
C. Transformation
D. Resilience
E. Reconciliation

🧩 YOUR MATCHES:
1 e-/clipse →
[_____]
[_____]

2 LUMIN- →
[_____]
[_____]

. . .

3 TRANS/FORM →

[_____]
[_____]

4 RE/SIL →

[_____]
[_____]

5 RE/CONCILI →

[_____]
[_____]

✎ CHALLENGE PROMPT:

Pick one of these words and write a metaphor using it.

Example: "Her resilience was like a tree bending but never breaking in the storm."

[_____]
[_____]

📖 COMPREHENSION QUESTIONS

1 What do the animal forms in this chapter symbolize about the kids' emotions and fears?

[_____]
[_____]

2 WHY IS IT IMPORTANT THAT CEDRIC SEES HIS YOUNGER SELF?

[_____]
[_____]

. . .

3 WHAT HAPPENS TO THE PARK, AND WHAT DOES IT NOW REPRESENT?

[_____]
[_____]

CHARACTER CHANGE REFLECTION

Character: Maya

Before: Unsure
Action Taken: Leads cleanup
How Maya Changed:

[_____]
[_____]

CHARACTER: CEDRIC

Before: Angry and rigid
Action Taken: Steps back and reflects
How   Cedric   Changed:
[_____]
[_____]

DRAW + WRITE ACTIVITY

Draw It:

Draw your favorite moment from this chapter — a powerful turning point.

[_____]
[_____]
[_____]
[_____]
[_____]
[_____]
[_____]
[_____]

. . .

WRITE IT:

Now write a *Unity Chant* that could bring people together.

[_____]
[_____]
[_____]
[_____]
[_____]
[_____]
[_____]
[_____]

PROVERB REFLECTION

"Wisdom does not come overnight."

What does this mean now that you've finished the story?

[_____]
[_____]
[_____]
[_____]

IF YOU HAD A TOKEN

If you could choose one magical token from the story, what would it be?

What would it represent for you?

How would you use it in your life?

[_____]
[_____]

[_____]
[_____]

☑ EXIT TICKET

1 What's one thing you'll always remember from this story?

[_____]
[_____]
[_____]

2 WHAT IS ONE WAY YOU WILL UNLEASH GREATNESS IN YOUR OWN life?

[_____]
[_____]
[_____]

✎ CER WRITING

Title: Chapter 26 – From Shadows to Light

PROMPT: HOW DID THE HEROES BRING REAL CHANGE TO THEIR community after returning home?

◄ CLAIM:

I believe that

[_____]
[_____]

✎ EVIDENCE:

In the story, it says

[_____]
[_____]

One example is when

[_____]
[_____]

. . .

REASONING:
This shows that

[_____]
[_____]

THIS PROVES THAT

[_____]
[_____]

THIS MEANS

[_____]
[_____]

FINAL UNIT JOURNAL – *FROM SHADOW TO SUNLIGHT*

Page 1: Looking Back
• What was the most powerful chapter for you? Why?

[_____]
[_____]
[_____]
[_____]

• WHAT WAS YOUR FAVORITE MOMENT FROM THE JOURNEY?

[_____]
[_____]
[_____]

PAGE 2: LESSONS FROM WAKADUO
• What is a leader?

[_____]
[_____]

• How did Scatter help others grow?

[_____]
[_____]
[_____]
[_____]

• What's the difference between being smart and being wise?

[_____]
[_____]
[_____]
[_____]
[_____]

Page 3: Wakaduo in the Real World
    • What lessons can help you at school or home?

[_____]
[_____]

• When have you seen kindness or leadership in real life?

[_____]
[_____]

Page 4: My Hero's Journey
    • Write about a challenge you've faced.
    • Who helped you?
    • What's your next step?

[_____]
[_____]

[_____]
[_____]
[_____]
[_____]

🐾 BONUS PAGE: MY ANIMAL FORM

Draw yourself as a magical animal. Name your animal kingdom.

[_____]
[_____]
[_____]
[_____]
[_____]
[_____]
[_____]
[_____]

WHAT POWERS WOULD YOU PROTECT IT WITH?

[_____]
[_____]

📜 POETRY PACK – CHAPTER 26: *LEGACY OF UNITY*

Poem Title: *Legacy of Unity*
(A Sonnet – Reflection and Growth)
In lands of myth, our spirits danced and grew,
Each trial faced, with hearts both brave and true.
From Wakaduo's fields to playgrounds near,
We carried forth our quest, devoid of fear.
Through games and stories, leadership took root,
In every act, our values absolute.
With courage gleaned from lands both fierce and grand,
We stand as one, a hopeful, steadfast band.
Our journey's not confined to tales of yore,
In every challenge faced, we open doors.

For wisdom's not a gift of fleeting night,
But morning's glow, a slow but spreading light.
So here beneath the stars, we pledge anew,
To live the lessons learned, and dreams pursue.

✿ STUDENT POETRY ACTIVITIES
ACTIVITY 1: Legacy Footprints 👣

Draw footprints leading from Wakaduo to a place you care about (home, school, park).

Inside each footprint, write one lesson:
• Courage
• Kindness
• Leadership
• Unity

[_____]
[_____]
[_____]
[_____]
[_____]
[_____]
[_____]
[_____]
[_____]
[_____]

ACTIVITY 2: SONNET STAR WORDS

Pick 2 big words from the poem (like legacy, courage, or wisdom).

Write what each word means to you and use it in a sentence.

• Word 1: _____

Meaning:

[_____]
[_____]

- •   Sentence:

[——————————————————————————]
  [——————————————————————————]

- WORD 2: _____
  Meaning:

  [——————————————————————————]
  [——————————————————————————]

- SENTENCE:

  [——————————————————————————]
  [——————————————————————————]

ACTIVITY 3: COMPLETE THE THOUGHT

"Our journey's not confined to tales of yore, because..."

  [——————————————————————————]
  [——————————————————————————]
  [——————————————————————————]
  [——————————————————————————]

ACTIVITY 4: DREAM PLEDGE

What will YOU do with the wisdom from this story?
  "I   pledge   to

[——————————————————————————]
  [——————————————————————————]
  [——————————————————————————]
  [——————————————————————————]
  "

POETRY PROMPT – LEGACY & LIGHT
Title Options:

- "One Token, One Light"
- "From Eclipse to Dawn"
- "I Am Wakaduo"

Theme Suggestions:
- Light breaking darkness
- The strength of unity
- Remembering where you came from
- Passing the torch (legacy)

✐ Sample Starters:

In the shadow of the oak, we stood still—
Until the light from our tokens bent the night to our will.

Or:

I was just a whisper once, a shadow in the crowd,
But Wakaduo taught me to speak my truth out loud.

[_____]
[_____]
[_____]
[_____]
[_____]
[_____]
[_____]
[_____]

🎓 **FINAL REFLECTION PROMPT: "LEGACY MAP"**

Write a final stanza or short poem that maps where you've been and where you're going next. Use nature or light metaphors.

I crossed fire and storm to find my name.
I carry it now—a light, not a flame.
The circle is closed, but my path begins—
With quiet courage and gentle wins.

[_____]
[_____]
[_____]
[_____]
[_____]

FINAL WORD TO OUR READERS

You've walked through deserts, crossed rivers, solved riddles, and faced fears. You've followed heroes, forgave mistakes, and stood up for what's right. Just like Scatter, Maya, and their friends, *you* have grown—page by page—into someone stronger, wiser, and more ready to lead.

As this story ends, remember: the journey never truly stops.

Every choice you make… every kind word… every brave step…

is part of *your* own Circle of Unity.

CARRY YOUR COURAGE. SHARE YOUR LIGHT. AND NEVER FORGET—
Wakaduo lives inside you. Always.

KEEP GOING, HERO. THE WORLD NEEDS YOUR STORY NEXT!

JOURNAL 6: AFTER CHAPTER 26 – FROM SHADOWS TO LIGHT

Chapters 25–26 Summary: Final transformation. Unity is declared. The real-world consequences of Wakaduo's journey unfold in the children's neighborhood.

Page 1 – Reflect & Write

Prompt 1:

"I used to think… but now I think…"

➤ About how change happens in communities

_____
_____

Prompt 2:

Which character's growth inspired you most? Why?

_____
_____

Prompt 3:

What does it mean to carry a place or lesson inside your heart?

_____
_____
_____

Page 2 – Create & Connect

• **Draw** your "Token of Change" — what would it look like and what power would it hold?

• **Write** a letter to your future self explaining what Wakaduo taught you

☙ "FINAL CHALLENGE: SHOW WHAT YOU'VE LEARNED!

"You've come so far! This final challenge helps you see just how much you've grown. Show your best thinking!"

📘 POST-TEST
◆ Section 1: Reading Comprehension

Read the passage and answer the questions.

Excerpt from Chapter 21: The Predators' Plot

"Tonight, we need to make a brave decision," Hugger hissed. "If we can make them scared enough to leave, Wakaduo will be ours. They will run from their home and right into our hands."

Dirty Donald laughed. "Imagine all the food! Just a little scare, and they're gone!"

Kael's golden eyes flicked nervously. "But... Tau told us not to bother them. If he finds out—"

"Tau?" Dirty Donald scoffed. "Where is he now? Or do you see us?"

Hugger's voice grew darker. "Fear will do the work for us. Let them believe a disaster is coming. That is how we win."

1. Why does Hugger believe fear will help them win?

A. Because fear will make the prey animals stronger

B. Because fear will cause the prey animals to flee

C. Because fear will help them talk to Tau

D. Because fear will convince Tau to join them

2. Which word best describes Dirty Donald's attitude in this scene?

A. Nervous

B. Joyful

C. Sneaky

D. Serious

3. What can you infer about Kael based on his reaction?

A. He is excited to join the plan

B. He is unsure and scared of the consequences

C. He wants to take over as the leader

D. He doesn't understand what's happening

4. What does the phrase "Fear will do the work for us" mean?

A. The predators will not need to act

B. The prey animals will ask for help

C. Fear will make them stronger

D. The predators will have to work harder

◆ Section 2: Vocabulary in Context

5. What does the word "looming" mean in the sentence below?

"The looming threat of the storm made all the animals uneasy."

A. Something already happening

B. A danger that might happen soon

C. Something to laugh at

D. A memory from long ago

6. What does "treacherous" most likely mean in this sentence?

"They journeyed into the treacherous jungle, unsure if they would make it out."

A. Peaceful and safe

B. Hot and boring

C. Dangerous and full of hidden threats

D. Dry and lifeless

7. Choose the sentence that best uses the word "contemplated."

A. She contemplated a big meal quickly.

B. He contemplated his decision before speaking.

C. They contemplated a loud laugh during lunch.

D. I contemplated my running shoes in the mud.

◆ Section 3: Short Constructed Response

8. Why is the idea of unity important in Chapters 20–23? Use at least two vocabulary words from the glossary in your response.

✍

✍

✍

▨ Morphology Section

Aligned to Science of Reading (SoR) principles – decoding, affix/root meaning, and word construction

Standards-Aligned Skills:

• Identifying root meanings

- Constructing words from parts
- Understanding word formation through affixes and context

Directions: Use the word parts and their meanings to answer each question.

Word Parts:

- **cor** = heart
- **guard** = to watch or protect
- **-ian** = one who
- **trans** = across
- **-ation** = action or process
- **en-** = to put into
- **chant** = to sing or speak rhythmically
- **pro-** = before
- **form** = shape

9. Which full word means "a person who protects"?

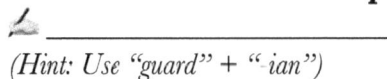 _____

(Hint: Use "guard" + "-ian")

10. Which full word means "a change in form"?

_____

(Hint: Use "trans" + "form" + "-ation")

11. What is the meaning of "enchantment"?

_____

(Hint: Use "en-" + "chant" + "-ment")

12. What root word is used in "courage" that means "heart"?

_____

13. What prefix in "prophecy" means "before"?

_____

✍ Extended Writing Prompt
Text-Dependent Analysis Prompt | 4th Grade Writing Standard W.4.1 & W.4.4

Directions: Use evidence from the story and glossary to support your writing.

14. Prompt:
In *Chapters 20–23*, both Adira and Scatter face major challenges that test their leadership and bravery.

Choose **one character** and explain how they showed **courage**, **wisdom**, or **cleverness**.

Use **at least two vocabulary words** from the chapter glossaries to support your ideas.

✍ Paragraph Response:
(Students should write 5–7 sentences, with a topic sentence, details from the story, vocabulary usage, and a closing idea.)

[_____]
[_____]
[_____]
[_____]
[_____]
[_____]
[_____]
[_____]
[_____]
[_____]
[_____]
[_____]
[_____]
[_____]
[_____]
[_____]

FINAL REFLECTION + CREATIVE CORNER

WHAT'S NEXT?

You've reached the end of the journey—but your story is just beginning.

The heroes of Wakaduo showed us that greatness isn't measured in strength alone. It lives in the choices we make—especially when we lead with courage, wisdom, and kindness.

Ask Yourself:
- What legacy do you want to leave behind?
- What does it mean to unleash your own greatness?

Reader Reflection
Write your own Final Reflection.
- What surprised you most about this story?
- What lesson will you carry into your real life?
- If you could speak to one character, what would you say?

Creative Corner: Your Inner Kingdom
Design your own kingdom of values.
Draw or imagine:

• A flag or crest that represents YOU
• Three core values that define your leadership (e.g. Kindness, Honesty, Bravery)
• A personal motto
Example: "Lead with your heart, walk with the wise."

Books That Inspire Courage

If you loved this story, check out:
• *The Wild Robot* – Peter Brown
• Echoes of Greatness: The Malcolm Middle Chronicles - R. G. Waugh
• *A Wish in the Dark* – Christina Soontornvat
• *One Crazy Summer* – Rita Williams-Garcia
• *Haroun and the Sea of Stories* – Salman Rushdie

Keep the Conversation Going

For classrooms, families, or book clubs:
• Host a Circle of Unity gathering
• Write a class or group "Chant of Values"
• Make a mural, banner, or memory capsule

FINAL REFLECTION & CREATIVE CORNER

"Now that you've completed your journey through Wakaduo, this is your space to look back — and dream forward."

A final quote-based reflection:

"Ask Yourself: What legacy do you want to leave behind? What does it mean to unleash your own greatness?"

A prompt labeled **Reader Reflection** with three questions:
• What surprised you most about this story?

• What lesson will you carry into your real life?

• If you could speak to one character, what would you say?

Reader Reflection with three questions:
- What surprised you most about this story?

- What lesson will you carry into your real life?

- If you could speak to one character, what would you say?

The **Creative Corner**: "Design your own kingdom of values" with a flag/crest, core values, motto, and example.

CERTIFICATE OF COMPLETION

Congratulations!

❧ CERTIFICATE OF COMPLETION ❧

Presented to: _____

For courage, creativity, and leadership on the path through Wakaduo.

You have shown:

- ☑ *Courage to face challenges*
  - ☑ *Wisdom to learn and grow*
  - ☑ *Kindness to lift others up*
  - ☑ *Leadership to make a difference*
  - ☑ *Creativity to dream big*

*Your adventure doesn't end here –
It's just the beginning of your journey to
Unleashing Your Greatness in the world!*

Date Completed: _____

Teacher's Signature: _____

Student's Signature: _____

We are so proud of the hero you are becoming!
Keep going. Keep growing. Keep unleashing your greatness!

"We rise by lifting others." – African Proverb

GLOSSARY

"This glossary includes new, powerful, and beautiful words. Each chapter's glossary helps you grow your vocabulary, understand big ideas, and recognize how language paints a world. The glossary contains every key word from the novel, organized by chapter. Use it to study, review, or prepare for writing and discussion."

Word Quest Chapter 1 Glossary – *Embracing the Unknown*
Categorized for Clarity | Optimized for Learning

Vocabulary (General Academic & Descriptive Words)
- **Affirmed** – Declared something to be true with confidence.
- **Amplifying** – Making something louder, stronger, or more noticeable.
- **Apprehension** – A nervous feeling that something bad might happen.
- **Awareness** – Knowing about something or understanding what's happening.
- **Beckoning** – A motion or signal inviting someone to come closer.

- **Bold** – Confident and willing to take risks.
- **Captivated** – So interested or fascinated that you can't look away.
- **Clutched** – Held something tightly.
- **Confidence** – A belief in your own abilities.
- **Crucial** – Very important or necessary for success.
- **Curiosity** – A strong desire to learn or know more.
- **Decisions** – Choices made after thinking about options.
- **Electric charge** – A feeling of energy or excitement.
- **Electric charge of transition** – A strong, exciting feeling during a big change.
- **Encourage** – To give someone support or praise.
- **Enthusiasm** – Excitement or eagerness for something.
- **Extraordinary** – Very unusual or special; better than ordinary.
- **Fascination** – Strong interest or attraction to something.
- **Fluttered** – Moved quickly and lightly, like wings or paper in the wind.
- **Incredible** – Amazing or hard to believe.
- **Instinct** – A natural way of thinking or reacting without needing to think about it.
- **Intensifying** – Getting stronger or more powerful.
- **Introverted** – Quiet and more comfortable being alone than in groups.
- **Irresistibly** – So appealing that you can't say no to it.
- **Judgment** – The ability to make good and careful decisions.
- **Momentarily** – For a short time.
- **Mused** – Thought carefully or deeply about something.
- **Narrative** – A story or series of events.
- **Ominous** – Something that feels like a warning of danger or trouble.
- **Participating** – Being part of an activity.
- **Pulsating** – Moving or beating with energy or rhythm.
- **Recognition** – Realizing or knowing someone or something.
- **Resilience** – The ability to bounce back after something hard.

- **Resolute** – Firm and determined, not giving up.
- **Restore her spirits** – To help someone feel happier or stronger.
- **Spark of determination** – A sudden feeling of strong will to keep going.
- **Steady beacon** – A calm and guiding presence during confusion.
- **Threshold** – The beginning of a new experience or phase.
- **Timbre** – The special sound or tone quality in a voice or noise.
- **Tension** – A nervous or uncomfortable feeling before something important.
- **Transformed** – Changed in a big or dramatic way.
- **Urgent** – Needing quick action or attention.
- **Valuable lesson** – An important thing learned from an experience.
- **Whirlwind** – A chaotic or fast-moving experience.
- **Wisdom** – Knowledge gained from experience that helps you make good choices.

Literary & Figurative Language

- **Canvas** – A surface for painting, used here as a metaphor for imagination or life.
- **Crossroads of their own destinies** – A moment when choices decide the future.
- **Crystallizing** – Making ideas or feelings very clear and defined.
- **Creativity knew no bounds** – A way of saying someone has endless imagination.
- **Gravity of the moment** – The serious importance of what is happening.
- **Moral compass** – Your sense of right and wrong that guides decisions.
- **Nexus of their fate** – The central point where everything important comes together.

- **Resonating the pulse of the earth** – A poetic way of describing a deep connection to nature or life.
- **Vortex** – A spinning force like a whirlpool, used metaphorically for chaos or strong emotion.

Science Concepts (Natural World, Energy, Phenomena)

- **Eagle-owl** – A large African owl with powerful vision and hunting skills.
- **Eclipse** – When one celestial body moves into the shadow of another (like the moon blocking the sun).
- **Electric charge** – A scientific term that also describes energy or excitement.
- **Honey badger** – A small, fearless African animal known for being tough and clever.
- **Pouched mouse** – A rodent with pouches in its cheeks to store food.
- **Wildebeests** – Large African animals known for long migrations.
- **Animal senses awakening** – Becoming more aware like animals who rely on instinct.

Cultural References, Social-Emotional Learning, Proverbs

- **African-American** – People in the U.S. with family roots in Africa, often connected to a deep cultural history.
- **Apprehension** – Emotional awareness of fear or hesitation in uncertain moments.
- **Bullying** – Repeated harmful behavior toward someone who is weaker.
- **Camaraderie** – A deep friendship and trust, like being part of a close team.
- **Confidence** – Believing in your own strengths.
- **Counselor** – A trusted adult who helps with problems or feelings.
- **Creative spirit** – The part of you that thinks outside the box and makes new things.

- **Curiosity** – Wanting to explore or learn more.
- **Destiny** – What is meant to happen in your life.
- **Empathy** – Understanding and sharing someone else's feelings.
- **Emphasize** – To give importance to something.
- **Encourage** – Support someone with kind words or actions.
- **Enthusiasm** – A joyful excitement for something you care about.
- **Flicker of hope** – A small feeling that things might get better.
- **Gang** – A group of people, often in trouble, who may stick together.
- **Imagination** – The ability to picture or create things in your mind.
- **Inspire** – To make someone want to do something great.
- **Intentions** – What someone plans or wants to do.
- **Leadership** – The skill of guiding others with strength and care.
- **Maturity** – Acting with emotional and mental

📖 Chapter 2 Glossary – *Adira's Awakening*
Categorized for Clarity | Optimized for Young Learners

🔲 Vocabulary (General Academic & Descriptive Words)
- **Abundance** – A large quantity of something; more than enough.
- **Access** – The ability or right to use, enter, or get something.
- **Battered** – Worn out or damaged from frequent use or hardship.
- **Challenges** – Difficult tasks that test your ability, strength, or courage.
- **Confused** – Not understanding something clearly; feeling puzzled.
- **Enchanted** – Magical or under a spell; filled with wonder.
- **Essence** – The most important quality or core of something.

- **Investigate** – To look into something carefully to find out more about it.
- **Introduce** – To present something or someone for the first time.
- **Language** – A system of words or symbols used for communication.
- **Mysterious** – Strange or hard to explain or understand.
- **Noble** – Showing high moral character; brave, kind, or honorable.
- **Potion** – A magical liquid often used in stories to bring about change or healing.
- **Respect** – A feeling of admiration for someone or something because of their good qualities or actions.
- **Responsibility** – The duty to take care of something or someone and do the right thing.
- **Sanctuary** – A safe place where people or animals are protected from danger.
- **Scarcity** – When something is limited or in short supply.
- **Springs of Wakaduo** – Imaginary magical springs in Wakaduo that may have special powers or meaning.
- **Surge of Energy** – A sudden burst or increase of strength or excitement.
- **Terrifying** – Very frightening or scary.
- **Unusual** – Not common or expected; different.

Literary & Figurative Language
- **Ebb and Flow** – A phrase that describes things that rise and fall, come and go—like waves in the ocean or feelings over time.
- **Move with effortless strength** – A poetic way to describe graceful yet powerful motion.
- **The Ways of the Water** – A poetic phrase referring to how water behaves or flows in nature.
- **True Nature of Things** – The real or most important qualities of someone or something.

Science Concepts (Animals, Geography, Natural World)

- **Hyena** – A wild African animal known for its loud, laughing-like sounds and strong jaws.
- **Land Bridge** – A natural strip of land connecting two larger land areas, often used by animals or people to cross between places.
- **Leopard** – A large wild cat with spots, excellent at climbing, found in Africa and parts of Asia.
- **Savanna** – A wide, flat grassy area with few trees, found in warm regions like Africa.
- **Tortoise** – A land-dwelling reptile with a hard shell, known for moving slowly.

Cultural References, Wisdom & Traditions

- **Ancient Rituals** – Traditional ceremonies that have been practiced for many generations.
- **Wise** – Showing good judgment and understanding based on experience or age.

Chapter 3 Glossary – *The Mysterious Quest*
Organized by Category | Cleanly Alphabetized | 4th Grade–Friendly

Vocabulary (General Academic & Descriptive Words)

- **Clever** – Quick to understand or figure things out; smart in a creative way.
- **Compass** – A tool used to find direction (like north, south, east, west).
- **Connected** – Joined together or closely related to something or someone.
- **Convinced** – Feeling sure or certain about something.
- **Kindled** – To start or ignite something, like a fire—or an idea or feeling.
- **Nervousness** – A feeling of being worried or anxious about what might happen.
- **Prosperity** – A state of being successful and having good fortune, often with money or health.

• **Reaction** – A way someone responds to something that happens.

• **Resolve** – To make a firm decision or commitment.

• **Reveal** – To show something that was hidden or unknown.

• **Sacred** – Very holy or deeply respected.

• **Spark of Hope** – A small sign that something good may happen.

• **Symbols** – Objects or signs that represent something else (like a heart for love).

• **Testament** – A clear sign or proof that something is true.

• **Thrive** – To grow, succeed, or live in a healthy way.

Literary Terms & Figurative Language

• **Imagine** – To picture something in your mind, especially something creative or not real.

• **Mystical** – Having a magical, mysterious, or spiritual quality.

• **Tall Tale** – A story that exaggerates facts in a funny or unbelievable way.

Science & Nature Concepts

• **Honey Badger** – A small but fierce animal known for being brave and clever.

• **Mandrill** – A large type of monkey known for its colorful face and behind.

• **Pouched Mouse** – A small rodent with cheek pouches for carrying food.

Cultural References & Social Themes

• **Ancestors** – Family members from generations before you, like great-grandparents.

• **Destiny** – What is meant or supposed to happen to someone in the future.

• **Quest** – A long and adventurous journey to find or achieve something important.

• **Unity** – The state of working together as one group or team.

• **Wisdom** – Knowledge gained through life experience that helps in making good decisions.

Chapter 4 Glossary – Scatter's Story

Organized by Category | Cleanly Alphabetized | 4th Grade–Friendly

Vocabulary (General Academic & Descriptive Words)

Abandoned – Left alone or given up on.

Amazed – Very surprised or impressed by something.

Connects – Joins together or relates one thing to another.

Curiosity – Wanting to learn or know more about something.

Destiny – A special future or purpose that someone or something is supposed to have.

Disbelief – A feeling of not being able to believe something because it's surprising or hard to accept.

Doubt – Feeling uncertain about something or not fully believing.

Echoing – Repeating or resounding a sound.

Exchanged – Gave something to someone and received something else in return.

Glimpse – A very quick look at something.

Grateful – Feeling thankful for something or someone.

Growing belief – Slowly starting to believe in something more and more.

Hopeless – Feeling like there is no chance for improvement or success.

Inheritance – Something passed down from older family members to younger ones, like traits or belongings.

Mood – The way you feel at a certain time.

Mysterious – Something that is not fully understood or known, often exciting curiosity.

Newfound respect – A fresh or recently developed feeling of admiration for someone or something.

Nuzzled – Gently pushed or rubbed with the nose.

Our history – The events or stories from the past that belong to us or our community.

Preparation – The act of getting ready for something.

Proud – Feeling pleased with oneself or someone else's achievements.

Purpose – The reason for doing something or the goal someone is trying to achieve.

Skeptically – Doubtfully or with a questioning attitude.

Sneered – Made a mean or mocking smile or comment.

Spirits – Feelings or moods; can also mean ghosts or magical beings in stories.

Started to see her differently – Began to understand or appreciate someone in a new way.

Surviving – Staying alive, especially in tough conditions.

Tears of doubt – Crying caused by feeling unsure or uncertain.

Unsure – Not certain or confident about something.

Valley – A low area of land between hills or mountains, often where a river flows.

Voice quivering – Speaking with a shaky or trembling voice, often from emotion.

Wonder – Feeling amazement or admiration, often caused by something beautiful or unexpected.

Literary Terms & Figurative Language

Ability to make a difference – Having the power or skills to cause a positive change.

Inspire us to rise above our doubts and fears – Motivate us to overcome our uncertainties and worries.

Mock – To make fun of or laugh at in a mean way.

Mockingly – Teasing or making fun of someone in a mean way.

More to this story than meets the eye – Saying there are hidden facts or deeper truths not immediately obvious.

My anchor – Something that provides stability or confidence in difficult situations.

Stepping into the Unknown – Moving forward into something new and unfamiliar.

Tale of Courage – A story about being brave.

The Power of Believing – The strength that comes from having confidence or faith in something.

United group – A team or collection of individuals working together as one.

Science & Nature Concepts

African Climbing Mice – Small mice that are good at climbing, found in Africa.

African Porcupine – A large rodent with sharp quills that can be raised when threatened.

Colobus Monkey – A type of monkey with black and white fur, known for jumping between trees.

Guinea Fowl – A type of bird often found in Africa, known for its spotted feathers.

Insects – Small animals with six legs, like ants, bees, and butterflies.

Kudu – A large African antelope known for its long spiral horns.

Mosquito – A small flying insect that bites and can make you itch.

Savuti Banded Mongoose – A small mammal found in Africa known for living in groups and hunting together.

Snout – The long nose and mouth area of some animals, like pigs.

Species – A group of living organisms that are similar and can produce young together.

Spotted Eagle-Owl – A large type of owl with spots on its body, known for its powerful eyesight at night.

Volcano – A mountain that can erupt with hot lava, ash, and gases.

Cultural References & Social Themes

Ancestors – Family members from past generations, like great-grandparents.

Chorused – When a group says something all at the same time.

Legendary – Famous or well-known, often from old stories or myths.

Symbol – Something that stands for or represents something else, often an idea or quality.

Unison – Doing something all together at the same time.

Chapter 5 Glossary – The Gathering

Organized by Category | Cleanly Alphabetized | 4th Grade–Friendly

Vocabulary (General Academic & Descriptive Words)

Ability – The skill or means to do something.

Attention – Focusing thought or care on something.

Commitment – The state or quality of being dedicated to a cause or activity.

Contemplated – Thought about something deeply.

Cunning – Having or showing skill in achieving one's goals by tricking or deceiving others.

Deceived – Tricked or lied to someone.

Debate – A formal discussion where people express different opinions.

Diverse – Showing a great deal of variety.

Earnestness – Serious and intense belief or feeling.

Emphasizing – Giving special importance to something when speaking or writing.

Evening – The part of the day after the afternoon and before night.

Face reality with eyes wide open – To accept the truth clearly and fully.

Fortified – Strengthened or made more secure.

Guarded looks – Looks that show caution or worry.

Hazards – Dangers or risks.

Heated discussions – Intense or passionate conversations or arguments.

Honor – High respect or admiration.

Insights – Deep understanding about something or someone.

Journey – A long trip from one place to another.

Leadership – The act of guiding or leading a group.

Lush – A place filled with a lot of green plants.

Mission – A specific task or duty someone is meant to do.

Morrow – An old-fashioned word meaning "tomorrow" or "the next day."

Mysterious allure – An interesting or magical quality that's hard to explain.

Nervous – Feeling anxious or worried about what might happen.

Opinions – Personal thoughts or beliefs, not always based on facts.

Participating – Taking part in an activity or event.

Pondering – Thinking about something carefully.

Possessed – Owned or had a quality or trait.

Proclaimed – Officially or publicly announced.

Reality – What actually exists or happens—not just thoughts or dreams.

Realization – A moment of clearly understanding something.

Reason – A cause or explanation for something that happens.

Reflection – Serious thought or careful thinking.

Regal – Like a king or queen; royal and impressive.

Relentless – Continuing strongly or without giving up.

Seriousness – The quality of not joking; being thoughtful and focused.

Shared mission – A goal or task that a group works on together.

Shared purpose – A common reason or goal for doing something.

Stakes – The outcome or consequences that depend on what happens.

Stakes at hand – The important issues that are happening right now.

Strategies – Careful plans made to reach a goal.

Survival – The act of staying alive or continuing to exist.

Threshold – The starting point of a new experience, or the entrance to a place.

Transformation – A big or important change in form or appearance.

Transcended – Rose above or went beyond normal limits.

Triumphant – Having won or succeeded at something.

Urgent purpose – A very important reason to act quickly.

Vanished – Disappeared suddenly and completely.

Vied – Competed with others to win or succeed.

Voice steady as stone – Speaking in a calm, strong, and firm way.

Weighing the myths – Thinking carefully about old stories or legends.

Well – A deep hole in the ground where water can be found.

Wisdom – Knowing what is right or best based on experience or learning.

Literary Terms & Figurative Language

A good point – A smart or valid thing to say in a discussion.

Bridged – Brought things or people closer together; made a connection.

Common purpose – A goal that a group of people share.

Face reality with eyes wide open – To fully accept and understand what's true, even if it's hard.

Hidden from the eyes of outsiders – Something kept secret or protected from people not in the group.

Painting streaks of earnestness across the tranquil scene – Adding serious feelings or purpose to a peaceful moment.

Pledge their allegiance – Promise to stay loyal to a group or cause.

Shadows got longer – When the sun is setting, shadows stretch out.

Voice steady as stone – Speaking in a strong and unshakable way.

Weight of leadership – The heavy responsibility a leader carries.

Science & Nature Concepts

Bat-eared Fox – A small African fox with big ears that help it hear very well.

Baboon – A large monkey with a dog-like face, found in Africa.

Banded Mongoose – A small animal with dark stripes across its back, known for living in groups.

Bongo – A large forest antelope with spiral horns and striking stripes.

Desert – A dry area with very little rain and few plants.

Grassland – A wide open area covered mainly in grass, with few trees.

Grey Parrot – A smart, talking parrot that's mostly grey and known for mimicking human speech.

Tortoise – A slow-moving land animal with a hard shell.

Cultural References & Social Themes

Caravan – A group of travelers moving together, especially across deserts.

Debate – A discussion where people express different opinions, sometimes in front of others.

Destiny – The future that is meant to happen to someone or something.

Leadership – The ability or role of guiding others toward a goal.

Quest – A long adventure or mission to find something important.

Shared mission – A common task or duty that a group agrees to work on.

Chapter 6 Glossary – The Tree of Life

Organized by Category | Cleanly Alphabetized | 4th Grade–
Friendly

▪ Vocabulary (General Academic & Descriptive Words)

Aggressively – In a forceful or intense way, sometimes too
strong.

Alternative – Another option or choice.

Amazement – A feeling of great surprise or wonder.

Anticipation – The feeling of looking forward to something.

Approached – Came near or closer to something or someone.

Attitude – The way you think or feel about someone or
something.

Capture the essence – To show the most important part of
something clearly.

Challenges – Difficult tasks or problems that test your abilities.

Community – A group of people living in the same place or
having something in common.

Cramped passage – A small, tight space that's hard to move
through.

Cravings – Strong desires for something.

Crucial detail – An extremely important piece of
information.

Devised – Planned or invented something carefully.

Determination – The will to keep going even when things are
hard.

Disrespect – Not showing politeness or honor.

Disturb – To interrupt or bother someone or something.

Diversity – A mix of different people, things, or ideas.

Dwindled – Became smaller or fewer.

Echoed – A sound that repeats or bounces back.

Every fiber of her being – All of her effort, feelings, or
strength.

Expedition – A journey with a special purpose.

Eyes filled with wonder and resolve – Looking amazed
and determined at the same time.

Flute – A musical instrument you blow into, held sideways.

Fragrance – A sweet or pleasant smell.

Gratitude – Thankfulness.

Greater purpose – A higher, more meaningful reason for doing something.

Hollowed trunk – The inside of a tree that has been emptied or carved out.

Immediately – Right away, without delay.

Impatience – (Opposite of patience) Wanting something to happen quickly.

Incredible gift – An amazing or special talent or present.

Indulge – To let yourself enjoy something.

Instantaneously – Happening right away.

Interjected – Interrupted by saying something suddenly.

Jeopardizing – Putting something important at risk.

Jested – Made a joke or said something funny.

Keen eyes – Very good at seeing or noticing things.

Legends – Old stories that may be true but are often magical or exaggerated.

Lightning – A bright flash in the sky during a storm.

Living fully – Enjoying life with meaning and excitement.

Majestic – Beautiful and grand in a powerful way.

Materialized – Appeared suddenly or unexpectedly.

Mingled – Mixed together.

Newfound – Recently found or discovered.

Observed – Watched carefully.

Patience – The ability to wait calmly without getting upset.

Peril – Great danger.

Permission – Being allowed to do something.

Possess – To have or own something.

Radiating – Shining or sending out energy or light.

Recognized – Noticed or remembered something.

Recognizing the risks involved – Understanding that something might be dangerous.

Reflection – Careful thought about something.

Regret – A sad feeling about something wrong or a mistake.

Revealing – Showing something that was hidden.

Reverberated – Echoed or bounced back in sound.

Sacred energy – A special, powerful feeling or force that is deeply respected.

Shimmered – Shined with soft, flickering light.

Small vial – A tiny bottle, often used to hold liquid.

Soft applause – Quiet clapping to show appreciation.

Steadfast – Very loyal or determined.

Subtly – In a quiet, not obvious way.

Subsided – Became less strong or intense.

Summarized – Explained the main points briefly.

Summon – To call someone to come.

Temptation – Wanting to do something that might not be wise.

Token – A small object that stands for something else, like a symbol.

Trepidation – A feeling of fear or worry about what might happen.

Trials – Hard situations that test your strength or character.

Twitched – Made a small, quick movement.

Undivided attention – Focusing completely without distractions.

Unique – One of a kind; unlike anything else.

Voice full of emotion – Speaking with strong feelings.

Voice growing firmer – Speaking with more strength and confidence.

Well-being – Feeling healthy, safe, and happy.

Wind danced through the leaves – The wind moved in the trees as if dancing.

Wisdom – Using knowledge and experience to make good choices.

Literary Terms & Figurative Language

Air seemed charged – The air felt full of energy, like something important was about to happen.

Capture the essence – To clearly express the most important or meaningful part.

Depth of our connections – How close or meaningful our relationships are.

Despite her desires – Even though she wanted something.

Eyes filled with wonder and resolve – Showing amazement and strong determination.

Recognizing the risks involved – Realizing something might be dangerous before doing it.

The land itself sensed their important quest – It felt like even nature knew something big was happening.

The tree holds our hopes – The tree stands for our dreams and beliefs.

Tree's heartwood – The strong, inner part of a tree, often used to represent strength or wisdom.

Voice full of emotion – Talking with deep feeling.

Science & Nature Concepts

Baobab Fruit – A fruit from the African baobab tree; it has a hard shell and nutritious seeds.

African Killer Bees – A kind of aggressive bee that defends its hive fiercely.

Beehive – The home where bees live and make honey.

Cobra – A poisonous snake known for spreading a hood around its head when threatened.

Honey – A sweet, sticky food made by bees from flower nectar.

Honey Badger – A small but fearless animal known for being tough and brave.

Grassland – A wide, open area mostly covered with grass.

Wasteland – A dry or empty area where little can grow.

Nectar – A sweet liquid made by flowers that attracts bees.

Cultural References & Social Themes

Bowing – Bending your body forward to show respect.

Covert mission – A secret task or operation.

Greater purpose – A bigger, more meaningful reason for doing something.

Humbly – Acting in a way that shows modesty, not showing off.

'Your majesty' – A respectful way to speak to royalty like a king or queen.

Queen bee – The leader bee in a hive; can also mean a powerful woman.

Regal gesture – An action that is noble or royal in style.

Respectful / Respectfully – Acting with politeness and care for others.

Spirits – The mood or emotional feeling of people or a place.

Unison – Doing something at the exact same time as others.

Chapter 7 Glossary – The Desert of No Return
Organized by Category | Cleanly Alphabetized | 4th Grade–Friendly

Vocabulary (General Academic & Descriptive Words)
Adapting – Changing to fit new conditions.

Bestowed – Given as a gift or honor.

Blessings – Good wishes or approval.

Collective wisdom – Knowledge gained by a group of people over time.

Curiosity – Wanting to learn about something.

Distinctive – Easy to recognize because it's different from others.

Encouraged – Given support, courage, or hope.

Endless dunes – Hills of sand that stretch out as far as you can see.

Face our fears – To be brave and deal with what scares us.

Familiar – Something you know well from seeing it often.

Insights – Deep understanding of something important.

Lingered – Stayed in one place longer than needed.

Mirage – Something that looks real (like water in the desert) but isn't really there.

Nervously – Acting or feeling worried about what might happen.

Oases – Special places in the desert where water and plants can be found.

Promise of discovery – The chance to find something new or exciting.

Relief – A feeling of calm after being worried or scared.

Seriously – In a serious or not joking way.

Subtle signs – Small hints that are easy to miss.

Transformed – Changed in shape or appearance.

Trudging – Walking slowly and heavily, usually when tired.

Vast – Very large or wide.

Ventured – Went somewhere new or risky.

Vigilant – Always watchful and alert.

Visions of their history – Images or ideas that show a group's past.

Weary – Very tired.

Wavering heat – Heat that makes the air look like it's shaking or moving.

Withered – Dried up and shrunk.

Literary Terms & Figurative Language

Each step weighed down by his absence – Feeling heavy or sad because someone is missing.

Face our fears – To deal with something scary with courage.

Sadness etched on their faces – Faces that clearly show deep sadness.

Scanned the horizon – Looked carefully across the distance to see what might be ahead.

Spirits of the past – Feelings or memories from long ago.

Subtle signs – Tiny clues that are not easy to notice.

Sun cast long shadows – In the late day, the sun makes long, stretched-out shadows.

Symbol of endurance – Something that stands for strength and the ability to keep going.

The desert changes to protect its secrets – A way to say the desert seems to hide its mysteries.

The desert showed its softer side – A time when the desert feels less harsh or more gentle.

Treacherous desert – A very dangerous or tricky desert.

Science & Nature Concepts

Baobab Tree – A large African tree with a wide trunk and fruit, known to live for a long time.

Desert's mysterious nature – The strange and hard-to-understand qualities of a desert.

White Rhinoceros – A large, thick-skinned animal with one or two horns on its nose.

Queen Bee – The main bee in a hive that lays all the eggs.

Sable – A dark-colored antelope found in Africa.

Spotted Hyena – A wild animal that looks like a dog and makes laugh-like sounds.

Sentinels – Guards who keep watch over a place.

Ridge – A long, narrow raised area of land.

Torches – Sticks with fire on top used to light the way.

Cultural References & Social Themes

Ancients – People who lived a very long time ago.

Countless generations – Many families over a long stretch of time.

Desert's mysterious nature – The desert being hard to understand or full of secrets.

Fate – What is meant to happen to someone, often out of their control.

Legends – Old stories passed down that may not be completely true.

Queen Bee – Can also mean a powerful or important woman, in addition to the insect meaning.

Sacred Site – A place that is very special or holy, often connected to religion or tradition.

Sage Advice – Very wise and helpful advice.

Chapter 8 Glossary – The Mountains of the Moon

Organized by Category | Cleanly Alphabetized | 4th Grade–Friendly

▦ Vocabulary (General Academic & Descriptive Words)

Adapting – Changing behavior or ideas to fit new conditions.

Agility – The ability to move quickly and easily.

Amidst – In the middle of or surrounded by.

Art gallery – A place where artwork is displayed.

Awe – A feeling of wonder mixed with respect or fear.

Barrier – Something that blocks movement or progress. *(Optional add-on based on "Obstacles" if needed)*

Breathtaking view – A view so amazing it takes your breath away.

Burst of energy – A sudden feeling of energy and excitement.

Dawn – The early morning when the sky begins to lighten.

Descended – Moved or fell downward.

Determination – The strong will to keep going or achieve something.

Dual nature – Having two different sides or qualities.

Enveloped – Surrounded or covered completely.

Essence – The basic or most important part of something.

Exclaimed – Said something suddenly and excitedly.

Fatigue – Great tiredness or exhaustion.

Foretelling – Predicting what will happen in the future.

Glimpse – A quick or brief look at something.

Haven – A safe or peaceful place.

Horizon – The line where the earth or sea seems to meet the sky.

Insurmountable – Too difficult to overcome.

Intelligence – The ability to learn and understand.

Magnificent – Very beautiful and grand.

Marveled – Felt great surprise or wonder.

Mirrored their deepest fears – Reflected or showed what they were most afraid of.

Motivated – Feeling encouraged or inspired to take action.

Murmured – Spoke in a quiet, soft voice.

Mystical appearance – Something that looks magical or mysterious.

Obstacles – Things that make it hard to move forward or succeed.

Pride – A feeling of satisfaction or joy about achievements.

Profound insight – A deep and meaningful understanding.

Radiating – Sending out light or energy; showing clearly.

Reassured – Made someone feel less worried or scared.

Reflecting on their experiences – Thinking deeply about what has happened and what was learned.

Relief – A feeling of comfort after worry or stress is gone.

Reinforcing – Making something stronger or more certain.

Respite – A short break or rest from something hard.

Sanctuary – A safe place of peace and protection.

Sense of pride – A feeling of being proud or pleased.

Sense of purpose – A strong feeling of having a goal or reason for doing something.

Serene – Calm and peaceful.

Shielding – Protecting something from danger.

Stark contrast – A very clear and obvious difference.

Summit – The very top of a mountain.

Taking its toll – Causing harm or difficulty over time.

Terrain – Land, especially in terms of its features or surface.

Towering – Very tall, like a mountain or big structure.

Transformed – Changed completely in form or appearance.

Tranquility – A state of peace and quiet.

Triumphs – Big wins or successes.

Turning point – A moment when things begin to change in a big way.

Undeniable – Something that is clearly true.

Undying hope – Hope that never ends or goes away.

Vivid – Very clear, bright, or strong in detail.

Vivid contrast – A strong, easy-to-see difference between two things.

Visionary – A person with creative or forward-thinking ideas.

Literary Terms & Figurative Language

Dreams that connected their animal and human forms – Dreams that showed a link between their two natures.

Feeling the weight of their adventures – Feeling tired or changed from everything they've gone through.

Mirrored their deepest fears – Showing on the outside what they feel afraid of inside.

Pull of the mountains – A strong feeling of being drawn or called toward the mountains.

Shared destiny – A future connected with others.

Stood majestically – Standing in a proud, grand way.

Turning point – A moment that brings big change in a story or life.

Science & Nature Concepts

Barren desert – A dry, empty place where almost nothing grows.

Horizon – The far-off line where the land or sea meets the sky.

Animal instinct – Natural behavior animals use to survive.

Predator – An animal that hunts and eats other animals.

Summit – The very top of a mountain.

Terrain – The land and its physical features like hills, rocks, or valleys.

Cultural References & Social Themes

Art gallery – A place where creative works are displayed.

Collective growth *(Optional addition to parallel "shared destiny")* – When a group grows or learns together.

Reflecting on their experiences – Thinking about what they've been through and how it changed them.

Sense of purpose – Knowing why you are doing something.

Shared destiny – A future that is affected by being part of a group or team.

Chapter 9 Glossary – Ugalla

Organized by Category | Cleanly Alphabetized | 4th Grade–Friendly

■ Vocabulary (General Academic & Descriptive Words)

Destination – The place someone is going to or being sent.

Good Fortune – Something lucky or helpful that happens by chance.

Hardships – Tough or painful experiences that make life difficult.

Shimmering – Shining or sparkling with a soft, flickering light.

Shielding – Protecting something or someone from harm or danger.

Struggling – Having a hard time doing something or facing a tough challenge.

Triumphant – Feeling joyful or proud after winning or succeeding.

Trumpet – A loud call or sound, often made by animals like elephants or used to celebrate.

▨ Literary Terms & Figurative Language

Edge of the clearing – The outer part of an open space in a forest or field; often used in stories to describe a place of transition or discovery.

Feathers ruffled – A phrase that means someone is upset or disturbed, like how a bird fluffs its feathers when bothered.

Tests of Courage – Situations that show how brave someone is when facing fear or danger.

■ Science & Nature Concepts

(No new entries for this category in this chapter—unless you'd like to classify *"trumpet"* under animal behavior, such as elephants. Just say the word and I can adjust!)

■ Cultural References, World-Building & Social Themes

Mountain of Dreams – A special mountain in the story that stands for big hopes, challenges, and discoveries.

Ugalla – A fictional place in the story that becomes the characters' new home.

Wakaduo – A magical or important place in the story that holds deep meaning for the characters.

Chapter 10: Glossary – Gurr

Organized by Category | Cleanly Alphabetized | 4th Grade–Friendly

Vocabulary (General Academic & Descriptive Words)

Apprehension – A nervous or uneasy feeling about something that might happen.

Braced – Got ready or prepared for something difficult.

Clever – Smart and good at solving problems quickly.

Compelled – Felt a strong need or desire to do something.

Curious – Wanting to know or learn more about something.

Daring Plan – A bold and risky idea or strategy.

Embrace – To hug someone or accept something new or different with open arms.

Formidable – Very strong, impressive, or a little scary.

Forged – Created or built, especially through hard work or difficulty.

Legendary – Very famous or admired, often from old stories or myths.

Magnificent – *(Optional addition if desired—frequently overlaps with "legendary" in tone.)*

Realms – Kingdoms or large areas ruled or known for something.

Reassured – *(Optional addition from Chapter 8—useful carryover if still relevant.)*

Referencing – Talking about or pointing to something as proof or support.

Regretful – Feeling sorry about something you did or didn't do.

Respectful – Showing politeness and honor toward others.

Risk of the Unknown – The danger of doing something when you don't know what will happen.

Severed – Completely cut off or ended.

Shimmering – Sparkling or shining with a soft, moving light.

Signaling – Giving a sign or signal to let someone know something.

Sensation – A feeling from your body, like warmth, tickling, or pain.

Sense of Urgency – A strong feeling that something must be done quickly.

Soothing – Calming and relaxing, especially when you're upset or tense.

Spread Like Wildfire – Something that spreads or moves very quickly, like news or gossip.

Subtle Reminder – A small or gentle hint to help someone remember something.

Tattered – Torn and worn out, often from use or age.

Tense Mood – A feeling of stress or nervousness in the air.

Unwavering – Strong and steady, not changing or giving up.

Literary Terms & Figurative Language

Air Heavy with Unspoken Thoughts – A moment when people are quiet, but you can feel they have a lot on their minds.

Cracks in Their Unity – Small signs that the group is not fully getting along or working together.

Countless Trials – Many challenges or hard times.

Dreams Brimmed with Possibility – Hopes or dreams that are full of opportunity and excitement.

Etched on Her Features – Clearly shown on her face.

Fragile Thread of Hope – A very small or delicate feeling of hope.

Sent Shivers Down the Spine – Caused a feeling of fear or excitement to run through someone's body.

Teeming with Life – Full of living things like plants, animals, and energy.

Unforgiving Disasters – Very harsh events that cause big problems and are hard to recover from.

Science & Nature Concepts

Baobab Tree – A large African tree with a wide trunk that can store water and has branches that look like roots.

Jasmine – A small flower that smells sweet, often white or yellow.

Mane – The long hair around the neck of animals like lions or horses.

Lush Valley – A valley that is very green, with lots of plants and trees.

River Route – A path or trail that follows along a river.

Seers – People believed to see or predict things before they happen.

Wellspring of Knowledge – A source full of information, learning, or wisdom.

Cultural References & Social Themes

Ancestors – Family members from generations in the past.

Betrayal – When someone breaks trust or is disloyal to someone else.

Dreams Brimmed with Possibility – Hopes or ideas that are full of promise for the future.

Gurr – *(Optional placeholder for story significance—if it's a location, title, or character reference, we can expand in companion guides.)*

Recounted – Told about something that happened in the past.

Rekindle – To restart or bring back something that was lost, like a friendship or feeling.

Shared History / Shared Struggles *(Optional expansion of themes reflected in unity/disunity.)*

Chapter 11 Glossary – The Returning Heroes

Organized by Category | Cleanly Alphabetized | 4th Grade–Friendly

Vocabulary (General Academic & Descriptive Words)

Altered – Changed in some way.

Daunting Obstacle – A very difficult challenge that seems hard to get past.

Destiny – What is meant or supposed to happen to someone in the future.

Duty to Protect – The responsibility to keep someone or something safe.

Fearsome Power – A strong and scary ability that makes others feel afraid.

Felt the Weight of Their Decisions – Realizing how important their choices were and what might happen because of them.

Flash of Insight – A sudden and clear idea or understanding.

Immense – Very big or powerful.

Looming Entrance – A large or scary doorway or opening that seems close.

Lurking – Hiding quietly, often because of a secret or bad reason.

Mind Racing with Possibilities – Thinking quickly about lots of different ideas or outcomes.

Navigate – To find your way around, especially in an unfamiliar place.

Patience – Staying calm while waiting, even when it's hard.

Perilous – Very dangerous.

Reassess – To think again about something to decide if it still makes sense.

Remorse – Feeling very sorry for something you did.

Rethink Their Strategy – To change or come up with a new plan.

Resonate – When something feels meaningful or connects with your feelings or thoughts.

Reunited – Coming back together after being apart.

Literary Terms & Figurative Language

Circle of Life – The idea that everything in nature is connected in a repeating cycle: birth, growth, death, and renewal.

Ghostly Voice – A spooky or soft voice that sounds like it could come from a ghost.

Legendary Guardian – A famous protector from old stories or myths.

Master Their Fates – To take control of what happens to you, instead of leaving it to chance.

Mind Racing with Possibilities – A way to describe when someone is thinking fast about many different options.

Renowned Resolve – Being known for staying strong and determined, even when things are hard.

Timeless Dance of the Wild – The ongoing, never-ending movements and behaviors of animals in nature.

Science & Nature Concepts

Instincts – Natural feelings or reactions that help animals (or people) survive, without needing to think.

Mother Nature – A way of talking about the Earth and nature as if it were a caring person.

Natural Predator – An animal that hunts and eats other animals as part of nature.

Prey – Animals that are hunted by other animals.

Predators – Animals that hunt and eat other animals.

Wetlands – Areas of land filled with water, like swamps or marshes, where many animals and plants live.

Cultural References & Social Themes

Ancient Tales – Very old stories passed down through time.

Loyalty – Being faithful and sticking with someone, even through hard times.

Misunderstandings – When people don't understand each other correctly, which can cause problems.

Chapter 12 Glossary – The Wonder Hole

Organized by Category | Cleanly Alphabetized | 4th Grade–Friendly

Vocabulary (General Academic & Descriptive Words)

Admonished – Firmly warned or scolded someone.

Assessed – Looked at or judged something carefully.

Banter – Light and playful teasing conversation.

Bellowed – Shouted loudly with a deep voice.

Camaraderie – Friendship and trust among people who spend time together.

Challenges – Difficult tasks or problems that test your abilities.

Courage – The strength to do something even when it's scary or difficult.

Echoing – A sound that repeats because it bounces off surfaces.

Energized – Given energy, motivation, or excitement.

Examined – Looked at something carefully to learn more.

Exclaimed – Spoke loudly and with strong feeling.

Ferocious – Very fierce or intense.

Force of her fury – Very powerful anger that shows strongly.

Frustration – Feeling upset when things don't go as hoped.

Impending Peril – Danger that is about to happen soon.

Lingering Smell – A scent that stays in the air for a long time.

Menacingly – In a threatening or dangerous way.

Mettle – Strength of spirit; the ability to keep going during hard times.

Miracles – Amazing and hard-to-believe events that seem magical.

Moss – A soft, green plant that grows in damp areas.

Mushrooms – A type of fungus that grows on the ground, often edible.

Nonsense – Silly or foolish talk that doesn't make sense.

Patience – Being calm while waiting without getting upset.

Pondered – Thought about something carefully.

Proud – Feeling pleased about something you or someone else has done well.

Relented – Finally gave in or agreed after saying no.

Resignation – Accepting something difficult or unpleasant without fighting it.

Resilience – The ability to recover from hard situations.

Resist – To hold back from doing something you're tempted to do.

Scroll – A rolled-up piece of paper or parchment used for writing.

Solution – The answer to a problem.

Succeed – To do what you were trying to do or reach your goal.

Teamwork – Working together with others to reach a shared goal.

Tinge of Dread – A small feeling of fear or worry.

Tone – The sound or feeling in someone's voice.

Tapering Off – Slowly becoming less or smaller until stopping.

Vivid – Bright, clear, and easy to imagine.

Literary Terms & Figurative Language

Ancient Secrets – Mysterious and old knowledge that has been hidden for a long time.

Eerie Shadows – Spooky or strange shadows that create a mysterious feeling.

Paint True Portraits of the Tale – Describe a story honestly and clearly, as if painting it with words.

Renewed Sense of Hope – Feeling hopeful again after a time of doubt or difficulty.

Spirits Unbroken – Staying strong and positive even when times are tough.

Tone Laced with Skepticism – Speaking in a way that shows you don't believe what was said.

Tone Light but Edged with Tension – Talking in a fun way, but with some stress or nervousness underneath.

Science & Nature Concepts

Minerals – Natural substances found in the earth that are good for health, like calcium or iron.

Moss – A soft, green plant that grows in damp and shady places.

Mushrooms – A fungus that grows from the ground, often in dark or damp places.

Pollen – A fine yellow powder made by flowers to help them grow seeds.

Predators – Animals that hunt and eat other animals.

Snake Scales – The small, hard plates that cover a snake's body.

Wafted – Moved gently through the air, like a smell or breeze.

Cavernous – Very large and deep, like a cave.

Cultural References & Social Themes

Guardian – A person or creature who protects others from harm.

Potion – A magical liquid often used in stories for healing or power.

Queen Bee – The most important female bee in a hive; can also mean a leader.

Riddle – A tricky question or puzzle that needs a clever answer.

Retorted – Replied quickly, often in a sharp or sassy way.

Sneered – Smiled or spoke in a mean or mocking way.

Sinister – Seeming evil or likely to cause harm.

Taunting – Making fun of someone in a mean way.

Chapter 13 Glossary – The Swamp of the Mists

Organized by Category | Cleanly Alphabetized | 4th Grade–Friendly

Vocabulary (General Academic & Descriptive Words)

Affected – Changed or influenced by something.

Annoyed – Feeling irritated or bothered.

Approaching – Coming closer.

Cautiously Resumed – Carefully started doing something again after pausing.

Character – The traits that make a person or thing different from others.

Confessed – Admitted to doing something wrong or secret.

Confidently – Doing something with self-assurance and belief in yourself.

Confronted Our Fears – Faced scary or difficult things head-on.

Confuse – To make someone unsure or mixed up about something.

Creatures – Animals or living beings.

Determined – Having a firm decision or purpose and not giving up.

Desperately – Trying very hard, especially when things are difficult or urgent.

Disbelief – Not being able to believe something is true.

Distraction – Something that pulls your attention away from what you're doing.

Do Not Stand in a Place of Trusting in Miracles – A warning not to wait for good things to happen without taking action.

Exclaimed – Spoke loudly and suddenly, often from surprise or emotion.

Familiar – Something well known because you've seen or experienced it before.

Feeling the Strain on Their Friendship – Sensing tension or pressure in a friendship.

Glee – Great happiness or delight.

Gratitude – Thankfulness or appreciation.

Guilt – The feeling that you've done something wrong.

Intentions – Reasons or plans to do something.

Maintained – Kept at the same level or state.

Maneuver – To move or act skillfully or carefully.

Observed – Watched carefully.

Outpace – To move faster than someone or something else.

Overwhelmed – Feeling like there's too much to handle—emotionally or physically.

Painful Truth – A fact that is hard to accept because it causes emotional hurt.

Pity – Feeling sorry for someone else's situation.

Quickened His Pace – Started walking or moving faster.

Regret – Feeling bad or sorry about something that happened or something you did.

Revealed – Showed something that was hidden.

Revelation – A surprising or important discovery.

Responsible – Being in charge of something and making sure it's done right.

Scroll – A rolled-up piece of paper or parchment used for writing.

Selfishly – Thinking only about yourself and not about others.

Sharing a Silent Understanding – Knowing how someone feels without needing words.

Slither – To move smoothly and quietly like a snake.

Survival – The act of staying alive in tough conditions.

Tempting – Something that makes you want to do it even if it's not a good idea.

Tinged with Alarm – Having a small amount of worry or fear.

Tree Limbs – The large branches of a tree.

Trials – Difficult tests that show your strength or character.

Literary Terms & Figurative Language

Betrayal Haunting Them – A betrayal that still affects someone long after it happened.

Confronted Our Fears – Faced the things we're afraid of directly.

Do Not Stand in a Place of Trusting in Miracles – A saying that warns against waiting for luck without effort.

Feeling the Strain on Their Friendship – Showing how pressure or problems can damage a friendship.

Scars of Betrayal – Emotional wounds left behind by someone breaking your trust.

Sharing a Silent Understanding – Knowing what someone else is feeling without having to say it.

Science & Nature Concepts

Ironwood Tree – A very strong and heavy tree known for its tough wood.

Murky – Dark and hard to see through, often describing water.

Orchid Moonflowers – A fictional flower, likely pretty and blooming at night like an orchid.

Ecosystem – A system where living things like plants and animals live and interact together with their environment.

Undergrowth – Small plants and bushes growing near the ground in a forest.

Palpable – So strong or real it feels like you can touch it (often used for feelings or atmosphere).

Cultural References & Story-Specific Creatures

Nile Lizard – A fictional lizard, possibly inspired by real reptiles from Africa.

Crocodile – A large reptile that lives in rivers or lakes, known for its strong jaws and sharp teeth.

Water Mongoose – A fictional or semi-realistic animal that lives near water and may resemble a mongoose.

Black-Nose Swamp Vulture – A fictional bird that lives in the swamp, likely scavenging like a vulture.

Guardians – Beings (real or mythical) who protect others or sacred places.

Predator Cravings – The strong desire animals (or characters) have to hunt or catch prey.

Chapter 14 Glossary – Trapped and Tricked

Organized by Category | Cleanly Alphabetized | 4th Grade–Friendly

Vocabulary (General Academic & Descriptive Words)

Always Thinking Ahead – Planning in advance for what might happen.

Anxiously – Acting with worry or nervous excitement.

Audacity – Boldness or bravery, often in a daring or risky way.

Beacon – A guiding light or signal, often used to warn or show the way.

Battered but Unbowed – Hurt or damaged but not defeated or giving up.

Careful Planning – Taking time to make a smart and thorough plan.

Create an Opportunity – Make a chance for something to happen.

Devised – Thought of or invented a plan or method.

Disarray – A state of confusion or mess.

Distract – To take someone's attention away from what they're doing.

Emerging – Coming into view or becoming known.

Exhausted – Extremely tired or worn out.

Fend Them Off – To defend against attackers or threats.

Heart Pounded with Dual Beats of Fear and Determination – Feeling both scared and brave at the same time.

Homage – Public honor or respect shown to someone or something.

Inspired Awe – Caused a feeling of wonder and respect.

Launch – To start or send something into motion.

Makeshift – Made quickly from whatever is available, usually temporary.

Navigating – Finding a way to move through or across something.

Obstacle – Something that gets in your way or makes it hard to move forward.

Perfectly Described – Explained in a very clear and complete way.

Pursuit – The act of chasing or following someone or something.

Quicksand – Wet, sinking sand that can trap people or animals.

Realizing – Becoming aware of or understanding something.

Reluctantly – Doing something even though you don't really want to.

Revealed – Showed something that was hidden.

Risky – Dangerous and uncertain.

Saga – A long, detailed story, often full of adventure or drama.

Scrambled – Moved quickly and clumsily, often using both hands and feet.

Shrouded – Hidden or covered so it can't be seen clearly.

Sprinted – Ran quickly for a short distance.

Strategy – A carefully made plan to reach a goal.

Sustained – Continued for a long time without stopping.

Tense with Fear – Feeling very nervous or afraid.

Tough Lesson – A hard experience that teaches something important.

Trick – *(Optional, if you'd like to define the title term for younger readers —let me know.)*

Tumultuous – Noisy, wild, or full of confusion.

Underbrush – Small bushes and plants growing beneath taller trees.

Under the Gaze of the Wild – Being watched or surrounded by nature or wild animals.

Voice Full of Concern – Speaking in a way that shows care or worry.

Literary Terms & Figurative Language

Amidst the Chaos – In the middle of confusion or wild action.

Banner of Defiance – Showing resistance or bravery, even in a bold or risky way.

Cause Harm from Afar – To hurt or damage something from a distance.

Depth of Their Bravery – The great strength of their courage.

Desperate Attempt – Trying something hard or risky when you have few options.

Desperate Gambit – A bold and risky move made in a hopeless situation.

Devastating Loss – A loss that causes great emotional pain or destruction.

Filled with Hidden Threats – Full of dangers that aren't easy to see.

Heart Pounded with Dual Beats of Fear and Determination – A poetic way to show someone is both scared and brave at once.

Raging Waters – Wild, fast-moving water.

Relentless Pursuit – Chasing or following something without ever giving up.

Rethink Our Approach – To change how you plan to do something after reconsidering it.

Test of Our Courage and Skills – A challenge that shows how brave and capable you are.

Voice Full of Concern / Doubt in His Voice – Ways someone's tone can show how they feel inside.

Water Roared with the Laughter of the River God – A poetic way of saying the water was loud and powerful, as if a god were laughing.

Wrathful Embrace – Holding something tightly, filled with anger or force.

Science & Nature Concepts

Lioness – A female lion.

Giant Tiger Fish / Tiger Fish – A fierce freshwater fish with sharp teeth, found in African rivers.

Predators – Animals that hunt and eat other animals.

Riverbank – The land next to a river.

Perilous Rapids – Very dangerous parts of a river where the water moves quickly and wildly.

Dense Wetlands – Thick, swampy land with a lot of plants and water.

Vines – Long, thin plants that grow up and around trees or buildings.

Cultural References & Social Themes

Goat – A small farm animal with horns, known for milk and meat.

Rethink Our Approach – To think again about how to handle a situation.

Hunting Party – A group of people working together to hunt animals.

Courageous Act – Doing something brave, even when it's scary.

Always Thinking Ahead – Planning wisely for what's to come.

Strengthened Their Bonds – Grew closer or more united, especially through hard experiences.

Renewed Sense of Loyalty – Feeling faithful or devoted to someone again after a difficult time.

Rallied the Spirits of His Band – Inspired or cheered up the group.

Chapter 15 Glossary – Lake Eyasi

Organized by Category | Cleanly Alphabetized | 4th Grade–Friendly

Vocabulary (General Academic & Descriptive Words)

Anticipated Path – The route or direction that was expected.

Balance of Vigilance and Trust – Being careful and alert while also showing faith in others.

Beauty Laced with Danger – Something that is beautiful but could be risky or harmful.

Calm Presence Anchored Him – Being near someone peaceful helped him feel safe and steady.

Challenges – Hard situations that take strength and effort to handle.

Despite – Even though something might make it hard, it still happens.

Discord – Conflict, disagreement, or lack of harmony.

Encouraged – Gave someone support, hope, or confidence.

His Instinct Was to Flee – His natural reaction was to run away from danger.

Honored – Treated with great respect or admiration.

Imperfect – Not perfect; having some flaws or mistakes.

Intervened – Stepped in to help or stop something from happening.

Memory – The ability to remember things from the past.

Mischievous – Playfully naughty or causing minor trouble.

Navigate – To find your way or plan your route.

Reassured – Made someone feel less worried or more confident.

Reinforced – Made something stronger or supported it further.

Revealing – Showing something that was hidden or unknown.

Resilience – The ability to recover quickly from difficulties.

Restless – Unable to relax or stay still.

Spirits Buoyed – Feelings were lifted or became more cheerful.

Symbolizing – Representing something, often through an object or action.

Vigilance – Staying alert and watching carefully for danger.

Literary Terms & Figurative Language

Beauty Laced with Danger – A phrase that means something looks beautiful but can be harmful.

Calm Presence Anchored Him – A figurative way of saying someone peaceful helped him stay grounded.

Lifted Their Spirits – Made them feel happier and more hopeful.

Spirits Buoyed – Another way of saying their mood or hope was lifted.

Science & Nature Concepts

Eagle-Owl – A large owl known for its size and strong features.

Lake Eyasi – A real salt lake in Tanzania, known for its unique environment.

Brown Hyena – A scavenger animal with scruffy fur, found in parts of Africa.

Sacred Ibis – A bird with cultural and religious significance in some traditions, especially in Egypt.

Mystic Ferns – Fictional or magical-feeling plants with delicate leaves.

Glowcap Mushrooms – Fictional mushrooms that likely glow in the dark.

Silvertip Tree – A made-up tree, possibly with shiny leaf tips.

Azure Crane – A fictional bird, likely blue in color and graceful in flight.

Predators – Animals that hunt other animals for food.

Cultural References & Social Themes

Old Legends – Stories from long ago that have been passed down through generations.

Honored – Treated with respect and praise for actions or importance.

Anticipated Path – A predicted direction or plan for where to go.

Balance of Vigilance and Trust – The idea of being careful but also having confidence in others.

Chapter 17 Glossary – Trapped

Organized by Category | Cleanly Alphabetized | 4th Grade–Friendly

Vocabulary (General Academic & Descriptive Words)

Ability to Adapt – The skill to change or adjust when facing new situations.

Advantage – A helpful or better position compared to others.

Alter – To change something slightly.

Anticipation – Looking forward to something with excitement or worry.

Assured – Confident and certain.

Brief Respite – A short break or rest from something difficult.

Canopy – The top layer of trees in a forest that forms a covering.

Chaos and Confusion – Total disorder and lack of organization.

Close Presence – Being physically near someone or something.

Consequences – The results of an action or decision.

Crucial – Very important and necessary.

Decay – The slow breaking down or rotting of something.

Decreed – Officially ordered or announced.

Deceived – Tricked or misled into believing something false.

Desperation – A hopeless feeling that can lead to extreme actions.

Determination Shining Through His Fear – Showing strong willpower even while feeling scared.

Elusive – Difficult to find or catch.

Frustration – Feeling upset because something is hard or not going your way.

Fleeting as the Morning Dew – Describes something that disappears quickly, like morning dew.

Guilt – The bad feeling after doing something wrong.

Intrigued – Very interested or curious.

Knowledge Without Wisdom Is Like Water in the Sand – A saying that means facts are not helpful unless you understand how to use them wisely.

Lingered – Stayed longer than necessary.

Menacing Grin – A threatening or scary smile.

Misled – Given the wrong idea or made to believe something untrue.

Mix of Hope and Caution – Feeling both optimistic and careful at the same time.

Necessarily – Something required or needed.

Negotiate – To talk through a disagreement to reach a deal or solution.

Narrowly Escape – To almost get caught or hurt, but avoid it just in time.

Observed – Watched something closely.

Overshadowed – Made something else seem less important.

Potential Value – The possible worth something may have.

Quest – A long and challenging search for something important.

Reassured – Made someone feel more confident or less worried.

Relentless Attack / Onslaught – A non-stop and intense fight or effort.

Resilience – The ability to recover from hardship or challenges.

Resolve Hardened – The decision or determination became stronger.

Retraced Their Steps – Went back the same way they came.

Revealing – Showing something hidden.

Reuniting – Coming back together after being apart.

Scene Unfolded – Events happened and became visible or clear.

Sense of Purpose – A strong feeling of having a goal or mission.

Skeptical – Doubting or not easily convinced.

Summoned – Called or gathered people together.

Terrified – Extremely scared.

To Run Is Not Necessarily to Arrive – Moving quickly doesn't always mean you're going in the right direction.

Unfortunate – Having bad luck.

Urgency – A feeling that something needs to be done quickly.

Wilderness – A wild, natural area where few people live.

Worriedly Suggesting – Giving an idea or advice while feeling concerned.

Literary Terms & Figurative Language

Amid the Painful Chaos – In the middle of confusion and emotional difficulty.

Amidst the Whispers of Strategy and Survival – Surrounded by quiet planning to stay alive.

Bravado – Acting bold to impress others, even if you're scared.

Cycle of Life and Death – The natural pattern of living, dying, and renewing.

Determination Shining Through His Fear – Showing courage even when afraid.

Fleeting as the Morning Dew – Something beautiful or meaningful that disappears quickly.

Heavy Burden – A great responsibility that is emotionally or mentally difficult.

Knowledge Without Wisdom Is Like Water in the Sand – A proverb meaning facts without understanding are useless.

Menacing Grin – A smile that shows threat or danger.

The True Nature of Heroism – What it really means to be brave and selfless.

The Weight of a Kingdom in His Gaze – Looking serious and responsible, as if carrying great responsibility.

Their Spirits Lifted – They began to feel more hopeful or happy.

To Run Is Not Necessarily to Arrive – A saying that means speed doesn't guarantee success.

Science & Nature Concepts

Cheetah – A large wild cat known as the fastest land animal.

Wild Dog – A canine that lives and hunts in the wild, not kept as a pet.

Hare – A fast-moving mammal similar to a rabbit, but bigger.

Golden Cat – A rare wild cat with golden fur, found in African forests.

Dense Forest – A thick area filled with many trees.

Nature – The physical world, including animals, plants, landscapes, and weather.

Cultural References & Social Themes

Betrays / Betrayal – Revealing something secret or being disloyal to someone's trust.

Confessed – Admitted to doing something wrong or telling the truth after hiding it.

Condemning – Saying strongly that something is wrong or bad.

Deceit – Lying or hiding the truth to fool someone.

Intruders – People who enter where they don't belong.

Navigating the Feelings – Dealing with or understanding your emotions.

Within Their Ranks – Among their own group or team.

Swarmed with Purpose and Fury – Rushed in with strong emotion and intention.

Prospect of Betraying – The idea that someone might be unfaithful or disloyal.

Chapter 18 Glossary – A Hero's Welcome

Organized by Category | Cleanly Alphabetized | 4th Grade–Friendly

Vocabulary (General Academic & Descriptive Words)

Anticipated – Expected or looked forward to.

Brimming – So full that it's almost overflowing.

Dominance – Being more powerful or in control than others.

Emerge – To come out or become visible.

Menacing Grin – A scary or threatening smile.

Orchestrated – Carefully planned or arranged to reach a goal.

Palpably – In a way that is easily felt or clearly noticed.

Restored – Brought back to a better or original condition.

Shocked – Feeling surprised or upset because of something unexpected.

Tense Standoff – A situation where two sides face each other and neither moves first.

Usher – To guide or lead someone to a place.

Ventured – Took a risk or tried something new.

Literary Terms & Figurative Language

Cold Betrayal – A disloyal action that feels especially heartless or uncaring.

Do Not Dwell on Your Mistakes – A phrase meaning not to stay stuck thinking about past wrongs.

Harmony of Their Fellowship – The peaceful and friendly way a group of people gets along.

Laughter Floating in the Air Like Music – A comparison showing how joyful sounds spread gently like a song.

Prisoners of Your Own Fate – A poetic way to describe being trapped by the results of your own choices.

Sharing Secrets with the Wrong Person Is Like Carrying Grain in a Bag with a Hole – A saying that means your secrets will be lost or misused if you tell them to someone untrustworthy.

Standing Strong When Things Get Tough – A phrase meaning to be brave and steady during hard times.

Weight of His Past Decisions Pulled at His Steps – A metaphor that means he felt burdened or slowed down by choices he had made before.

Science & Nature Concepts

Marula Trees – A tree native to Africa with fruit enjoyed by both people and animals.

Cultural References & Social Themes

Cold Betrayal – A theme where someone breaks trust in a particularly harsh or emotionless way.

Harmony of Their Fellowship – The good feeling and unity within a close group.

Standing Strong When Things Get Tough – A theme of resilience and inner strength.

Prisoners of Your Own Fate – A reflection on personal responsibility and consequence.

Chapter 19 Glossary – Interlude

Organized by Category | Cleanly Alphabetized | 4th Grade–Friendly

Vocabulary (General Academic & Descriptive Words)

Cunning Strategies – Smart and sometimes sneaky plans used to achieve a goal.

Delicate Balance – A situation that must be handled carefully so that everything stays in harmony.

Disrupt – To interrupt or mess up the normal way something works.

Enduring Power of Unity, Courage, and Wisdom – The lasting strength that comes from being united, brave, and smart.

Examination – A close look at something to learn more about it.

Formidable – Strong, powerful, and impressive or a little scary.

Fresh Perspective – A new way of looking at or thinking about something.

Impact Their Roles – To affect or influence how people act or what part they play.

Intricate World They Navigated – A complicated and detailed place they explored and lived in.

Journey of Self-Discovery – Learning more about who you are and what you're capable of.

Misinformation – Wrong or incorrect information that confuses people.

Reflection and Discussion – Thinking deeply about something and talking about it with others.

Resist – To stand against something and not give in.

Sustained Peace – A long-lasting time of calm without fighting or conflict.

Testament – Proof or sign that something is true or important.

Undermine – To slowly weaken or damage something.

Literary Terms & Figurative Language

Connects the Past with the Present – Shows how earlier events relate to what's happening now.

Epic Tale – A long, exciting story filled with heroic events.

Heroes' Saga – A big story about the adventures and brave actions of heroes.

Inspire, Recognize, and Embrace Their Inner Greatness – Motivate someone to see and accept how special and powerful they really are.

Legacies – What people leave behind after they're gone, such as ideas, stories, or the ways they helped others.

Reflection and Discussion – Looking back and thinking deeply about something, and sharing ideas with others.

Story's Climax The most exciting or important moment in the story when the big problem gets solved.

Triumph of Spirit – A victory that shows how strong and determined someone is on the inside.

Science & Nature Concepts

Tortoise – A slow-moving land animal with a shell, known for living a long time.

Cultural References & Social Themes

Epilogue – A short section at the end of a book that explains what happens after the main part of the story.

Collective Strength – The power that comes from working together as a group.

Complex Relationship – A relationship with many feelings or issues that make it hard to understand.

Themes of Governance – Ideas in the story about how leadership and rule work in a society or group.

Triumph of Spirit – Showing strength and bravery in hard times.

Journey of Self-Discovery – Learning about yourself through experiences.

Chapter 20 Glossary – Adira, the Tortoise and Tau the Lion

Organized by Category | Cleanly Alphabetized | 4th Grade–Friendly

Vocabulary (General Academic & Descriptive Words)

Ability to Adapt – The ability to change or adjust when needed.

Anticipation – Looking forward to something that is going to happen.

Authority – The power or right to make decisions and give orders.

Bounty – A large amount of something valuable or desirable.

Brief Respite – A short break or time of rest.

Canopy – The top layer of trees that forms a cover in the forest.

Commanding Respect – Gaining admiration from others because of good behavior or leadership.

Conceded – Admitted that something is true, often after first denying or resisting it.

Contemplated – Thought deeply about something.

Contemplation – Careful and deep thinking.

Delicate Balance – A situation where things must stay just right to keep from falling apart.

Desperation – A feeling of hopelessness that can lead to risky actions.

Devour – To eat something quickly and hungrily.

Eerie Shadow – A strange and slightly scary shadow.

Falter – To lose strength or pause uncertainly.

Glen – A small, narrow valley.

Governed – Controlled or ruled.

Gratitude – Thankfulness or appreciation.

Guarantee – A promise that something will definitely happen.

Howling Gusts – Loud, strong winds.

Imagine – To form a picture or idea in your mind.

Impending – About to happen soon.

Investigate – To look into something carefully to discover the truth.

Looming Threat – A danger that is near or expected to happen soon.

Maintaining Order – Keeping things organized and peaceful.

Mere – Used to show how small or simple something is.

Navigating the Feelings – Understanding and managing emotions.

Overshadowed – Made to seem less important.

Peace Was Preserved – Peace was protected and kept safe.

Presided – Was in charge of or led a meeting or place.

Prohibited – Not allowed.

Propose – To suggest a plan or idea.

Realm – A kingdom or region under someone's control.

Refuge – A safe place or shelter.

Reign – The time someone rules, like a king or queen.

Relentless Attack / Onslaught – A never-ending and intense attack or assault.

Resolved – Made a firm decision.

Reuniting – Coming back together after being separated.

Sanctity – The quality of being very important and respected.

Scanned the Horizon – Looked far into the distance.

Sense of Urgency – A strong feeling that something must be done quickly.

Silence Spoke Volumes – When saying nothing says a lot or makes a strong impression.

Submit – To give in or agree to what someone else wants or decides.

Thrived – Grew strong, healthy, and successful.

Tightly Knit Ecosystem – A closely connected environment where everything depends on everything else.

Treacherous – Dangerous and unpredictable.

Unresolved – Not yet settled or decided.

Ventured – Took a risk to try something new or unknown.

Weight of Wisdom and Caution – The responsibility of being wise and careful.

Weathered – Got through something difficult.

Yearned – Felt a strong desire or longing.

Yield – To give up or let someone else have their way.

Literary Terms & Figurative Language

Amid the Painful Chaos – In the middle of confusing and emotional trouble.

Bound by a Sense of Community and Shared Purpose – Connected by a common goal and feeling of belonging.

Disrupting the Delicate Balance – Disturbing something that needs to stay calm and steady.

His Mind a Battlefield of Instinct and Intellect – His thoughts are full of conflict between natural feelings and careful thinking.

How Do You Propose We Calm the Coming Storm? – A poetic way of asking: What's your plan to solve this big problem?

My Pride Grows Restless – My group (especially lions) is feeling uneasy or agitated.

Our Lands Have Danced to the Tune of Peace – Our territory has been peaceful, like moving with soft music.

Peace Was Preserved – Peace was saved or maintained.

Silence Spoke Volumes – A quiet moment that said a lot.

The True Nature of Heroism – What it really means to be brave and selfless.

Thoughts Burdened with Worry – Thinking about problems in a way that feels heavy or stressful.

Unravel Our Threads of Peace – To ruin the peaceful connection that holds a group together.

Unity Born of Necessity – People or groups coming together because they have to, not just because they want to.

When the Music Changes, So Does the Dance – When life changes, we must also change how we respond.

Science & Nature Concepts

Tortoise – A land animal with a shell that moves slowly and lives a long time.

African Crowned Eagle – A strong bird of prey from Africa with a striking appearance.

Tightly Knit Ecosystem – A natural system where plants, animals, and places are closely connected.

Howling Gusts – Powerful and noisy winds.

Cultural References & Social Themes

Authority / Governed / Reign – Concepts tied to leadership, power, and control.

Bound by a Sense of Community and Shared Purpose – Working together for a common good.

Peace Was Preserved / Unity Born of Necessity – Social themes about maintaining harmony and coming together when needed.

Regal Demeanor – Acting with the dignity of a king or queen.

Bravado / Desperation – Emotional reactions in the face of crisis or danger.

Within Their Ranks – Among their group or team members.

Chapter 21 Glossary – The Predators' Plot

Organized by Category | Cleanly Alphabetized | 4th Grade–Friendly

Vocabulary (General Academic & Descriptive Words)

Achieve – To successfully complete a task or reach a goal.

Dire News – Very bad or serious information.

Endangering – Putting someone or something at risk of harm.

Forbid – To order someone not to do something.

Goal – A desired outcome or something you're trying to achieve.

Honorable – Deserving respect for doing the right thing.

Imagine – To create a picture in your mind of something that's not real or hasn't happened yet.

Impending Doom – The feeling that something terrible is about to happen.

Jealous – Feeling upset because someone else has something you want.

Mount Tanganyika – A fictional mountain, possibly inspired by real African geography.

Nervous – Feeling anxious, worried, or scared about something.

Panic – Sudden fear that makes people act without thinking.

Rumors of Disaster – Unconfirmed stories or talk about something terrible happening.

Stay Vigilant – To remain alert and watchful for danger.

Turmoil – A state of confusion, disorder, or chaos.

Literary Terms & Figurative Language

'Do Not Look Where You Fell, but Where You Slipped' – A saying that means we should focus on what caused the problem, not just the result.

Fear Became Their Most Potent Ally – A poetic way of saying fear helped them succeed, giving them power or control.

Fear Moved Like Shadows Through the Bushes – A simile comparing fear to shadows spreading quietly and quickly.

Send Chills Down the Spine – A phrase used to describe something so scary it makes your body react.

Sinister Ruse – A sneaky trick designed to hurt or deceive someone.

Treachery Brewed on the Horizon – A phrase showing that betrayal is beginning and will soon show itself.

Wicked Plan – An evil, harmful, or very mean strategy.

Science & Nature Concepts

Black Eagle – A large bird of prey with dark feathers, known for sharp vision and strength.

Brown Hyena – A type of hyena with shaggy dark fur, found in African regions.

Baobab Tree – A giant African tree with a thick trunk, known for its long life and cultural significance.

Cultural References & Social Themes

Deceit – Dishonesty meant to trick or mislead someone.

Endangering – Taking actions that put others in danger.

Impending Doom / Turmoil / Treachery Brewed – Themes of darkness, suspense, and chaos that suggest something dangerous is rising.

Stay Vigilant – A message about the importance of awareness and mental readiness in uncertain times.

Rumors of Disaster – An example of how fear and false information can spread quickly in a community.

Chapter 22 Glossary – Alice and the Stone Bracelet

Organized by Category | Cleanly Alphabetized | 4th Grade–Friendly

Vocabulary (General Academic & Descriptive Words)

Admiration – Respect and warm approval.

Attempting – Trying to do something.

Cautious – Being careful to avoid danger or mistakes.

Commanding – Having a strong and powerful presence.

Confusion – A state of not understanding what is happening.

Cunning Offer – A clever or tricky suggestion or deal.

Daunting – Seeming difficult or scary to face or do.

Dense – Thick and tightly packed, like a dense forest.

Drama Unfolding – Exciting or intense events happening one after another.

Erupted – Burst out suddenly, like with emotion or action.

Explorers – People who travel to unknown places to learn about them.

Feeling Grateful for Her Concern – Being thankful that someone cared.

Frantic – Acting wild or panicked due to strong emotion.

Hoping to Gain Favor – Trying to make someone like or approve of you.

Kind Gesture – A small act of kindness.

Mercy – Kindness shown to someone who is in your power.

Momentarily – For a very short period of time.

Mysterious – Not easy to understand; full of mystery.

Optimistically – Thinking positively and expecting good things to happen.

Perch – A high place to sit or stand on.

Pendant – A piece of jewelry that hangs from a necklace.

Proposed – Suggested an idea or plan.

Sincerity – Being honest and genuine.

Stealthy – Moving quietly and secretly so as not to be noticed.

Swirling Secrets – Secrets being shared in a confusing or mysterious way.

Toothy Grin – A big smile showing many teeth.

Treacherous Jungle – A dangerous forest full of hidden threats.

Trials They Had Overcome – Difficult events that were faced and conquered.

Literary Terms & Figurative Language

'Something Doesn't Smell Right' – A phrase meaning something seems suspicious or wrong.

'To Get Lost Is to Learn the Way' – A saying that means we grow and learn by making mistakes.

Each Tree Telling Its Own Ancient Story – A poetic way to imagine that nature holds many memories of the past.

Fear Moved Like Shadows Through the Bushes *(related phrase from Ch. 21)* – Optional reference if discussed across chapters.

Shadows of the Night Grew Longer – Describes the darkening evening as time goes on.

Their Hearts Swelled with Joy – They felt deeply happy and full of emotion.

Token of Our Trust / Token of Thanks – Small gifts or signs that show appreciation or belief in someone.

Under the Cover of Night – Something done secretly or in darkness.

Whispers of Ancient Secrets – Quiet talk or hints about mysterious and old knowledge.

Science & Nature Concepts

Chimpanzee – A smart and playful great ape that lives in African forests.

White Collared Mangabey – A type of monkey with a white neck, known for being playful.

Treacherous Jungle / Dense Forest – Wild, plant-filled areas that are hard to travel through.

Dawn Broke – The moment when the sun rises and the day begins.

Cultural References & Social Themes

Symbol of Survival and Courage – An object or action that stands for strength through tough times.

Bonds Strengthened – Friendships or relationships that became stronger through experience.

Token of Thanks / Kind Gesture – Small ways of showing appreciation and kindness.

Sincerity / Admiration / Mercy – Positive human qualities and emotional intelligence.

Explorers / Proposed Plans / Gaining Favor – Leadership and social navigation.

Cunning Offer / Drama Unfolding – Social manipulation or rising tension.

Chapter 23 Glossary – Next Day

Organized by Category | Cleanly Alphabetized | 4th Grade–Friendly

▮ Vocabulary (General Academic & Descriptive Words)

Advised – Gave helpful ideas or suggestions about what someone should do.

Alert – Paying close attention and ready to act if needed.

Allies – Friends or partners who support each other, especially in difficult times.

Appease – To make someone less angry or upset, often by giving them something they want.

Assured – Feeling confident and certain about something.

Blessings Echoing in Their Hearts – Feeling deeply thankful that stays with them.

Bonds They Had Forged – Strong relationships that were built through shared experiences.

Cautious – Being careful and trying to avoid danger or mistakes.

Chimpanzees' Crazy Taste for Monkeys – A reference to some chimpanzees occasionally eating monkeys.

Complex Web of Deceit Spun by Their Enemies – A complicated trap of lies and trickery made by those working against them.

Confidence – Belief in your own abilities and choices.

Confront Their Fears – To face things they are afraid of.

Cowered – Shrunk down or moved back in fear.

Crouched – Bent your knees and lowered your body close to the ground.

Daunting – Feeling hard or scary to face.

Deceitful – Dishonest or lying.

Disproportionate – Too big or too small compared to what it should be.

Distraction – Something that pulls your attention away from what you're doing.

Ended the Curse – Stopped a period of bad luck or misfortune.

Ensured Their Safety – Made sure everyone stayed safe.

Enthusiastically – Doing something with a lot of excitement and energy.

Erupted in Celebration – Suddenly began cheering or rejoicing.

Expression – The look on someone's face that shows what they are feeling.

Eyes Fixated – Staring intently at something without looking away.

Fake Symbol of Friendship – A false or dishonest sign that pretends to show kindness.

Feeling Guilty – Feeling bad about something wrong or hurtful you've done.

Frustration – The feeling of being upset or annoyed because something is difficult or not going as planned.

Graciously – In a kind, respectful, and polite way.

Heartfelt Gratitude – Deep and sincere thankfulness.

He Used to Help a Noble – He once worked with or supported someone very important.

He Was Torn – He was feeling unsure between two different choices or feelings.

Her Confidence Was Evident – It was clear that she felt sure of herself.

Hooted Loudly in Protest – Made loud sounds to show disagreement.

Immediate – Happening right away, without delay.

In Unison – When everyone acts or speaks at the same time.

Jubilant – Extremely happy and joyful, especially because something good happened.

Keen Instincts – Strong natural feelings or abilities that help someone understand things quickly.

Losing Patience – Becoming annoyed or tired of waiting.

Maze – A confusing path or puzzle where it's hard to find your way out.

Mockingly – In a mean or teasing way, making fun of someone.

Navigate – To find your way or move through a space.

Newfound Allies – Friends or supporters who were just recently made or discovered.

Peril – A situation of serious danger.

Pinpointed – Found or identified something exactly.

Queen Bee – A powerful or central female figure, originally the egg-laying leader of a bee colony.

Reassuring Smile – A smile that helps someone feel safe or less worried.

Refreshed – Feeling rested and full of energy again.

Saluted – Gave a respectful gesture, especially to show honor or recognition.

Serious Situation – An important or possibly dangerous moment or problem.

Significance – The importance or special meaning of something.

Survival Was the Most Precious Victory – Just staying alive was considered the greatest success.

Tantalizing Her Senses – Exciting or tempting her feelings.

Their Hearts Racing with Apprehension – They felt very nervous or scared about what might happen.

The Forest Was Alive with Secrets – A poetic way of saying that the forest felt full of hidden stories and mystery.

To Get Lost Is to Learn the Way *(From Ch. 22)* – A saying that means making mistakes can help you learn.

Vanished – Disappeared completely and quickly.

United by Their Shared Caution and Determination – Working together because they were all being careful and strongly focused on a goal.

Literary Terms & Figurative Language

Blessings Echoing in Their Hearts – A poetic way to say they kept feeling thankful.

Chimpanzees' Crazy Taste for Monkeys – A striking way to show unexpected behavior in nature.

Complex Web of Deceit – A metaphor for a tricky, tangled situation full of lies.

Ended the Curse – A figurative way to describe breaking a streak of bad events.

Fake Symbol of Friendship – A false or misleading gesture meant to look kind but is not real.

He Was Torn – A common phrase showing inner conflict or being pulled in two directions.

Her Confidence Was Evident – Describes someone clearly feeling sure of themselves.

Survival Was the Most Precious Victory – A figurative way to say staying alive mattered more than anything else.

The Forest Was Alive with Secrets – A poetic expression showing how mysterious the forest felt.

Science & Nature Concepts

Chimpanzee – A great ape with high intelligence, found in African forests.

Keen Instincts / Navigate / Maze – Brain and sense-driven navigation and survival skills.

Cultural References & Social Themes

Newfound Allies / Bonds They Had Forged / United by Shared Caution – Relationships formed through experience and trust.

Heartfelt Gratitude / Reassuring Smile / Graciously – Themes of kindness, communication, and emotional intelligence.

Deceitful / Fake Friendship / Complex Web of Lies – Social warning signs and lessons in trust.

Confront Fears / Ensured Safety / Survival – Acts of bravery, protection, and growth.

Chapter 24 Glossary – Tested by Fire

Organized by Category | Cleanly Alphabetized | 4th Grade–Friendly

Vocabulary (General Academic & Descriptive Words)

Arrogantly – Acting in a way that shows too much pride and not enough respect for others.

Authority – The power or right to give orders and make decisions.

Cautious – Being very careful to avoid danger or mistakes.

Challenging Path – A difficult road or journey that takes effort and bravery.

Commanded – Gave a strong and direct order.

Cultivated – Carefully developed or improved over time.

Doubting His Loyalty – Questioning whether someone is truly faithful or trustworthy.

End of the Straits – A metaphor meaning the end of a difficult or narrow situation.

Epic Journey – A long and amazing adventure filled with big challenges.

Eyes Scanning the Horizon – Looking far away to see what's coming or to find something.

Fear of Failing Those Who Depended on Her – Being scared of letting down people who rely on her.

Final Approach – The last stage or step in a big journey or effort.

Focused – Paying very close attention to one thing.

Frustrated – Feeling annoyed or upset because things aren't going well.

Instructed – Gave directions or taught someone what to do.

Lake Kilangiri – A fictional lake in the story.

Loomed Ahead – Appeared as a large or unclear shape, often a sign of something important or threatening.

Permeated – Spread all through something.

Poised – Ready and in position to act.

Reign – A period of rule or control, often used for kings and queens.

Savanna – A grassy flat land found in warm places, with few trees.

Sharp Smell of Sulfur – A strong and stinky smell, like rotten eggs, often near volcanoes.

Signaled All Clear – Gave a sign that things were safe again.

Silhouette – A dark shape seen against a light background.

Spewing – Pouring out or throwing out something with force (like lava or gas).

Spirits Buoyed – Feeling happier and more hopeful.

Strategized – Made a smart and careful plan.

Teased – Made fun of someone in a playful or mean way.

Tested Their Mettle – Challenged them to show their courage and strength.

Threshold of Destiny – A moment when something big and life-changing is about to happen.

Unbreakable Determination – A strong decision or will that cannot be broken or changed.

Volcano – A mountain that can erupt with lava, smoke, and ash.

Literary Terms & Figurative Language

"In a Moment of Crisis, the Wise Build Bridges and the Foolish Build Dams" – A saying that teaches that smart people try to solve problems by working together, while others make things worse by blocking progress.

"Her Resolve as Firm as the Earth Beneath Their Feet" – A comparison showing how strong and steady someone's decision is.

"We're Being Tested by Fire" – A metaphor meaning they are going through something very difficult to prove their strength or character.

"Threshold of Destiny" – A symbolic phrase meaning a person is right at the edge of something very important in their life.

"Loomed Ahead" – Used to describe something large or threatening that's coming soon, often in a dramatic way.

Science & Nature Concepts

Volcano – A mountain that can erupt with lava, gas, and ash.

Lava – Melted rock that flows from a volcano.

Sharp Smell of Sulfur – A smell that often comes from volcanic gases or burning materials.

Savanna – A warm area of land with grasses and few trees.

Cultural References & Social Themes

Strategized / Cultivated / Focused – Planning, thinking, and developing inner strength.

Tested Their Mettle / Unbreakable Determination / Challenging Path – Courage, resilience, and endurance during adversity.

Fear of Failing / Doubting Loyalty / Frustrated – Emotional challenges in leadership and trust.

Threshold of Destiny / Final Approach – Pivotal turning points and preparing for transformation.

Chapter 25 Glossary – The Circle of Unity

Organized by Category | Cleanly Alphabetized | 4th Grade–Friendly

Vocabulary (General Academic & Descriptive Words)

Acceptance – Saying "yes" to something offered or agreeing to it.

Acknowledging – Recognizing or accepting the truth or importance of something.

Agony – Extreme physical or emotional pain.

Alliance – A partnership or agreement between people or groups working together.

Anticipation – Looking forward to something with excitement or anxiety.

Approaching – Coming closer in time or space.

Balance – A condition where different elements are equal or work well together.

Celebratory Run – A joyful event or action to celebrate a special moment or success.

Chaos – Total confusion and lack of order.

Cleverness – Being smart and good at solving problems.

Conclusion – The end of something.

Confidence – Belief in your own abilities or decisions.

Confusion – A state of not being clear or understanding something.

Cooperation – Working together toward a common goal.

Crucial – Very important.

Debris – Broken or scattered pieces left over from destruction.

Determination – Not giving up; staying focused on a goal.

Destinies Intertwined – Lives or futures that are connected closely.

Distress – Deep sadness, anxiety, or pain.

Diverging – Going in different directions.

Energized – Full of energy and excitement.

Enveloped – Completely surrounded or covered.

Exhilaration – Great excitement or happiness.

Expression – The way someone shows how they feel, often on their face.

Face the Final Obstacle – Confront the last big challenge in a journey.

Feeling Inspired – Being filled with new ideas or motivation.

Firm Resolve – A strong decision that doesn't change easily.

Forged Friendships – Built strong friendships, especially through shared experiences.

Gestured – Moved your hands or body to show something.

Hobbled – Walked with difficulty, usually due to pain or injury.

Improvised – Made or did something using what was available, without planning.

Impacted – Affected strongly by something.

Impending Battle of Wills – A conflict where two sides will try to outlast each other with determination.

Inner Strength – Personal power that helps you stay strong inside, even during tough times.

Inhabitants – The animals or people who live in a place.

Intense Trials – Very hard or difficult tests or challenges.

Intensity – Extreme strength or feeling.

Interfere – To get involved in something that's not your business or that changes the outcome.

Legends – Traditional stories from the past.

Lit the Fire of Hope – Caused hope to start growing again.

Manageable Ascent – A climb that is difficult but possible.

Menacing Voice – A scary or threatening way of speaking.

Miraculously Recovered – Got better in a surprising or amazing way.

Motivated by Duty and Honor – Acting because of responsibility and respect.

Murmured – Spoke softly, often not clearly.

Mutual Respect – A shared feeling of admiration and value for one another.

Navigating the Obstacles – Finding a way through difficulties.

Newfound Harmony – Peace and unity that has just been found or formed.

Not Playing by the Rules – Acting unfairly or dishonestly.

Partnership – A team or group working together toward the same goal.

Peak of Their Ordeal – The hardest or most intense moment in a struggle.

Peril – Serious danger.

Physical Aid – Help given with the body, like support or carrying.

Plummeting – Falling straight down very fast.

Proverb – A short saying that teaches a truth or lesson.

Quest – A long or difficult journey to find or achieve something important.

Recognition – Realizing and accepting something is important or true.

Reject – To say "no" to something; not accept it.

Respect – Treating someone or something with honor or value.

Respect for All Life – Believing every living being deserves care and kindness.

Right of Proxy – Having permission to act or speak for someone else.

Solidified – Became firm or strong; no longer likely to change.

Sorrow – Deep sadness.

Stark Contrast – A strong and obvious difference between two things.

Tense Pace of the Struggle – A quick and stressful speed of conflict.

Threshold – The beginning of something new or important.

Tiger Fish – A fierce fish known for its sharp teeth.

Transformation – A big change in someone or something.

Triumph Coursing Through Their Veins – A strong feeling of pride and success filling them up.

Uncertainty – Not being sure about something.

Victorious – Having won or succeeded.

Wishful Thinking – Hoping something will happen even if it's unlikely.

Literary Terms & Figurative Language

"Air Got Tense" – The atmosphere felt full of nervous energy or stress.

"Chaos and Debris" – Used together to show destruction and confusion after conflict.

"Her Heart Heavy" – A way to show someone is feeling deeply sad or burdened.

"Leaving a Lasting Impact" – Doing something that people will remember or that will affect the future.

"Lit the Fire of Hope" – A phrase to show hope is returning or growing.

"Moment Seemed to Stop in Time" – Everything felt still, like something very important was happening.

"The Peak of Their Ordeal" – The hardest part of a long, difficult experience.

"Triumph Coursing Through Their Veins" – A vivid way to show how victory feels exciting and powerful.

"Embodying the Power of Unity" – Representing the strength that comes from being united.

"Everlasting Truths of Africa" – Timeless wisdom or values that continue through generations in African culture.

Science & Nature Concepts

Mother Nature – A way to describe the natural world as if it were a nurturing and powerful being.

Hot Cracked Lava – Cooled molten rock that formed sharp cracks after a volcano eruption.

Tiger Fish – A sharp-toothed fish known for being fierce.

Cultural References & Social Themes

Leadership / Inner Strength / Alliance / Unity – Powerful themes of character, connection, and courage.

Empathy / Mutual Respect / Cooperation / Acceptance – Important emotional and social values.

Inhabitants / Respect for All Life / Mother Nature – Highlighting the importance of harmony with nature and all living beings.

Transformation / Destiny / Legends / Everlasting Truths – The deep cultural and spiritual takeaways of the chapter.

Chapter 26 Glossary – Reflections and Revelations
Organized by Category | Cleanly Alphabetized | 4th Grade–Friendly

Chapter Twenty-Six: *Reflections and Revelations* is a beautifully grounded and future-focused ending—bridging the magical journey of the Kingdom of Shadows with the very real experiences of youth in today's world. With themes like **empowerment, literacy, resilience, and leadership**, this glossary captures a rich mix of **figurative language**, **real-life applications**, and **emotional growth**.

Vocabulary (General Academic & Descriptive Words)

Agents of Change – People who take action to make the world better.

Agitated – Feeling nervous, upset, or uneasy.

Aspirations – Strong hopes or dreams to achieve something great.

Authority – The power or right to lead, give orders, or make decisions.

Basketball Clinic – A training event where people learn basketball skills.

Calculated – Planned carefully with thought.

Canvas – A strong cloth that artists paint on.

Captivated – Completely interested or fascinated.

Commitment to Excel – A promise to try hard and do your very best.

Diverse Backgrounds – People coming from different cultures, communities, or life experiences.

Drawing Parallels – Showing how two things are similar.

Emphasized – Showed that something is especially important.

Empowered – Given the strength or power to do something confidently.

Endeavor – A serious effort to do or achieve something.

Enriched – Made better or improved in quality or value.

Equipped Them – Gave them the tools or skills they needed.

Excel – To do very well at something.

Expressive – Clearly showing thoughts or feelings.

Facing Real-World Challenges with Bravery and Intelligence – Handling real-life problems with courage and smart thinking.

Fantastical Valley – A magical and imaginary place.

Gangs – Groups of people who may be involved in dangerous or illegal activities.

Illegal Drugs – Harmful substances that are against the law.

Impact of Violence and Neglect – The harmful effects of abuse or lack of care.

Incredible – Amazing and hard to believe.

Influence – The ability to affect how someone thinks or acts.

Inhabitants – The people or animals who live in a place.

Initiatives – New projects or plans started to make change.

Inspired – Filled with the urge to do something creative or good.

Instinctively – Doing something naturally without needing to think about it.

Instantaneously – Right away, with no delay.

Leadership Skills – The ability to guide and support others.

Legacy of Unity – The memory or impact of people working together in peace.

Local Library – A community place where people can borrow books and learn.

Mantle of Change – Taking on the responsibility to help make the world better.

Messages of Inspiration – Words that make others feel hopeful or encouraged.

Mural Project – A big picture painted on a wall that tells a story or shares a message.

Mystical World – A place that feels magical and full of mystery.

New Grace – A new way of moving or acting that feels kind, calm, or beautiful.

New Initiatives – Fresh ideas or projects meant to make a positive change.

Non-Violence Talks – Conversations about solving problems peacefully.

Overcome Their Own Obstacles – Found ways to get through personal challenges.

Parallels – Similarities between two things.

Patience – Staying calm when things take time.

Reflections and Revelations – Looking back and discovering important truths.

Resilience – The strength to recover from problems or hard times.

Reaffirmation – Saying or showing again that something is still true or important.

Renewal – The process of becoming fresh or new again.

Revelations – Surprising truths that are discovered or told.

Sense of Purpose – The feeling that you have a reason or goal in life.

Shy and Reserved – Quiet and not very outgoing.

Sportsmanship – Being fair and respectful in games or competition.

Strategic Play – A smart plan for winning or reaching a goal, especially in sports or games.

Team Dynamics – How people in a group interact and work together.

Transformation – A big or important change in someone or something.

Transformed – Changed in appearance, form, or behavior.

Vibrant Scenes – Lively, colorful, and full of energy.

Vivid – Clear, bright, and easy to imagine.

Vitality – Energy and strength.

Youth Workshops – Classes or group sessions where young people learn new things and grow.

Literary Terms & Figurative Language

"Celebrate Diversity in Your World" – A phrase that means to appreciate and honor the many different kinds of people and cultures around you.

"Facing Real-World Challenges with Bravery and Intelligence" – Using courage and smart choices to handle tough situations.

"Ignite" – To spark or start something powerful, like an idea or movement.

"Leadership Was Gentle Yet Firm" – A poetic way of saying someone led with both kindness and strength.

"Reaffirmation of Their Commitment to Excel" – A strong restating that they are ready to try hard and succeed.

"Reflections and Revelations" – Looking back and discovering truths or lessons.

"Sense of Purpose" – Feeling like you have a mission or goal in life.

"Teach a Kid to Read Well and Give Them the Freedom to Conquer the World" – A metaphor about how learning to read can open up endless opportunities.

Real-World Concepts & Applications

Children's Book Club – A group where kids gather to read and talk about books.

Local Library / Literacy / Reading Empowerment – Real-life places and practices that open doors to knowledge and growth.

Art Therapy / Mural Project / Canvas – Using creativity to heal, express, and connect.

Basketball Clinic / Strategic Play / Sportsmanship – Learning through games and teamwork.

Youth Workshops / Team Dynamics / Leadership Skills – Developing important life skills through group learning.

Social Themes & Emotional Intelligence

Empathy / Diversity / Resilience / Patience – Important traits for understanding and helping others.

Inspire Change / Agents of Change / Equipped to Lead – Themes of social responsibility and leadership.

Non-Violence / Community Healing / Overcoming Obstacles – Facing and resolving real-life struggles with peace and purpose.

These definitions aim to enhance comprehension of the themes and events in Chapter One through Chapter Twenty-six of the book.

Total = 1489 vocabulary terms

TEXT-BASED SYMBOL CARDS

Text-Based Symbol Cards (Flashcard Style)

You can copy/paste these into your Vellum document. Each card can be placed in a box or line-spaced for printing/cutting.

Prefix: re-
> **Meaning:** again
> **Helps you understand:** *resolve, resonate*

Root: son
> **Meaning:** sound
> **Helps you understand:** *resonate*

Suffix: -th
> **Meaning:** a state or quality
> **Helps you understand:** *stealth*

Root: solve
> **Meaning:** to decide or figure out
> **Helps you understand:** *resolve*

Prefix: am-
    Meaning: toward
    Helps you understand: *ambush*

Root: bush
    Meaning: hide or cover
    Helps you understand: *ambush*

Root: guile
    Meaning: trick or cleverness
    Helps you understand: *guile*

How to Use:
- Print on cardstock and cut out
- Use in matching games, sentence building, or morphology puzzles
- Add blank cards for students to draw their own symbols or add new root words

SCATTER'S LEADERS TOOLKIT

SCATTER'S LEADER'S TOOLKIT

"The journey may end, but the tools of leadership stay with you. Keep this guide close when real life feels like a challenge. Each symbol reminds you that you're already becoming the leader Wakaduo believes in."

1. ⚈ The Lion's Tooth of Passage
Represents: Wisdom earned through trials
Use it when: You're scared or uncertain
Try this: Write down 3 moments when you showed courage. These are your "Lion's Teeth."

2. 🐚 Adira's Wisdom Shell
Represents: Patience, insight, reflection
Use it when: Emotions run high or conflict arises
Try this: Pause. Ask, "What would a wise leader do right now?"

3. 🐚 The Bracelet of Trust

Represents: Earning and offering trust

Use it when: Rebuilding relationships or creating new ones

Try this: Make a gesture of trust—keep a promise, offer forgiveness, or ask a thoughtful question.

4. 🎺 The Trumpet of Courage

Represents: Speaking up, standing strong

Use it when: You need to advocate for yourself or others

Try this: Write a message of courage for yourself or someone who needs it.

5. 🌐 The Circle of Unity

Represents: Community, collaboration, empathy

Use it when: You're leading a group or solving a challenge together

Try this: Invite someone into your circle today. Include someone who feels left out.

Your Leader's Oath

Complete your journey by writing your own oath:

I am a leader when I _____.

I carry forward _____.

And I will always choose _____.

"Your leadership doesn't start someday. It starts now."

AFTERWORD: THE STORY
DOESN'T END HERE

Afterword: The Story Doesn't End Here

Dear Reader,

By the time you've reached this page, you've traveled far.

You've crossed deserts and mountains. You've outsmarted monsters and doubts. You've walked beside Scatter, Tusker, Ernie, and Henry—not just watching their journey, but growing alongside them.

But here's the secret: *Wakaduo isn't just a story world.*

It's a mirror.

A reflection of who we are—and who we could become.

Each African proverb in this book holds a truth deeper than its words. My hope is that one of them reached you, challenged you, or whispered something to your heart.

Maybe it was:

"If you think you're too small to make a difference, then you haven't spent the night with a mosquito."

Or perhaps:

"If you want to go fast, go alone. If you want to go far, go together."

Or even:

"To get lost is to learn the way."

Whatever proverb stays with you... carry it. Let it guide you the way Scatter's ring guided her.

This book is part of a bigger journey—a movement to change how we see reading, how we teach it, and how we use it to build strength, not just in our minds, but in our communities.

I leave you with one final thought:

"Wisdom does not come overnight."

Keep reading. Keep dreaming. Keep growing.

And remember—your greatness is not just in the pages of a book.

It's in you.

With pride and belief in your journey,

R. G. Waugh

Author | Educator | Literacy Advocate